THE FRENCH EXILES
1789–1815

Margery Weiner

THE FRENCH EXILES

1789–1815

William Morrow and Company

NEW YORK   1961

A. W.
E. W.

Patri matrique dilectissimis
filia haud ingrata

Contents

Illustrations

between pages 84 and 85

A contemporary cartoon

The first emigration, 1. Madame de Polignac, 2. le Comte d'Artois, 3. le Prince de Condé, 4. le Baron de Breteuil

Jean-François de La Marche, Bishop of St. Pol de Léon from the original drawing by H. P. Danloux *British Museum*

The Chapel of the Annunciation in 1890 after the water colour by T. Appleton (now in the Ashbridge Collection; reproduced by permission of St. Marylebone Public Libraries Committee)

Le Comte Auguste de La Ferronays *Photo. Méneux*

Le Duc de Berri

Louis XVIII

La Duchesse d'Angoulême *Radio Times Hulton Picture Library*

Le Duc d'Angoulême *Radio Times Hulton Picture Library*

Charles-Philippe, Comte d'Artois

Louise, Comtesse de Polastron

ix

Acknowledgements

The author wishes to express her most grateful thanks to the following authors and publishers for permission to quote from the works cited:

G. K. Fortescue, *Cambridge Modern History*, Volume VIII, the Syndics of the Cambridge University Press.

Mrs. George Bambridge and Macmillan and Co. Ltd., *Rewards and Fairies—A Priest in Spite of Himself*—by Rudyard Kipling.

Lord Beveridge, *Voluntary Action*, George Allen and Unwin, Ltd.

Bonamy Dobrée, *The Letters of George III*, Cassell and Co., Ltd.

Général de Gaulle, *Mémoires de Guerre—l'Appel*, Librairie Plon.

Fernand Baldensperger, *Le Mouvement des Idées dans l'Emigration Française*, Librairie Plon.

Avant Propos

This book sets out to portray something of the life during the French Revolution and Empire of French émigrés in London; how they came here, how they lived, their relations with the English and with each other. More especially it is concerned with the small group which stands a little apart from the other émigrés because they lived in the orbit of the French Princes, the Comte d'Artois and the Duc de Berri, in the parish of St. Marylebone. Of this group I have singled out as the convinced Royalist who never wavered in his allegiance the Comte Auguste Ferron de La Ferronays, who was gentleman in waiting to the Duc de Berri. Some material for his life has come from the memoir written by the Marquis Costa de Beauregard, based on the La Ferronays papers, but I have also had the advantage of using the unpublished manuscript of the Comtesse Auguste de La Ferronays.

I have made no attempt to write a general history of the emigration in England where, at one time or another, there were some twenty-five thousand French émigrés, of whom a large proportion were clergy, scattered over a wide area from the Channel Islands to Berwick, although the majority were settled in London.

The last general history of the émigrés was written over seventy years ago by H. Forneron but little use has been made in it of English original sources. Ernest Daudet's work on the emigration deals mainly with the émigrés on the Continent and more particularly with Louis XVIII. Other basic works treat only of special aspects of émigré activity, like F. X. Plasse's exhaustive study of the clergy in England which only touches on émigré society as a whole. Since these books were published numerous memoirs written by the émigrés themselves have appeared although a still larger number remains in manuscript.

I have been unable to trace any previous detailed examination of the large sums voted annually by the British Government from

1794–1814 for the 'relief of the suffering French clergy and laity', or any analysis of the striking amount of private charitable endeavour on their behalf.

While I have devoted an introductory chapter to the causes of the emigration I have not dealt with the causes of the French Revolution, which are largely irrelevant to my purpose, nor have I attempted any appreciation of the extremely involved political relations between the leaders of the émigrés and the British Government except in so far as they affected the daily lives of my characters.

Since the world has grown used nowadays and even indifferent to the spectacle of large numbers of people uprooted from their homes and country and forced, under threat of persecution and annihilation, to flee for their lives, it might be argued that this story of over a hundred and fifty years ago is no longer of great interest because during our own lifetime we have witnessed greater disasters and seen more violent upheavals.

This argument might have some validity if human suffering were real only in terms of actuality and if the lessons to be learned from dignity in misfortune, generosity in distress and courage in adversity were valuable only when in one's direct line of vision. In raking over the ashes of history it is always possible to re-kindle a flame.

These lessons, and many more, can be studied in the history of the French émigrés in England and it is not wholly idle to suppose that the real *entente cordiale* between France and England dates back to the gratitude engendered in thousands of French men, women and children who, under adverse circumstances, learned to love and respect England.

My most grateful thanks are due to the Rev. Arthur Barnett, Minister Emeritus of the Western Synagogue who, by introducing me to the French Chapel Royal in Carton Street and telling me something of its history, first fired me to read further into the subject of the émigrés and their institutions; to the Vicomte Augustin de Rougé, who not only most generously lent me the unpublished memoirs of his great-grandmother, the Comtesse Auguste de La Ferronays, but to whom I am deeply indebted for the privilege of visiting the last resting-place of the La Ferronays family; to Canon E. A. Swinton and Lieutenant-Colonel the

Honourable H. R. Alexander for taking so much trouble to give me information about their ancestors, Samuel and Félicité Swinton; to Monsieur Raymond Clavreuil, who has performed miracles in obtaining rare books for me and whose immense knowledge of the period has been invaluable; and last, but by no means least, to my sister, Joyce Weiner, who has suffered patiently the long intrusion into our household of so many ghosts, which have crowded us uncomfortably, but without whose wise assistance and moral support this book would not have been written.

My greatest debt is acknowledged in, but can never be repaid by, the dedication of this study.

St. Marylebone, 1959.

I

The Joyous Emigration

In the Musée Carnavalet in Paris there is a model of the Bastille carved from one of its massy stones. A sinister aura seems to emanate from the miniature medieval fortress as it must have done when the actual edifice lowered over the city of Paris as a formidable sign of feudal oppression. Yet, by 1789, as the Parisians must have known well, it no longer served its original purpose and plans for its demolition had been made by the Government. The fortuitous destruction on July 14th was not of an instrument but of a symbol of tyranny.

The storming of the Bastille in Paris, which had been preceded by local jacqueries, encouraged the mob all over France to renew its savagery on the objects or individuals which it found accessible, and the peasantry succeeded in surpassing in brutality the more sophisticated Parisians. Churches were desecrated with obscene songs and wilder dances, châteaux were burnt and the inhabitants assassinated, often with a variety of tortures. Those gentry who had treated their tenants best fared the worst.

These instances were not isolated nor were they excesses committed as reprisals. Louis XVI remained securely enthroned at Versailles and the orators of the National Assembly were still pouring out in eloquent periods the most unexceptionable principles.

There was nothing in the convocation of the States General which presaged a sequel of violence and anarchy. It was inspired by a legitimate desire for reform of outworn institutions, a desire which Louis XVI shared and which he was clumsily doing his best to implement. The noble concepts of liberty, equality and fraternity were the product of eighteenth-century French philosophical thought, as much respected by many among the privileged Estates, the nobility and clergy, as by the Third Estate, the commons. But the impatience of the crowd, for whom

4

the processes of constitutional reform were slow and incomprehensible, managed to undermine and ultimately to overbear the sober elements in the National Assembly.

Contagion of this nature cannot be countered by a *cordon sanitaire*. Violent changes of government or radical reversals of policy, which alone suited the mood of the mob avid for drama, provoke one of two reactions. If the opposition to the new doctrines is strong enough civil war can ensue, which is what happened in England in the seventeenth century. If the opposition is weak, and no one was more paralytically weak than the well-intentioned Louis XVI, then its weakness will invite a persecution seeking its justification in distinctions of caste, religion or privilege but whose fundamental motives are hatred and greed.

Hatred found an easy and early prey in the King's youngest brother, Charles-Philippe, Comte d'Artois. Tall, distinguished and handsome, except for a pendent lower lip, extremely elegant in dress and manner and of infinite grace and charm, Artois was born to all the privileges and pleasures of royalty but was required to have no share in its responsibilities.

He had desired a military career but was allowed only the empty honour of the Colonel-Generalship of the Swiss Guards. Since his eldest brother had not yet produced an heir and his second brother, the Comte de Provence, was incapable of so doing Artois satisfied the only demand made on him and, from a loveless marriage of state made at the age of sixteen to Marie Thérèse de Savoie, duly fathered two sons, the Ducs d'Angoulême and de Berri. He was henceforward free to devote himself to a life of unalloyed pleasure and self-indulgence in the gayest and most magnificent court in Europe. As chief *chevalier servant* to his sister-in-law, Marie Antoinette, in the entertainments of Trianon and Versailles, Charles-Philippe danced happily through life, carefree and careless.

The Parisians saw in him the personal qualities and amiable weaknesses which had so endeared Henri IV to them and, making him their darling, they admiringly dubbed him, too, the *vert galant*. To the courtiers he was the perfect chevalier, the paladin of high romance. They called him Galaor, after the brother of the famed Amadis de Gaul (though neither the ponderous Louis nor the

5

pedantic Comte de Provence qualified for this title). His own immediate circle considered him perfection itself.

Young, intoxicated with so much adulation and deficient in judgment, Artois had received no education which caused him to recognise any limits to his personal indulgence in high play, in dalliance or in disrespect to his kingly brother, until finally his excesses alienated his admirers and from regarding benevolently the caprices of a charming boy the nation came to detest the arrogance and giddiness of the public behaviour of the young man.

Unexpectedly Artois' way of life changed radically with the appearance at court of Louise de Lussan d'Esparbès, Comtesse Adhémar de Polastron, sister-in-law of the Duchesse de Polignac, the favourite of Marie Antoinette.

Louise was barely eighteen when she received her first Court appointment which almost overwhelmed one so timid and retiring by nature. An orphan, she had been educated at the famous Abbaye de Penthémont, the convent in the Faubourg St. Germain where girls of the highest aristocracy were brought up. It must have been a happy place for its pupils looked back on the days they spent there as the happiest in their lives.

When her formidable sister-in-law first presented her at Versailles Louise impressed everyone by her delicate beauty. Her large pale blue eyes were set in an oval face whose gentle sadness was irradiated by a smile of appealing sweetness. Her head, crowned by ash-blonde hair, was always inclined slightly over her shoulder, which added to the languid grace of her elegant and supple figure. Lamartine said of her much later that she was the incarnation of tenderness.

For two years her marriage was happy and she gave birth to a son, Louis, but Comte Adhémar cared more for the camp and his violin than for the pleasures of the Court. The young Louise was left much alone by him and when she captivated the Comte d'Artois by her beauty, charm and simplicity the sequel was inevitable.

Artois was passionately and profoundly in love and under the gentle influence of the Comtesse de Polastron he reformed. The nights of debauch at Bel-Air, the questionable *petits-soupers* at Bagatelle, the evenings at Opera balls, the scandalous liaisons and the high play at faro ended abruptly. There were moments when the old habits threatened to re-assert themselves but he saw that they displeased Louise and he soon settled with her into an almost domestic bliss.

It was too late, however, for Artois to eradicate the bad impression he had created or to diminish his present unpopularity. Indeed his new-found sobriety, leading him to choose politics as his sphere of interest, brought him only into worse disrepute since he displayed an unstatesmanlike inflexibility, born of his own inexperience, and ranged round himself the most intransigent and conservative elements in the court.

The rake reformed was even less acceptable than the rake unrepentant and, from being merely unpopular, Artois now became identified with reaction and an object of real enmity to the people. Love had turned to hatred with a vengeance. Had the Parisians guessed that, immediately after the fall of the Bastille, Artois, counselled by Talleyrand, urged the King, temperamentally inclined to appeasement, to use force to restore the situation, the price they insolently dared to put upon his head would have been still higher. But Louis would not listen (although events proved that Artois may well have been right) and the Parisians did not know.

What Louis did, fearing the unfortunate consequences of Artois' unpopularity, was expressly to order him to leave France until the troubles had blown over. On the night of July 16th–17th, 1789, Charles-Philippe and his family quitted France.

He did not go alone. A few days later he was followed by the junior branch of the Bourbon family, the old Prince de Condé, his son, the Duc de Bourbon, and his grandson, the young Duc d'Enghien, who would return to France only to meet a firing-squad at Vincennes. The Comtesse de Polastron naturally followed Artois, in company with her school-friends from Penthémont, chubby Madame de Poulpry and her adored Blimonette, Stéphanie d'Amblimont, Marquise de Lage, lady-in-waiting to the Princesse de Lamballe.

They had been preceded by the Polignacs and the Duchesse's faithful lover, the Comte de Vaudreuil, all of whom were execrated by the masses as favourites and evil geniuses of Marie Antoinette, at whose urging they had taken flight to escape the possible vengeance of the mob. Following these departures other courtiers decided to make excursions of pleasure in the provinces or abroad until the atmosphere at Versailles should be restored to its customary congeniality.

Many of the high French aristocracy who had frequently visited England in the past, repaying the kindnesses they had received by lavish entertainments at Paris and Versailles, came across the Channel for what they firmly believed was merely another short holiday, a time to enjoy again the hospitality of Carlton House, the Devonshires, the Bessboroughs, the Spencers, the Grenvilles and other families of the *ton*. This exodus, negligible in quantity, has been called the *émigration joyeuse*, a light-hearted withdrawal, temporary in intention, while the King and his ministers dealt with the unpleasant but surely unimportant manifestations of popular discontent.

The mood of these early arrivals in England was a carefree one. Although the Duc de Luxembourg had a price of 300,000 livres on his head his Duchesse's sole concern on arrival in London was to know if there was any mass.

Their friends flocked to town to see the illustrious exiles and their reception in no way differed from that which they had met with on previous visits although they arrived at a moment when events in France were being greeted with surprise and approbation by a large section of public opinion in England. One recalls Charles James Fox's exclamation that the fall of the Bastille was much the greatest and best event that ever happened. He might have been justified and France might have developed peacefully into a constitutional monarchy on English lines had the House of Commons shown a little more sympathy with one of the under-lying causes of French unrest.

A short time before the conclusion of the Parliamentary session in 1789 an application was made by the French Government for permission for the export from England of twenty thousand sacks of wheat flour for the relief of the inhabitants of their Northern provinces.

'As the price of corn, at this time in Great Britain, exceeded the exportation price, the matter was necessarily brought into Parliament. A committee was appointed to inquire into the case; who reported, that from a comparative view of the prices of wheat flour in France and in England, they were of opinion that 20,000 sacks of flour ought not to be exported.'*

Pitt and Wilberforce were anxious to agree to the French request but the House of Commons decided otherwise. Had it followed Pitt's lead the bread crisis in France might have been halted, giving time for hot heads to cool and empty stomachs to be filled. There might have been no march to Versailles in October and no bringing to Paris of the 'baker and the baker's wife,' a revolt perhaps but not a revolution.

But Parliament, having acquiesced in the committee's findings, adjourned in August for the summer recess. Many of the members, and hundreds of other curious English, took the opportunity of going over to France to view the National Assembly at close quarters and the general attitude of sympathetic interest in French affairs continued.

In addition to the young men making the obligatory Grand Tour after the end of the War of American Independence there had been a continuous tourist traffic between France and England.

Every night in the week, except Sunday, a coach left London which arrived at Dover early next morning. The cost to each passenger was one guinea. Six persons might hire a whole coach for a guinea a head, their luggage paid separately, while outside passengers paid ten shillings and sixpence. To hire a whole vessel which left every tide to Calais or Boulogne cost five guineas, while a single passage cost half a guinea.

Alternatively one might take the Paris diligence which set out from the Paris Office, Piccadilly, at five o'clock in the afternoon, every day except Friday and Sunday. Passage and meals included the cost to each person was five guineas. If the wind was fair the passage across the Channel took three hours and thirty-five minutes.

Whatever private opinion might be the policy of the Government from the outbreak of the Revolution was to keep a strict neutrality, resisting any attempt to embroil it in the internal affairs of France. From the Peace of Versailles in 1783 all Pitt's efforts had been concentrated on re-establishing England's place in the

* *Annual Register*, 1789.

9

councils of Europe. Always in the forefront of his mind were the objects of peace, retrenchment and reform and even in the face of the rising menace in France he clung tenaciously to these aims, rigorously eschewing any action which might imperil them.

In October, 1790, George III could write to him that:

'We have honourably not meddled with the internal dissension of France, and no object ought to drive us from that honourable ground.'

The English, therefore, need feel no scruples in satisfying their curiosity as to what was going on across the Channel but, while they were continuing their visits to France, the French were already leaving their country in a steady stream.

From the provinces, where pillage and murder were in some places already rife, the gentry, the squirearchy and the *petite noblesse* took to the roads to seek safety. Within two months after the fall of the Bastille thousands had applied for passports and the roads were choked with their travelling berlines. So great was the pressure on post-horses that some stages had to be done by oxen. This flight to safety became known as the *émigration de sûreté*.

Following the attack of the Parisians on Versailles in October still more people sought to leave France. Some went on foot with their belongings on the end of a stick, others in mud-bespattered coaches. Those who saw in the new era an opportunity to seek their fortune in Paris travelled in the same diligence as those in flight. During the journey they talked freely to one another but in Paris they separated, some to find fame and success, others a more painful destiny.

Soon, however, it became difficult to leave Paris. Passports cost as much as ten thousand livres and, even if one was prepared to pay this extortionate sum, there was the risk, on presenting oneself at the *mairie* to obtain papers, of being treated as a suspect.

Readers of Baroness Orczy's famous story are familiar with the scenes of venom and mob violence which attended the departure of aristocrats from Paris. They are authenticated by the Marquise de Larochejacquelein, wife of the famous Vendéen leader, who described the populace hurling round her carriage:

'À la lanterne! À l'Abbaye! Ce sont des aristocrates qui se sauvent.'

Everywhere along her route to the West her carriage was stopped by insolent soldiers, who insulted the occupants, crying: 'Massacre the émigrés! Kill them!'

Some ladies leaving for the east availed themselves of the generous impulse of Swiss men who came over to French municipalities, went through a form of marriage so that the women could be entered on their passports as Swiss citizens, and escorted them over the frontier. One such Scarlet Pimpernel was arrested at his eighteenth marriage.

The Swiss were not unique in their chivalry. After Charlotte de Rutant, a young aristocrat of Nancy, had been executed for suspected correspondence with the émigrés, a British officer, Major 'Punch' Bryan, to whom she had been engaged, went through a civil marriage with her younger sister, Augustine, which enabled him to get the rest of the family safely to London.

Artois and his friends of the *émigration joyeuse* had no such difficulties. The early stages of their prudent absence were all sunshine. After an idyllic month spent in Switzerland with Louise de Polastron he settled down with his family at the court of his father-in-law at Turin. It would have been impolitic to keep Louise too near him while enjoying family hospitality and the only shadow that darkened their lives was their enforced separation. From Rome, where Louise was installed, the Comte de Vaudreuil kept her lover fully informed by letter of her state of mind and health, which was always delicate and a source of anxiety, and there were delicious interludes at Venice and elsewhere in Italy when they were re-united.

The halcyon days were all too short. As the senior representative of the French Royal family abroad Artois felt it his duty to act. This new-found sense of political responsibility was not, unfortunately, matched by a high degree of political intelligence, and many of his enterprises served only to exacerbate French opinion and even that of the King and Queen.

With the Prince de Condé he formed a committee to study French affairs and to organise a European league against the enemies of the monarchy. From the safety of his father-in-law's summer palace at Turin he watched with anxiety the mounting tensions and particularly the consequences of the October days resulting in the King and Queen's enforced residence in Paris.

In England sympathetic interest in French affairs continued to grow until in 1790 the publication of Edmund Burke's *Reflections on the Revolution in France* brought the starry-eyed idealists face to face with reality. No man of honour and sensibility could fail to be stirred by Burke's passionate defence of Marie Antoinette which was not to be lightly dismissed as a piece of Irish rhodomontade. For the first time the English were invited to ask themselves whether events in France could have any influence on England, apart from the normal eighteenth-century reaction as to what advantage in the colonial and commercial sphere might result from a decline in French power abroad.

Burke's *Reflections* produced an immediate riposte from the opposition party with Sir James Mackintosh's *Vindiciae Gallicae* and with Thomas Paine's *The Rights of Man*. Sympathisers with the Revolution welcomed the works of Paine and Mackintosh and its other apologists but those to whom Burke's *Reflections* had given pause grew even more alarmed at this visible sign of a growing Radical party in England, calling for Parliamentary and every other kind of reform. *The Rights of Man* seriously frightened the governing classes to the extent of provoking a large number of Whigs to join Pitt in 1792.

Artois was either ignorant of or indifferent to the sway of public opinion in England, being far more nearly concerned with his efforts to enrol allies for his cause on the Continent. He undertook a series of démarches, which proved abortive, to the sovereigns of Europe, especially to Marie Antoinette's brother, the Emperor, inviting them to co-operate with him in aiding Louis XVI and the Queen. Money, too, now began to run short and Artois knew for the first time the humiliation of pawning his jewels. Hitherto his debts had been paid by his brother at the expense of the French Treasury.

As the situation continued to worsen he invited the nobility to emigrate and assist in opposing the new régime by organising help for the King from outside the frontiers of France.

The climax came with the attempted flight of the Royal family of France in June, 1791, summarily halted at Varennes. Only the Comte de Provence succeeded in escaping. The King and Queen and the Royal children were brought back to Paris to virtual imprisonment in the Tuileries.

Opinion in England again received a shock and indignation at the treatment of the King and Queen rose to a high pitch. As Horace Walpole wrote to his faithful correspondent, the Countess of Upper Ossory:

'The escape of the King and Queen of France came merely time enough [*sic*] to double the shock of their being retaken. An ocean of pity cannot suffice to lament their miserable condition. . . . How the tragedy is to end, or begin it is impossible to guess.'

And when the failure of the escape was confirmed in London he wrote again of his horror, this time to Miss Mary Berry:

'Of one thing I am certain, of pitying the Queen; which was so generally felt here as soon as the reverse of her escape was known, that I was told that, if money could serve her, an hundred thousand pounds would have been subscribed in a quarter of an hour at Lloyd's coffee-house.'

Many of the nobility, who had stayed as near the King's person as they could so long as there seemed any hope of supporting him, began to realise that hope was vain and, when his intention to escape became known (and it was perhaps one of the worst kept of secrets), they also decided to leave France.

Among them was the Comte de Montsoreau, a nobleman of great wealth, who was allied by birth and marriage to half the armorial of France. Although he held no Court appointment he lived in its orbit and his daughters had played with the Royal children. The Comte had stayed in Paris until his sister-in-law, the Duchesse de Tourzel, *gouvernante* to the Dauphin, warned him of the impending flight of the Royal family so, judging that he could be of more use to his King abroad than by remaining in France, he too left Paris. Madame de Montsoreau packed only one season of her missal and a few summer dresses, leaving her furs behind in Paris, for they were still convinced that their absence would be short. When the Comte learned of the King's arrest at Varennes he tried to turn back but once across the frontier there was no return.

To argue that men like Montsoreau should have remained at home to resist the rising forces of revolution is to pre-suppose that they were the ruling as well as the privileged classes. In an absolute monarchy such as that of the Bourbons the ruling elements, however, derive from the personal preferences of the sovereign so that there was no ruling class as such. The nobility, courtiers rather than peers in the English sense, had neither the means of restoring law and order when they disintegrated nor access to those means when law and order finally collapsed. Thus, when no longer protected by the laws of their country, when unable to render those laws their support, they had only one course, to flee from a land which had fallen under the sway of terror and violence.

Louis himself now realised that all hope of bringing the French to reason, of any action of his own free will or spontaneous movement on his part, was ended. His own attempt at flight tacitly set the seal of his approval on the emigration.

Not those that he was forced to utter in public but Louis' true feelings were expressed in a letter written to the Comte de Provence in which he foretold that the flight so necessary to him, which might have made his happiness and that of the people, would be the subject of a terrible accusation. He was threatened by cries of hatred, by talk of a trial. So long as he was allowed to believe himself King of France he would undertake no action which would dishonour himself. Once the Frenchman had loved his kings. What had he done to be so hated, he who had always cherished them? If he had been a Nero or Tiberius . . .

Louis had been neither. His crime was to be weak when the times demanded strength. In 1791 he was already conscious that the sands were running out for him. The wheels which started rolling to Varennes would go on turning relentlessly until they stopped on a cold January morning two years later in the Place de la Révolution.

A few days before he attempted flight he had been, on his own admission, a king, though but a vain phantom, the powerless chief of a people who tyrannised over their monarch who had become the slave of his oppressors. Now he was a prisoner in his own palace, deprived even of the right to protest.

'Séparé de ma famille entière, mon épouse, ma sœur, mes enfans gémissent loin de moi; et vous, mon frère, par le plus noble dévouement, vous vous êtes condamné à l'exil; vous voilà dans les lieux où gémissent tant de victimes que l'honneur appelait sur les bords du Rhin . . . S'ils sont malheureux, dites-leur que Louis, que leur roi, que leur père, que leur ami est plus malheureux encore!!'

Blow after blow now descended on Louis' bowed head. He was forced to take the oath to the Constitution in that autumn and he must have felt some bitterness that George III, under the influence of Pitt, who was steadfastly pursuing his policy of non-intervention in French affairs, was one of the first to recognise it.

In the previous year he had had to face a crisis which touched this pious man even more nearly. This was the Civil Constitution of the clergy. The National Assembly in its reforming zeal had attempted to remodel the Church of France. While not dissolving the connection between Church and State it rendered that connection intolerable to the vast majority of the clergy. First of all their political power had been reduced by the merging of the three Estates, then the Assembly laid greedy hands on their wealth. The ancient ecclesiastical dioceses and provinces were set aside and bishops reduced to mere civil servants.

The advocates of the Civil Constitution argued that it did not impinge on doctrine or worship but merely effected a necessary reform of discipline. Inevitably this argument brought the Assembly into conflict with the Pope who naturally condemned a constitution which extinguished his authority in France. The Assembly was not, of course, moved by papal opposition and proceeded to deprive of their office the clergy who refused to swear the new oath to the Constitution, finally removing all the non-juring priests from their benefices and confiscating their stipends.

Louis had dared to veto the decree against the non-juring clergy but already his actions scarcely counted. For the clergy nothing then remained but to leave a country which denied them the free exercise of their conscience, a country which was in effect neither a republic nor a monarchy but a state without society, an assembly of victims, of slaves and of murderers. They experienced no enthusiasm and no hope in quitting their posts, anticipating nothing but unhappiness, yet nevertheless all that was best in their order left France. Many of them would have defied the enemies who had now taken the Church as their especial target for persecution but they were given no choice since their emigration was enforced by compulsory deportation.

They fled in their thousands from Normandy, from Brittany and the North West of France to the Channel Islands and to England, many dragged from prison and led like galley slaves to the ports. Those in the east hastily crossed the frontiers into Belgium and Switzerland. Victims of every kind of violence, they had as their sole possessions the garments in which they stood up and their breviaries. At the final moment of departure they were searched, the few remaining coins they had with them confiscated and derisively replaced with worthless *assignats*.

The Bishop of Avranches had to flee from his diocese with his Grands Vicaires and his servants. They managed to reach Rouen where they spent several days in hiding until they were discovered by the populace, escaping only in disguise to Dieppe. They arrived during the night and, at the time appointed for the sailing of the packet, ran to the water's edge. Providentially it was high tide and they were able to get out of reach of their pursuers who ran after them to the shore itself shouting imprecations. After the fury of the rabble the fury of the storm. The Bishop, together with some seventy-six other ecclesiastics in his boat making for Brighton, were blown eastward to Hastings.

When Malouet, a liberal aristocrat, sailed from Calais he saw, once out at sea, the Bishop of Coutances and some other gentlemen emerge painfully from the hold where they had been hidden under mattresses.

The Bishop of St. Pol de Léon, Jean-François de La Marche, defied the civil authority and continued to administer his diocese until the police came to arrest him. Courteously asking for permission to dress himself properly he went into his study, the police officer having assured himself that there was no possible exit, but St. Pol de Léon slipped through a door hidden behind the bookshelves. He was pursued by the *maréchaussée* but managed to reach Mount's Bay in Cornwall, landing in November, 1791.

The plight of the monks and nuns, particularly of the enclosed orders, was even more pathetic. Turned out into a world of which most of them had only the haziest recollection, forced to put off their robes and habits and don the unfamiliar garments of secularity they were even more than the priesthood, as we have been able to glimpse in Bernanos' *Les Carmélites**, victims of anguish and bewilderment.

But if their emigration was enforced it was also fortunate. They were at least saved from the bitter fate that awaited those who stayed behind.

* *Dialogues des Carmélites*

II

'Le Chemin de l'Honneur'

Before the French Revolution gave the word another connotation an emigrant was defined as a man who, voluntarily and permanently, renounced his own country in favour of another, taking with him his family, his household goods, his means of livelihood, his fortune and his savings, either because the political climate of his own country no longer appealed to him or because he saw the opportunity of a better future in another land.

The French émigrés of the Revolution desired no other home but France which they left, not of their own free will, but under compulsion, and with the intention of returning at the earliest possible moment. In the terms of this definition they were not emigrants but the misnomer has stuck and is now consecrated by usage.

The Marquis de Lally-Tollendal summed up their situation irrefutably in his *Défense des Emigrés*. He was a supporter of a constitution based on the English model and, as such, anathema to the Comte d'Artois and his party, who would admit of no encroachment on the Royal rights, but in spite of this liberalism he was a firm adherent of the monarchy. Although he emigrated to Switzerland in 1790 when his own brand of constitutionalism became unpopular, he returned in 1792 in the hope of rendering some aid to Louis XVI, whom he had hailed in 1789 as 'the restorer of liberty.' For this attempt to help the King he was thrown into the prison of the Abbaye but was released and managed to escape to England although his nerves were so shattered that he continued to start when anyone opened the door and was constantly looking over his shoulder in the expectation of being again apprised.

It was Lally-Tollendal who exclaimed passionately that it was not voluntarily that one left the sun of one's childhood, the cradle and the tombs of one's fathers, the sanctuaries of one's

family, and of one's friends, the foundations of one's life, the
pleasures of one's heart, in sum all that makes the support, the
pride and the charm of one's existence, to go forth under an
alien sky, across barbaric regions in search of some corner of a
hospitable country where one was pursued by one's memories,
overwhelmed by one's isolation, at the very least menaced by
poverty, aided sometimes but rarely respected:

'Non, ce n'est pas volontairement qu'on a pu échanger de si
douces et paisibles destinées contre un exil si amer et des
combats si déchirans.'

The ultimate crime of the émigrés, both aristocrats and bourgeoisie, was that, in the opinion of the demagogues, they represented the 'haves' while the rest of the nation were the 'have-nots'.
First the lands of the clergy, then the possessions of the nobility
had excited their greed. The definition of the 'haves' was rapidly
extended to the Third Estate, to those members of their own
order more fortunate than themselves, since the stocks of a small
shop, an artisan's tools, a forge or a mill were prizes of equal if
not superior value to a *château fort* or the gewgaws of an aristocrat.
Out of an assessed total of a hundred and twenty thousand émigrés
just over half belonged to the *tiers état*.

'Confiscation' summed up the revolutionaries' theory of financial reform and, since men will not stand idly by, watching
dispassionately the spoliation of their property, their potential
resistance had to be crushed or their persons eliminated. Whoever
estimated the gross fortune of the nobility at three milliards
unconsciously signed the death warrant of thousands and sent
many more on the road to exile, ensuring in either case that they
did not return to dispossess their dispossessors.

'Vast interests depended on the maintenance of the laws
against the émigrés. Their property, with that of the clergy and
the national domains, formed the security on which the assignats
were issued, and many thousands of purchasers had been found
for their confiscated estates. If a general amnesty were granted
and the émigrés were allowed to reclaim their lands and houses,
the assignats would become waste-paper and the whole social
fabric would fall to pieces.'*

* G. K. Fortescue, *Cambridge Modern History*, Vol. VIII, Chapter XVI.

Decree after decree between 1791 and 1795 was enacted against the émigrés, 'those tigers savaging their mother's bosom,' to ensure that the tranquillity of their despoilers remained undisturbed. First they became liable to death for assembling beyond the frontiers, then they became liable to death for returning to France, then they became liable to death for going to the colonies, then they became liable to death for not returning to France. Next came a ferocious persecution directed against their wives and children and other relatives whom they had left behind. Followed the persecution extended to any of their debtors who paid their debts to them. Children of over ten were to be counted as émigrés. Marriage was rendered null and void by emigration. Those who denounced the émigrés were to be rewarded.

Every possible penalty was invoked to make the withdrawal from France permanent, in the sacred name of liberty, equality, fraternity—or death. One did not even have to be an émigré in fact. Many who stayed behind were entered on the fatal lists and became subject to the same penalties as those who had gone.

Since hatred of the émigrés, particularly against those now assembling in arms across the Rhine, was so violent, it might be assumed that those who remained at home, tamely allowing themselves to be destituted of their property and their rights, would receive some distinguishing marks of consequence, their very act of presence entitling them to be admitted to the fraternity of liberty and equality.

This premise does not take into account the workings of the revolutionary mind. Freedom the aristocrats should have, freedom from the cares of this world; equality, which all find in the grave; brotherhood, in a fate shared with their kin.

To be dragged to the guillotine with no consideration of age or sex, to be drowned in the *noyades* with the added indignity of the *mariage républicain*, to be tortured in the *glacière* of Avignon, to be pursued in their hiding-places and starved in their homes, these were the alternatives pressed upon those who did not emigrate. Under the heady influence of the *carmagnole* and the *ça ira* lust for blood soon surpassed in ferocity greed for gold. Some seventeen thousand persons perished under the Terror alone and thousands more under the continuous pressure of persecution.

Were these not sufficiently compelling reasons to force thousands of Frenchmen of all classes to exchange a country and a way of life to which they were so attached for the uncertainties and the hardships of exile? There was indeed nothing in common between the voluntary abandonment of one's country and being chased from it by violence. To abandon and betray one's country are not the same thing as being abandoned and betrayed by it, yet this act of departure, this movement of self-preservation, brought contumely and vilification upon the heads of those who claimed this ele. nentary right. With an illogicality which in other circumstances might have been amusing the French revolutionaries hurled bitter reproaches at those who, as a consequence of these outrages, fled from a country which no longer offered them any security. But if vehement protests were made in public about the emigration in private there was great satisfaction. It was simultaneously made the pretext for declaring a war abroad which had already been decided upon and at home for seizing the fortunes the men of the Revolution coveted. They needed victims, not defenders. It was the presence, not the absence, of the landowners that was feared and the hypocrites of the Revolution repulsed the return of those whose departure they penalised.

Where the émigrés were in question right was engulfed in the Rights of Man which was a doctrine of extreme exclusiveness. Its principles applied only to the masses, who arrogated to themselves alone the privileges formerly enjoyed by their masters. The voice of reason was drowned in jubilant cries of 'We are the masters now!'

But there was a factor in the emigration far more compelling even than the instinct for self-preservation. This was the eighteenth-century aristocrat's conception of patriotism, differing fundamentally from that of the Revolution for which patriotism was attachment to its own principles.

The belief of the French aristocrat was that patriotism was bound up in the person of the King. In a monarchy one does not serve the prince by serving the country but, on the contrary, one serves the country by serving the prince. Between the two ideologies, that of the Royalists for whom France was the King, and that of the revolutionaries for whom France was the Revolution, lay an impassable abyss.

The revolutionaries, however, held the trump card, the person of the King, which made the duty of the émigrés even clearer. They must save the monarchy by intervention from without if it could not be saved from within.

This possibility became more of a probability after the Declaration of Pillnitz, made jointly in August, 1791, by the Emperor and the King of Prussia, promising intervention in France if that intervention was approved by all the European powers. Achieving this Declaration was in Artois' opinion a resounding diplomatic success brought about by two years of striving to enlist the aid of the Powers to the Royal cause. He had not perhaps read the document very carefully or else he was too unfamiliar with anodyne international pronouncements to perceive its hesitations and reservations.

What the sovereigns said was as follows:

'Their Majesties, the Emperor and the King of Prussia, having heard the wishes and representations of Monsieur (the Comte de Provence) and the Comte d'Artois declare jointly that they consider the situation in which the King of France is placed as an object of common interest to all the sovereigns of Europe.

'They hope that this interest will not fail to be recognised by the powers whose aid is invoked, and that in consequence they will not refuse to employ, conjointly with their said Majesties, the most efficacious means, having regard to the forces at their disposal, to place the King of France in a position to strengthen in perfect freedom the bases of a monarchical government, according equally with the rights of sovereigns and with the well-being of the French nobility.

'Then, and in that case, their said Majesties, the Emperor and the King of Prussia, are resolved to act promptly and in unison, with the necessary force, to achieve the common end proposed.

'While waiting they will give their troops suitable orders so that they are in readiness to take action.'

The French Princes brought this Declaration to their brother's notice by having it published in the newspapers, with the rider that Louis could not doubt that the other European sovereigns would agree with the Emperor and the King of Prussia. That, however, was unfortunately wishful thinking. The Princes reassured Louis and the French people that the sovereigns' interest was as pure and disinterested as the zeal with which they themselves had acted and involved nothing that could alarm either the State or the people, for to repress licence was to avenge liberty and re-establishing public order was liberating the nation.

Louis was in no position to act and for the moment France was not ready but the promise of Pillnitz did seem to offer a hope of deliverance which demanded the support and encouragement of all those devoted to the Royal cause.

For the officers of the Royal army and navy the question had already resolved itself with the same simplicity as for the clergy. When the National Assembly imposed on them an oath in which the name of the King had no place they held it to be contrary to their honour to subscribe to it and, believing that the only way in which they could now carry out their duty to him was to emigrate, they took the same road as the Princes. Not only the officers but whole regiments with bag and baggage went in this way.

To them and to the rest of the aristocratic caste honour was a very real thing. Bright honour was no mere scutcheon, no word alone, but a *mystique*, a buckler against fate, a way of life which they had inherited from their ancestors. It was their support and their reason for existence, by which they lived and for which they were ready to die.

One of the favourite sneers with which the émigrés were taunted was that they regarded themselves as new crusaders, as Tancreds and Bouillons, while they were in fact nothing more than the shabby remnants of a subservient feudalism.

His enemy's scorn was the pride of the émigrés. '*Dieu et le Roi*' was the device under which their forefathers had fought with St. Louis in the Crusades. It was to follow in their tradition, as well as in the footsteps of their Princes, that so many emigrated, driven as much by conscience as by care of their own safety.

After the Declaration of Pillnitz the Princes of the House of Bourbon-Condé wrote to the Comtes de Provence and d'Artois a letter, echoing the words of their hero and common ancestor, Henri IV:

'En suivant les pas de nos princes, nous sommes sûrs de marcher

avec fermêté dans le chemin de l'honneur; et c'est sous leurs
nobles auspices que nous renouvelons entre vos mains comme
princes de votre sang et comme gentilhommes français, le
serment de mourir fidèles à votre service.

'Nous périrons tous plutôt que de souffrir le triomphe du crime,
l'avilissement du trône et le renversement de la monarchie.'

When the Declaration and these letters became known in
France with the honourable opportunity they offered of restoring
dignity to the Crown, stability to the kingdom and happiness to its
people many more supporters of the monarchy decided to
emigrate.

Yet, if to take the *chemin de l'honneur* was the pressing duty of all
who wished to show their devotion to the King and to the
principles of monarchy, the decision to do so was not always an
easy one.

Happiest were the single-minded, those won over completely
by the *vertige d'honneur* which led them to leave their parents, their
chattels and their country without a backward glance, the young
men like the Comte de Neuilly who, at the age of seventeen,
found it all a splendid adventure. He and his family had already
suffered a not too rigorous imprisonment but on their release,
when his mother's offer of herself as a hostage for the Royal
family was refused, she emigrated with her son to Coblentz which
Provence and Artois had now made their headquarters.

'The moment we reached the yellow and black posts of the
frontier with their two-headed eagle the coachman and I tore
off our national cockades. When we stopped I used mine for
a purpose which it would be indelicate to mention,' wrote
Neuilly many years later.

The young Vicomte de Chateaubriand was in America when he
learned of the flight of Louis XVI. This ardent, imaginative,
mystical and adventurous Breton had succumbed to the popular
enthusiasm for savage countries and he had left the regiment of
Navarre, in which he was a lieutenant, and the society of men of
letters in Paris which he was beginning to frequent, with the
avowed intention of exploring the polar regions. He was still in
the civilised parts of the new United States when the news came of

Varennes and immediately he returned to Europe and joined the
émigrés across the Rhine.

To cogent arguments that the emigration was justified and
armed intervention at least as defensible as Lafayette's aid to the
Americans in gaining their liberty he listened but was not convinced, believing that it was *une sottise et une folie*.

'Je ne cédai réellement,' he wrote from his Embassy in London
in the *Mémoires d'Outre-Tombe*, 'qu'au mouvement de mon âge, au
point d'honneur.'

But not all the later émigrés were ardent young men, rushing
towards the unknown, bewitched by the pleasures of travel, eager
to escape from the dullness of home life in the provinces and
exalted by the cause of saving their King, finding even in the hard
life of the penurious exile a quality of adventure which outweighed
the hardship, when for a brief moment at least 'to be young was
very heaven.' Maturer minds were influenced less by the spirit of
adventure than by growing consternation at events at home.
Under the influence of the terrors of 1789 and 1790, and even
before the Terror of 1792 and 1793, those who had favoured
reform, like the Comte d'Haussonville, who had welcomed the
Revolution with enthusiasm, threw themselves into opposition,
not only renouncing their liberal views but forgetting that they
had held them. Persecution and bloodshed work powerfully upon
the minds of men.

Had they stayed at home and held to their opinions it would
have availed them nothing for the age was not one of moderation.
Very few nobles like Talleyrand, Bishop of Autun, managed to
weather all storms and even he in the end was forced to emigrate.
And the alternatives revolted their pride.

'N'émigrez point,' counselled the shrewd prelate to a lady, 'ni
Paris ni les châteaux ne sont tenables, mais allez dans quelque
petite ville, vivez-y sans vous faire remarquer.'

'Fi, Monsieur d'Autun, paysanne tant que voudra,' she replied,
'bourgeoise jamais.'

The Marquis de Falaiseau was convinced that the emigration
was mistaken but could not withstand the general contagion. He
was not a man of the Court but was brought up in the country,
preferring its simple pleasures to the sophistications of Paris. Marat
had been one of his tutors although he does not seem to have

influenced his ideas, possibly because he was found guilty of theft and was chased from the Falaiseaus' château.

The Marquis had married the great-niece of Dupleix of Indian fame, a marriage of inclination, a rare phenomenon in the eighteenth century, and the Falaiseaus were a devoted and rather intellectual couple, very popular on their estates. In spite of the fact that Falaiseau, who had served in the musketeers as a young man, was elected colonel of his local National Guard his country home was invaded by a band of revolutionaries, which determined the Falaiseaus to leave for Paris with thoughts of going further. Their friends wrote to them from across the frontier, urging them to leave, saying that in three months' time they would return and all would be as before.

Madame de Falaiseau's mother and family strongly disapproved of the émigrés, considering them to be fools who were ruining themselves and compromising their families but the point of honour prevailed over reason and, in spite of all his doubts and hesitations, the Marquis left for Coblentz, to be joined three months later by his wife.

The concerted efforts of the family did not prevent the appropriation of their estates and Falaiseau wrote to his wife:

'So our estates have been sequestrated. It is very sad news and I cannot view it with the indifference they do here. But I had made my decision. I have said for a long time that we are committing a great folly. My family had already lost, on account of its religion and emigration (Falaiseau came of Huguenot stock) a large part of its fortune. I shall lose the whole lot.'

Madame de Falaiseau's mother wrote to her:

'Since you keep on telling me that honour is above everything and that all personal interest must be sacrificed to it without question, then I should have to believe that those who haven't followed your example are dishonoured, which I am unable to do.'

But, although he had no enthusiasm for the part he had undertaken to play, Falaiseau, once engaged, could not in honour withdraw.

One for whom the issue was clear-cut and simple was the

Comte Eugène de La Ferronays, an intransigent Royalist on whose mind the cloud of politics had never fallen.

Since the days when Payen Ferron de La Ferronays had hired a boat with Bonabès de Rougé to sail with Saint Louis to the Crusades in each generation the old Breton family of La Ferronays had furnished a regiment to the King of France. Comte Eugène himself had spilled his blood and money with equal recklessness in the Seven Years' War and it was without question or hesitation that he offered his sword to the King's champions across the Rhine.

His absences with his regiment or at Court left him little time for his wife and children nor did their education concern him greatly.

'One is always well brought up,' he said, 'when one comes from good stock.'

His only son, Auguste, fed by romantic dreams and stories of his own family, grew up confounding the history of France with the history of the La Ferronays. Like his compatriot, Chateaubriand, with whose career his own would have such strange parallels, he breathed in with his native air of Brittany a soft melancholy, born of the eternal soughing of the sea upon its rocky coast. He inherited his father's Breton susceptibility to the point of honour and passion for the profession of arms. To his mother, neglected by her husband and yearning for the sunshine of her native Martinique, he owed his beautiful dark eyes and the ardour and the mysticism of his nature.

His bitter-sweet childhood ended abruptly when his uncle, the Bishop of Lisieux, grew alarmed at the exaltation of mind and spirit shown by his nephew. Through his intervention Auguste was sent to school in Paris, an unhappy period from which the Revolution, proving in this alone not his enemy, rescued him. Comte Eugène, emigrating in 1790, took his young son with him but, while he joined the Army of the Princes as soon as it was formed, Auguste was once more sent to school.

For men like the Comte Eugène de La Ferronays and the Comte de Montsoreau and for the children to whom they handed down their traditions and beliefs what enterprise was more glorious than to oppose their bodies between their King and the men who, on their debased altars, had sworn his ruin? What other sovereign ruler could there be for them, born defenders of his throne, than the King? What other banners could they carry than the lilies of France? What other emblem could they fight under than the white plume of Henri of Navarre? If this loyalty involved danger and hardship it only made their choice more glorious, their fidelity more fervent, their honour more shining. Honour, more than life, far more than the hope of regaining their lands and their property, the fantastical point of honour, was the supreme inspiration for which so many Frenchmen forsook their homes and their families to seek new destinies, not under the device of a subservient feudalism, but of an ancient chivalry.

> 'Mon âme à Dieu
> Ma vie au Roi,
> L'honneur à moi.'

Coblentz

Coblentz in May, 1791, dreamed in the Rhenish sunshine, only the great fortress of Ehrenbreitstein casting its shadow from across the river. Life was peaceful and *gemütlich* under the benevolent eye of the Elector Clement-Wenceslaus, Archbishop of Trier, who kept his court in the new palace which dominated the city.

By the end of June a complete change had come over Coblentz. More French than German was heard in the streets while the cafés were thronged with those émigrés who had responded to the appeal of the Comtes de Provence and d'Artois and the Prince de Condé to join them there to prepare an armed intervention on behalf of the King.

After two years of confused and purposeless journeying the original émigrés found a rallying-point in Coblentz and a cohesive society where their moral solitude ended. The new émigrés knew only the fear that they would be dishonoured by a late arrival at the post assigned by honour, to organise themselves into regular units to oppose the Revolution by force.

But if numbers were required to swell the military ranks of the *émigration d'honneur* the rules of admission were still severe. However ardent their desire to serve bourgeois were turned away. Quarterings were still more important than enthusiasm. Even the Marquis de Falaiseau had to inscribe himself at an office where he was given a certificate to show how he had presented himself. He was required to furnish the date of his departure from France and, in addition, a document signed by four gentlemen in his regiment who gave their word of honour that he was *dans les bons principes*. Then, and then only, could he be presented to the Princes.

For the Comte de Provence the experience of emigration was still a novelty but for Artois, after two years of rebuffs and reversals of fortune, Coblentz seemed a return to the old and sweet way of life. From the moment he made his entry into the city, surrounded by a suite of sixty cavaliers and greeted by a salute of a hundred guns, he opened like a flower touched by frost which revives under the sun's rays.

The Royal brothers set up their courts in the castle of Schönbornlust lent to them by their uncle, the Elector, and here, surrounded each by his own favourites and intimates, they recaptured something of the atmosphere, the glory and the luxury of Versailles.

With Provence were his wife and his *chère amie*, the Comtesse de Balbi, lady-in-waiting to the Comtesse de Provence. Madame de Balbi, who was a great *intrigante* and aspired to play a political rôle, enjoyed all the prestige and none of the disadvantages of mistress to the King's brother.

Artois had left his wife with her father in Turin and Louise de Polastron reigned over his household in company with her friends, the Comtesse de Poulpry and the Marquise de Lage, who had been granted leave of absence from her post by the Princesse de Lamballe. Comte Adhémar de Polastron had taken his squadron to Coblentz but it was too embarrassing for him to remain there in face of his wife's open liaison with the Comte d'Artois and he left for Worms to join Condé.

Soon Artois' familiar circle was practically complete with the arrival of the Comtesse de Montaut and her daughter (who became the Duchesse de Gontaut), and of the Duchesse de Guiche, daughter of the Duchesse de Polignac.

The Comte de Montaut had served with distinction in the Seven Years' War and had been one of the tutors of Louis XVI and his brothers. His widow and daughter were devoted Royalists and Madame de Gontaut was to remain intimately associated with the Comte d'Artois and his family all her long life, ultimately becoming *gouvernante* to his grandchildren. By a strange irony of fate Monsieur de Montaut had been instrumental in securing Napoleon Bonaparte's nomination to the Academy at Brienne and thus played a vital, if unknown, part in the history of the world.

In her childhood Madame de Gontaut had been one of the bevy of adoring young people round Madame de Genlis, governor of the children of the regicide Duc d'Orléans, but she and her mother were outraged to find them all in the early days of the

Revolution dancing to the revolutionary theme song, the *Ça ira*, while Madame de Genlis presided smiling in a dress in the national colours of the tricolour. It was apparent that this was no place for the King's adherents and Madame de Montaut immediately made up her mind to leave Paris as soon as possible but not before she had donated part of her fortune to aid the King's escape.

At Coblentz the atmosphere was infinitely more congenial, no wild songs, no hated tricolour. Everything was ordered as at Versailles. The Comte d'Artois kept royal state, covers for a hundred persons being laid every day while five nights a week he gave grand dinners for his entourage. He took great interest in the uniforms of the different regiments that were being formed and designed for his own corps an elegant dress of red and royal blue.

The young Comte de Neuilly, commissioned into Artois' *guet des gardes*, was so charmed with his green uniform reversed with scarlet and laced with silver and his captain's epaulettes that he would get up during the night to admire himself in the mirror.

Everything seemed to indicate that the days of exile would not now be prolonged and inevitably the émigrés from Versailles, who breathed only in an atmosphere of intrigue and jockeying for place, looked to consolidate the position they had won for themselves by their loyalty. If society was feverish it was because its temperature was raised by the prospect of an early cure for the *mal du pays*, from which the émigrés suffered acutely, and the tremendous moral shock they had sustained through the sudden disruption of an orderly and settled way of life into an existence of mental and material insecurity.

They made matters worse for themselves by the financially ruinous way in which many of them lived. Since they had for the most part left France with little money, thinking it not worth while to take large sums for the short time of their absence, they gaily sold their jewellery and other movable assets to keep pace with the style set by Artois. Rose Bertin, the Queen's dressmaker, found her old clients as eager to buy her fashions at extortionate prices in Coblentz as they had been at Versailles.

The twelve thousand livres that Madame de Lage received for her diamond chain was soon swallowed up in the silks and laces necessary for her crowded social life but it was of minor importance since she would undoubtedly soon be back in Paris!

Stéphanie d'Amblimont, Marquise de Lage de Volude, is one of the most attractive figures of the emigration. Her devotion to the Royalist cause and her great affection for Louise de Polastron show a most pleasing strength and sweetness of character. All through the years of exile she ran hither and thither across Europe to give the comfort of her presence to her friends and relatives in distress, and her attachment to the Bourbon cause ended only with the line.

The sober elements of the emigration and most of the professional soldiers, who were repelled by the frivolity and extravagance of Coblentz, preferred to join the corps being raised by the Prince de Condé at near-by Worms.

Louis-Joseph de Bourbon-Condé, the only living soldier among the Bourbons, was the grandson of the Great Condé, venerated as victor of Rocroi, and himself a victorious general of the Seven Years' War. He had the stability of character and the military experience which Artois lacked and he clung tenaciously to his plan of armed opposition to the Revolution through nine long years of reversals.

The rivalries and intrigues among the three parties of the emigration, headed by Provence, Artois and Condé, could only weaken the common cause. On one point alone were they early in agreement. The King could no longer be considered as playing any active part, especially after the voting of the Constitution in September, 1791. Henceforward they regarded him as powerless and, since he patently could no longer help himself, the duty of restoring to him those powers, which he had ceded under duress, devolved on his family and subjects across the frontiers of France.

Louis now did nothing to refute this belief. He blew hot and cold about the emigration, at one moment thinking with Marie Antoinette that its swelling size was to be deplored, at another that with it lay his only hope. It is understandable that, as more and more of their natural defenders crossed the frontiers and the shadows of their destiny grew longer, the King and Queen should feel themselves isolated although they must at the same time have been aware how powerless the nobility was to raise the standard for their defence within the kingdom.

Given so much vacillation on the part of the King, and lacking any sure directive from him, it did indeed seem that in the émigrés lay the sole hope for his deliverance and that of France.

Such at any rate was the thought of the young and the old who rushed to join the Army of the Princes in accordance with their instinct, their education and their *Weltanschauung*. If they set extravagant store on the puerilities of etiquette and the refinements of the point of honour this was the way in which they had been educated and they redeemed themselves from the charge of irresponsibility by the readiness with which they faced death. They met it with the same dignity and even gaiety with which their relatives and friends at home mounted the tumbrils, although some of them might come to think that even the guillotine was preferable to the long littleness of the emigration.

But, in spite of the doubters and the fact that underneath the gaudy surface there was already heart-breaking distress, all seemed justified in 1791 and 1792 at Coblentz. The émigrés were convinced that the sovereigns of Europe were thinking only of France. They were not mistaken. The Powers indeed had their eye on her but only to calculate how long her state of helplessness and anarchy would last and how they might profit thereby. Neither Catherine the Great nor Frederick William of Prussia nor even the Emperor was likely to lose the opportunity of modifying the map of Europe in their own interest while France was powerless to resist.

That, of course, was not the way the French émigrés saw it. Ignorant for the most part of politics and inexperienced in the ways of European diplomacy, like Artois they took the Declaration of Pillnitz, with its promise of intervention in their cause, at its face value, not understanding the implications of its provisos and reservations.

Little was permitted to daunt their belief in the triumph of their cause. Their native gaiety had not yet been diminished, although it would never be wholly extinguished, by misfortune. In community they found all the reassurance they needed. They had an over-riding compulsion to run after the latest rumours, the most recent news, even the most worthless opinions, because in unity lay strength and in reunion they could forget their bewilderment and the apprehension which sometimes lay under their brave exterior. The lightest expression of hope, the merest scrap of encouraging news, immediately re-inforced their gaiety, their courage and their exaltation, rekindling their desire to terminate their precarious situation, always providing that the way back home lay along the *chemin de l'honneur*.

The most enthusiastic, the most eloquent among them was the Comte d'Artois. Finding himself again at the head of a party and in a position of authority revived his ideas of his own value and consequence and when he returned from Vienna to Coblentz, proud of his diplomatic success with the Powers, he became an object of adoration among the émigrés. This was not only Artois' finest hour but the apogee of the emigration.

The Comte de Provence remained prudently in the background at this time, greeting his younger brother on his entry with a reception usually reserved for a conquering hero, although the adulation with which Artois was regarded was in fact little to his taste or to that of the cooler and wiser head of the Prince de Condé.

Provence had far greater political acumen than Artois but he also had too much sagacity to appear to run counter to the general opinion and he preferred to approve the conduct of his brother in public while making every effort to maintain his prestige as the elder.

He did allow himself a quip at Artois' expense.

'There are no two ways about it,' he exclaimed, 'the Comte d'Artois is a *pur* and I am not.'

A *pur* made no concession to any ideas of reform, of constitutional monarchy or of any infringement of Royal rights. The *purs* were the irridentist émigrés who would never return to France except with the white cockade and their legitimate sovereign and it was they who remained proudly in exile when the usurper and upstart Bonaparte facilitated the return of the proscribed.

Artois' high summer had reached its meridian and the long hours of sunshine now began to decline. Even the passive Elector tired of the intrigues and luxurious display of his nephews and their following and most especially of paying for them. Money grew shorter everywhere. The Duchesse de Fitz-James, living in another part of Germany, skimped and scraped out of the eightpence a day on which she had to live to send a louis or

two to her sons with the émigré armies. The troops drilled with
sticks instead of with guns and often they had scarcely enough
to eat.

Calonne, the former minister of Louis XVI, and Madame de
Polastron had laid their fortunes at Artois' feet but his expenses
were a gulf no amount of gold could fill. He had no experience of
finance, least of all the maintenance of an inactive army. Everyone
talked, for talk was the primary activity of Coblentz, everyone
discussed, but nobody took any action. All through this gale of
conversation Artois remained unruffled and optimistic.

'No one here,' wrote Louise de Polastron to Madame de Lage
who had returned to her post, 'indulges the least doubt.'

Poor languid Louise, whose great gift lay in providing Artois
with tender affection and the background and atmosphere in
which he liked to live, was not a distinguished political observer.
As the months of inaction went by demoralisation did begin to
creep in, especially among those who had hesitated as to the
wisdom of emigration. They did not doubt the justice of their
cause, only whether they could bring it to a successful conclusion.
The émigrés began uneasily to realise that the impasse they were
in offered slender chances of escape.

In Condé's army material distress started early, mainly because
it was largely made up of the less wealthy elements.

> 'We are completely without food and half of us haven't eaten
> to-day,' wrote the Marquis de Falaiseau from the camp to his
> wife in Coblentz. 'Everyone is so poor and everything is so
> badly organised that it is impossible to obtain the essentials.
> Fatigue is absolute. Our lives are much harder than those of the
> ordinary soldier as our commissariat and our marches are not
> assured. Last night we slept in the open, our stomachs empty.
> Before wrapping ourselves in our cloaks we cried three times
> at the top of our voices, *Vive le roi!*'

But an army is not made up of loyalty, of principles or of
sacrifices alone. It is made up of men, of trained soldiers of
similar age, size and strength. The Princes' army, according to
Chateaubriand, was very different; a confused mass of mature men,
of the old, of children scarcely out of their swaddling clothes,
speaking a confused mass of dialects, norman, breton, picard,

auvergnat, gascon, provençal, and the langue d'oc. (It must be remembered that it was far from being the courtiers of Versailles alone who made up the Princes' army. At most they numbered ten thousand men and women, not all of whom emigrated. It was the provincial nobility, the gentry and the squirearchy who swelled its ranks.)

'However ridiculous this motley collection appeared it still offered a spectacle at once honourable and touching because it was actuated by sincere convictions. It represented the old monarchy, a last display of a world which was vanishing.

'I have seen old gentlemen, grey-haired and of severe aspect, their clothing worn, knapsacks on their backs and their rifles slung over their shoulders, dragging themselves forward with a stick and supported on the arm of one of their sons; I have seen the father of my friend who was massacred at my side at Rennes marching sad and alone, bare-footed in the mud, and carrying his shoes on the point of his bayonet for fear of wearing them out.

'All this poverty-stricken troop made war at its own expense as it did not receive a sou from the princes, while at home the decrees completed their destitution and threw wives and mothers into prison.'

Preparations for war continued and Artois' justification and a revival of enthusiasm for all came in March, 1792, when France, taking the initiative, declared war on Austria. He saw himself, henceforward honoured as his country's saviour, at the head of the Allied armies, for Prussia marched with Austria, flanked by his two sons, the Ducs d'Angoulême and de Berri, crossing the French frontier at a gallop, the white plume of Henri of Navarre waving in his hat, and re-establishing the monarchy in its ancient glory.

Nor was it Artois' moment alone. The whole of the emigration which since 1789 had been waiting in the wings now sprang to take the centre of the stage.

Cruel deception! It was no part of the Allied plans to put the émigrés in the forefront either of their military operations or of their subsequent intentions. The Duke of Brunswick, who was in command of the Prussian army, naturally enough took offence at Artois' imperious,

'The Prussian army! We have no need of the Prussian army!'

A more experienced general than Artois, who had no experience at all beyond an abortive expedition to Gibraltar as a young man, Brunswick did not share his view that the forthcoming campaign would be a walkover and he regarded the émigrés as an entirely useless and additional burden of which he would willingly have been relieved.

Nevertheless, after the ceremonial blessing of their colours, the Army of the Princes set out on the march in July, 1792, *pour Dieu et le Roi*. Their pain at taking up arms against their compatriots was assuaged by their ardent hope of liberating their king. He who marched under the white flag of the Bourbons was a soldier armed not against France but against the felons of the Revolution. These so-called 'shabby remnants of a subservient feudalism' burned with the chivalry of their Crusading ancestors and though they deplored the ill-success of their own arms they were proud of the valour of their French opponents.

'The enemy is French,' they said, 'which is enough to say he did not falter.'

Nothing ever encroached upon or superseded their love of their country and they never neglected an occasion of protesting against any attempt to lessen the glory of France.

But chivalry and the will to fight do not make a fighting unit and the fundamental weakness of the Army of the Princes, its lack of military training and discipline, became apparent as soon as it left the shelter of the camp.

While events at home like the attack on the Tuileries in August, 1792, only reinforced their determination, their horror and their sorrow could not turn their inchoate mass into an army. They made matters worse for themselves by allowing the émigré ladies to accompany them on the early stages of the march so that the roads were choked with carriages, impeding their own progress.

The initial successes of Brunswick's army at Longwy and Verdun raised their hopes but simultaneously came the news of the September massacres in Paris, the cold-blooded and premeditated murder of prisoners awaiting trial, and then at the end of September the decisive victory of the revolutionaries at Valmy and the defeat of the Allied army.

A day later the Convention met in Paris and on September 22nd, 1792, the monarchy, for which they were enduring and fighting, and which they had been so confident of restoring to its old supremacy, was abolished. To defeat on the field was added the moral collapse of the complete dissolution of their hopes. Henceforward France would fight under the tricolour, the lilies trampled under the feet of the advancing armies of the Revolution, legality on the side of the victors.

The Prussians decided to retreat, showing as little consideration for the émigrés in defeat as they had shown in the advance. The émigrés stumbled on their way, beaten and battered, in long forced marches along roads deep in mire, hampered by the ladies in their carriages and the carts bearing the wounded, all bedevilled by the ceaseless rain, which beat down remorselessly, and the merciless mud.

It was the beginning of a new era of vicissitudes, of privations and of sacrifices. The disorder of the retreat was appalling and more than ever the folly made itself felt of going to war as to manœuvres.

For the young there was still the future but for the aged, dragging their grey hairs and sorrows in the interminable retreat, the fortunate supported by their sons, the others by memories alone, there was only the bitter joy of faithfulness to their cause and to their honour. More even than material and physical distress they felt the moral pain of the death of the ideas by which they had lived. In a world in which customs, tastes, pleasures and habits all took on a different complexion from those they had known their only feeling was one of bewilderment.

The case of the ladies who had set out so gaily to accompany their husbands, sons and lovers to victory was even worse than that of the men. There would be no rendezvous in Paris; it might be that they would never meet again. Nothing in their sheltered lives had prepared them for the rigours of these long days of horror and the more dreadful nights when they were obliged to find shelter where they could.

Writing at the age of eighty of this nightmare journey, the

Duchesse de Gontaut vividly recalled her experiences, as fresh in her memory as if they had taken place yesterday. She and her mother, the Duchesse de Guiche and Mesdames de Poulpry and de Lage had found for themselves a large barn with fresh straw on which they hoped to pass a restful night, under the protection of a chasseur of the Duchesse de Guiche, who stood outside with drawn sword.

They were summarily awakened by a woman's voice, demanding shelter, to see Madame de Calonne in full dress, powdered and painted as if she were going to a reception at Versailles, calling to her lackeys for lights.

When she saw bodies lying in the straw she cried out in horror, only to redouble her cries when she saw corpses hanging from the rafters. But the corpses were sheep killed ready for market and the bodies were not dead or wounded soldiers but her friends lying asleep, and all ended in laughter.

But laughter in those days was all too infrequent. What hope was now left to the émigrés? Their unwilling allies were in full retreat. The French revolutionary armies were across the Rhine and streaming into Belgium. For the Princes' army it was the end.

'When an army is disbanded it goes back to its home; but did the soldiers of Condé's army have homes? Where would the staff, which they had barely been allowed to cut from a German tree, lead them, now that they had laid down the muskets that they had shouldered for the defence of their King? They had to separate. The brothers in arms bade each other a final farewell and went their ways.'*

No longer an organised body they were left to their own resources, their leaders in equally sad case. In Belgium and in Holland they found a charitable reception but the Germans showed in their true colours. The French whom they had welcomed in their days of good fortune were spurned in the day of their disaster. So the émigrés stumbled always eastward from the State which said, 'Get out,' to the State which said, 'Don't come in.'

* Chateaubriand: *Mémoires touchant la Vie et la Mort du duc de Berri.*

At Cologne the Elector had signs put out banning from his territories Jews, outlaws and émigrés. He did not foresee the days when he, in his turn, would be proscribed and cast out. One of the Frenchwomen whom he had expelled said that, when she had seen him as an émigré, *she* had not jeered at his misfortune.

No race worships force as does the Teuton and it found in the beaten French fit objects to be humiliated, harassed, despoiled and exploited without pity and without shame. Not only the Germans subjected the émigrés to brutal treatment. In Berlin their worst enemies were the descendants of those French Huguenots who had been expelled from France in 1685 by the Revocation of the Edict of Nantes. Forgetting that their ancestors, too, had suffered in the same way and remembering only that they had been cast out from their fatherland, they called down on the heads of the Catholic French the bitterness of biblical curses, their vengefulness intensified by the German blood with which theirs was now mingled.

Perhaps the only person in this welter of misery who was reasonably happy was Chateaubriand. Although his physical sufferings were as great as anyone else's he was able to survey the scenes around him with the objective eye of the creative artist and to amuse himself by correcting the pages of *Atala* in the midst of the ruins. But his detachment was shared by few of his companions in arms. Bitterly might they echo his words if they had looked over his shoulder as he wrote:

'Happy are those who have not seen the smoke rising from the feasts of strangers and who have sat only at the rejoicings of their fathers. Long habits of love, so necessary to existence, you filled the days of those who have never left their native country.'

Henceforward for many long years the émigrés would sit only by alien fires, their rejoicings always tinged with sorrow, while they wept for their native land by the waters of many Babylons. Emigration had become exile.

IV

Journey to England

'The world was all before them, where to choose
Their place of rest, and Providence their guide'

but it was no Eden the émigrés were leaving. For them that lay
westwards to France but its gates were guarded by the flaming
swords of the rapacious and bloodthirsty men of the Revolution,
so intoxicated with the success of their arms that they now dared
to imprison their King and soon would bring him to trial.

Belgium, most nearly accessible and within the scope of purses
for the most part becoming intolerably slender, almost immediately became untenable for the émigrés. Many of them now turned
their eyes towards England where they might put the barrier of
the Channel between themselves and the pursuit of the Revolutionary armies. Faithful to his policy of neutrality, Pitt had refused
to take any part when France declared war against Austria and
later, still holding to his chosen course, he rejected overtures from
the French Princes to join the struggle so that in England the
émigrés knew that, whatever else might await them, they would
at least find physical safety.

The numbers who sought refuge here had been increasing in
1792. As Constituent Assembly succeeded National Assembly, to
be replaced first by the Legislative Assembly and then by the
Convention, the discredited members of these governments were
themselves proscribed. Fleeing from the terrors they had been
instrumental in provoking they eagerly took advantage of the
political asylum offered by England, although their arrival here
was viewed in informed circles with a certain distaste, especially
after the September massacres.

James Bland Burges, then Under-Secretary at the Foreign
Office, and a convinced antagonist of the Revolution, noted, however, in a letter to Lord Auckland, after the English had supped

full of the horrors of the massacres in the newspapers, that such a diet was often the only means by which public conscience is aroused.

'The late horrors in France have at least been attended with one good consequence, for they have turned the tide of general opinions here very suddenly. French principles and French men are daily becoming more unpopular and I think it not impossible that in a short time the imprudence of some of these levellers will work so much on the temper of our people as to make England neither a pleasant nor a secure residence for them.'

Lord Auckland's letters and those of his correspondents are an invaluable source of information about the sentiments of politicians and the *ton* towards the French émigrés. A friend of Pitt, who at one time was on the point of marrying his daughter, Eleanor, Auckland himself knew the French well. As Sir William Eden he negotiated the Anglo-French Commercial Treaty of 1786. He was Ambassador at the Hague from 1791 to 1793 where, and later at his country house at Beckenham when he was out of office, his friends kept him posted as to the *on-dits* of society in town, of which the topic of the émigrés, many of whom were personally known to these correspondents, was the first in importance.

At the Hague Auckland himself had plenty of opportunity of observing the French of whom he patently disapproved.

He had written to Mr. Burges:

'The levity and gaiety of the French in the midst of the calamities and the disgrace of their own country and in despite of the ruin of their own individual interests are beyond all belief.'

Evidently Lord Auckland had never heard of laughing that one might not weep. What is less understandable in a man of the eighteenth century is that he ignored that convention of good breeding which does not permit a display of one's personal feelings to the embarrassment of others.

Resentment against certain of the émigrés continued to run high. Anthony Storer, Whig, dilettante and man of fashion, reputedly the best skater and dancer of his time, wrote to Auckland:

'Even Noailles has taken refuge in England, the last country in which he ought to have shown his face. Lafayette and he, Noailles, were treated in England with a generosity and frankness that no foreigners ever before or since experienced, and yet they went, warm with our civilities, in the most treacherous manner, as if they had come here merely as spies, to attack us in America. The Town swarms with these ex-members of the Assemblée Nationale.'

In the eighteenth century the English were apparently not a nation of such short memories as Sir Winston Churchill has said they are in the twentieth and it is obvious that, as some of the more percipient émigrés feared, Lafayette's knight errantry in the American War of Independence was still remembered with animosity.

Auckland, too, deplored the presence of so many of the 'coxcombs of the Assemblée Constituante, who called themselves philosophers and legislators,' while Mr. Burges expressed himself with even greater acerbity:

'Of those who are known, I am sure not one, except a few harmless old women, deserve anything; for the whole class were Jacobins and persecutors so long as they were in power, and would be so still, were they not supplanted by others of the same stamp.'

Burges, who was married to a Frenchwoman, daughter of the Baron de Saint-Hippolite, ought really to have known better than to lump the whole of the French aristocracy and even the members of the Assemblies into so sweeping a condemnation.

Since he believed that the higher orders of the aristocracy were deeply implicated in the guilt of the Revolution he feared bad consequences from the residence of the émigrés here and felt he had good reason to think that they were visitors more for the purpose of doing mischief than from any other motives.

The émigrés themselves had other causes of anxiety. They knew that thousands of destitute people had landed in England before. There had been the influx of Flemings in the sixteenth century, fleeing from religious persecution, and of the Huguenots after the Massacre of St. Bartholomew and again after the Revocation of the Edict of Nantes in 1685.

When the Huguenots poured into England they had come as martyrs in a common cause to a Protestant country where they might reasonably expect, and did in fact find, a sympathetic welcome. Dared the Roman Catholic descendants of their oppressors, seeking asylum in a land which only grudgingly allowed the fewest possible rights to its own Catholic minority and where, fifteen years after the Gordon Riots, cries of 'No Popery' still lingered on the air, hope to find a comparable reception? Nor did they forget that France and England were traditional enemies and rare had been the periods when they were not actively engaged in war against each other. Was it to be expected that the English would show tolerance to those now seeking their protection and, when the ancient rivalries still persisted, welcome into their homes the French who were making a virtue of necessity?

It was yet another risk the émigrés had to take for there was no alternative. In spite of Mr. Burges's fears they were far more concerned with the hazards of their journey than with any projects of reinforcing the Radical movement in England or attempts to overthrow the Government, ideas which they did not entertain.

After the defeat of the Allies and the disbanding of the Princes' Army the Marquis de Falaiseau, his wife and family, made their painful way to Holland where they endured the hardships of a rigorous winter. Unable to speak the language, burdened with their young children and a prey to perpetual cruel anxiety as to the fate of their relatives and friends in France, they found Holland unfriendly and inhospitable. Inns and means of transport were at astronomical prices. From Nijmegen to Rotterdam the only place they could find on a boat was in a hold where the cables were stowed and here they travelled in the greatest discomfort, but only too glad to be putting some distance between themselves and the pursuing French army.

On New Year's Day, 1793, Madame de Falaiseau bitterly surveyed the present and the future:

'Separated perhaps for ever from my family, proscribed, a wanderer outlawed from my country, no longer possessing anything, far from all I knew and loved in my childhood, from

44

my days of happiness, I saw around me nothing but distress and no hope for the future at all.'

Added to the material discomforts of a wretched inn room in which were huddled seven people the Falaiseaus had to decide between two perils, the enemy behind and the unknown sea before them.

'We had to undertake at a rigorous and dangerous season a sea voyage for the first time, with a nursing infant, weakly, apathetic and worn out with changes of nurse and with all the vicissitudes it had been obliged to undergo; with a wet nurse whose temper was uncertain and bad, whose health was disturbed by the slightest crossing of her will, who was very nervous of the sea journey, and who threatened not to come with us on account of all the shipwrecks and sinister events which everyone said were liable to happen at this wretched season of the year.'

There were two ways of leaving Holland, one to take the packet from Helvoetsluys which was quicker but far dearer, and on which it was difficult to get a passage. The packets were often delayed for weeks because of storms and contrary winds and many people were forced to stay on board in appalling conditions. The second alternative, to embark at Rotterdam on a merchant ship which would take them direct to London, seemed more practical and cheaper to the Falaiseaus.

Finally the weathercock, which they had consulted a thousand times a day, turned to the north, resolving their doubts and hesitations, and the party embarked, accompanied by their faithful servants, whose service continued to be as devoted as it was disinterested.

The English never ceased to wonder at the degree of devotion manifested by the servants of the French émigrés, greatly admiring their unalterable attachment to their masters.

So many unhappy émigrés had waited for so long for this wind from the north, so many had exhausted the few resources they still possessed in an unfriendly and ruinously expensive country that all were wildly impatient. Two had killed themselves since they had spent their passage money to keep alive while waiting for the wind to turn.

Others embarked in hordes, packed closer and tighter than on a slaver. Some had forced their captains to leave with the first breath of wind, without waiting for it to strengthen, and were becalmed at the mouth of the river, unable to cross the sea, battered by the storm or marooned on sand bars and dying of hunger, with vermin and misfortunes of every kind.

The Falaiseaus, still lucky possessors of twenty-five louis, paid for a cabin on the ship, *Friendship*, a two-masted brig, normally carrying a cargo of coal, now filled with miserable émigrés and horses. Their cabin contained thirteen people. The hold had been equipped for a hundred émigrés, each paying a guinea, by constructing little stalls, two feet six inches wide and six feet long, divided by a partition a foot high, and filled with fresh straw. This was their home for three days—if the voyage did not take longer— three days of discomfort, monotony and danger.

A break in the monotony was not always welcome. One day a sail was sighted which the captain thought was that of a French vessel making towards him. The prospect for the émigrés of being taken off by a French ship and hauled to certain prison and the guillotine was terrifying. At last from afar the ship was seen to be taking the same direction as the *Friendship*. The wretched sea-sick émigrés breathed again.

Sight of the English coast brought a general cry of joy. The interest that the English were known to have demonstrated in the plight of the émigrés, the protection and generous hospitality they had given, in spite of privately expressed unfavourable opinions, inspired hope and confidence and for the moment other fears were forgotten.

'We passed,' said Madame de Falaiseau, as they anchored off Harwich, 'one of the sweetest nights I had spent for a very long time and above all our awakening had lost its customary bitterness.'

The day that dawned was one of astonishment, light and tenderness as it reunited her with her family in London, the Floyers of Portland Place, human beings who cared about her and about whom she cared. They earned her especial gratitude not so much for the material help they gave as for their expressed detestation of the Revolution and their respect and pity for the

46

émigrés. After the indifference or hostility they had encountered it was a welcome experience to find in relatives who were almost strangers so sympathetic an attitude to the cause for which they were suffering.

Yet the Falaiseaus would not stay in England. The Marquis was still tormented by the loss of his property, not for his own sake but for his children's. They determined to brave all the dangers of a return to France to see whether they could not get their names erased from the fatal list of émigrés.

In spite of all their efforts and those made by Madame de Falaiseau's mother and sister they were unsuccessful and, being in danger of denunciation, they were forced to take to flight. From Abbeville, where they had been hiding, they were conducted over the frontier by a friendly peasant, Madame de Falaiseau disguised in striped skirt and muslin kerchief with a mob cap and heavy black shoes and coarse stockings.

One more journey the Marquis made to England to leave the children in the care of friends, then he and his wife wandered across the Continent until finally they found a temporary home in Hamburg.

When Coblentz was evacuated the Duchesse de Gontaut and her mother succeeded with difficulty in finding a skiff in which to escape the bombs thrown from the fortress of Ehrenbreitstein. Once out of range they transferred to carts and, after a deplorable journey, they, too, succeeded in reaching Rotterdam, in that winter of bitter cold and disastrous floods.

The Comte de Gontaut-Biron, who was to be her husband, urged Mademoiselle de Montaut and her mother to go to England and in the spring they managed to make their way to Harwich. The first English word they heard on their arrival made the Duchesse's heart beat faster and the cordial reception they met with inspired her with an affection for England in which she never wavered.

But often, when the émigrés had succeeded with difficulty in embarking on a boat, the sailors would amuse themselves by frightening the poor creatures, in sight of escape from years of misery and persecution, of cold and hunger, of prison and approach to death.

What could have been the feelings of a man like Monsieur de

Crosne, Lieutenant of Police, who already had the rope around his neck but managed to escape when his executioners' attention was distracted by a new tumult, and others who had been in similar danger when, once out at sea, the men would point to the shores of France and England, jeering,

'There's a good wind blowing. In two hours we shall be in France.'

Purses were emptied and money pressed upon the laughing crews, who pocketed the coins—and sailed towards England. But achieving safety often meant the sacrifice of everything that might keep them alive once they reached it.

The proximity of Sheffield Park, near Lewes, to the Sussex coast where so many émigrés landed gave Lord Sheffield an earlier opportunity of hearing of French arrivals and proffering practical help than was possible for others.

As he wrote to Lord Auckland:

'I have been particularly occupied (I did not want extra work) in favour of the French clergy.'

Lord Sheffield held a far more tolerant view of the émigrés than did either Auckland or Burges. He was not only morally sympathetic but made great exertions on their behalf. Lady Sheffield, too, gave them considerable aid and her early death was in part attributed to her efforts on their behalf, particularly in looking after the sick.

As a friend of Gibbon perhaps Lord Sheffield looked on the decline and fall of the French monarchy with a historian's objectivity although there was nothing objective about the help he gave them.

'The Vicomtesse de Sesmaisons, (niece of that Bishop of Avranches who had so difficult an escape from Normandy),' he wrote to Lord Auckland, 'with four children, her preceptor and two servants, had an extraordinary escape and passage in an open boat to Eastbourne, where they found the utmost attention from the bathers.'

'On Sunday last (this was in October, 1792) notice was given me that a small French vessel with emigrants, women and children, was wrecked near Newhaven. I sent my Swiss servant to interpret and conduct them here. In the evening he brought

48

Madame de Balbany, sister to Madame de Sesmaisons, with her three children, from three to eight years old, as fine brats as ever were seen, their parish priest and man and maid.'

'As an instance how these poor creatures are pillaged, I mention that they were obliged to pay 2,500 livres for their passage before they sailed. As they are safe I am glad the vessel is entirely lost.'

Not so fortunate in finding an immediate protector was the Comtesse de Saisseval. Turned out of the Low Countries by the revolutionaries she threw herself into a boat in the middle of January, one of her children being only thirteen days old. Disembarking at Dover at three o'clock in the afternoon she begged for shelter from door to door until midnight. At each door she was turned away.

'Those nine hours of rebuffs and suffering seemed very long to me,' she said, 'as snow was falling and I saw my poor children dying of cold and hunger.'

At last a passer-by dropped a coin into the hand of one of the children, who ran to her mother, saying:

'Now, Mamma, I can say that I am hungry since we have something with which to buy bread.'

Pride is not the prerogative of the old.

At Brighton Lord Malmesbury watched a fishing-boat land. As he approached it a French sailor held out to him a baby in swaddling clothes, entrusted to him by its mother who had been unable herself to escape. Malmesbury took the child and sent money to its mother, the Vicomtesse de Noailles, who arrived in England a month later.

Those who, like the Falaiseaus, were allied by ties of blood or friendship to English families were assured of a welcome. To the English Harcourts the Duc d'Harcourt represented the senior branch of the family and was given a house at Staines for as long as he cared to use it. The Duke of Grafton invited the Duc de Liancourt to make Euston his home during his exile.

The Stuart supporters, who had followed James II and the Old Pretender to France, were welcomed home again by members of their families when they returned as Frenchmen to the country of their origin.

The Dillon family had been particularly faithful adherents of James II and nearly all the family emigrated with him to France. There they raised a regiment which fought in all the French wars of the eighteenth century until, by the curious quirks of fate, it was, after the Revolution, taken on the strength of the British army as an émigré formation.

Although Lord Dillon had become a Protestant when he returned to England to assume his title he made an annual allowance of a thousand pounds to his uncle, Arthur Dillon, the aged Archbishop of Narbonne. True, the Archbishop had found an income of 350,000 francs insufficient for his style of living in France but a thousand a year was far removed from penury.

Other members of the Irish Brigade were equally fortunate in finding kindly relatives, like the Walsh de Serrants whose uncle, Lord Southwell, wrote to them that he had not forgotten the happy hours he had spent in France with his wife's family and invited them to come to his home at Standen Hall to await the restoration of order and peace.

If the émigrés were apprehensive about their reception by the Protestants they need have no fears about their co-religionists. From all Catholics they received a cordial welcome and Thomas Weld, a relative of Mrs. Fitzherbert's, showed them particular generosity. To the French Trappist monks he gave his residence, Lulworth Castle, while the Jesuit fathers, forced to flee from Liège, were installed in his property at Stonyhurst in Lancashire.

There, almost on the borders of Scotland, country of the Stuarts, the young French émigrés, among them the Vicomte Walsh de Serrant, continued the education they had begun at Liège, finding at Stonyhurst far more romantic associations.

Charles I had stayed there and the room he occupied was preserved as he had left it, which greatly impressed the descendants of the Stuart adherents among the boys.

'We who were mourning Louis XVI and Marie Antoinette,' wrote Walsh, 'bared our heads while our hearts contracted in grief as we approached the bed, covered in red damask, in which had slept this other royal victim of decapitation.'

They found another source of pious interest in the priest-holes, where they were much moved to discover altar vessels and other traces of the rites celebrated by their occupants, and in one such hole they even found a skeleton which showed that a priest had died for his faith in hiding.

The Jesuits treated their pupils with the same kindness that they themselves had received. After Walsh's first four years at Stonyhurst his family found it impossible to continue to pay his fees but he did not learn this until later nor that many of his friends in like circumstances were kept at the charge of instructors who had so little to share.

By the time the Marquise de la Tour du Pin, niece of Lord Dillon, came to England in 1797 the journey from Paris to the coast took three days, not only because she and her party had to appear before all the local authorities situated on the route but because under the revolutionary régime the roads had so greatly deteriorated. She travelled under the escort of Madame de Genlis' brother since gentlemen, even if their acquaintance was of the slightest, would often delay their departure risking their own lives to protect the women.

'Heartbroken, ruined, furious,' wrote Madame de la Tour du Pin, 'we were still able to maintain our good humour and to laugh.'

On her arrival in London she was able to stay with her aunt, Lady Jerningham, at her house in Bolton Row, Piccadilly, and at her country home at Cossey. Feeling, perhaps, that he had done enough for his family all Lord Dillon offered her was the occasional use of his box at the Opera but another uncle, Lord Kenmare, allowed her six louis a month which was of more practical value.

Madame de Lage, who had left her friends in Coblentz and returned to France and many adventures, arrived in London from Lisbon, like

'one of the heroines of an old novel, quite alone, not knowing a word of the language, at a miserable tavern which one of the travellers in the mail coach had suggested to me, but my heart was so full of deep emotion that I saw nothing around me.'

In a disgusting room, smelling of beer and with the remains of someone's supper on the table, she waited for a messenger to find her father, the Comte d'Amblimont, alone and ill in a Soho garret. She had come to London to take care of him, to wait for her husband who was expected with his regiment and, perhaps more important, to see her lover, Comte Charles de Damas.

As she paced up and down that squalid coffee-room in the cold, unfriendly light of a winter morning it may be that her thoughts went back to the gay cavalcades from Versailles to Marly, to St. Germain, to Rambouillet and to Paris, or she may have remembered another arrival, only six years earlier but what worlds away, a May Day in Paris.

She was moving her apartments and on one pretext or another her friends—the gay circle round Marie Antoinette—had given her tasks to do in which none of them seemed inclined to help her. Finally she returned home, harassed and annoyed, to find her windows brilliantly lit and the anteroom and the stairs full of flowers.

The first person she met on crossing the threshold was the Princesse de Lamballe, the spectre of whose lovely head adorning a bloody pike must now haunt her dreams.

Around the Princesse a dozen friends were laughing and chattering as the enchanted Blimonette moved from room to room, admiring the charming gifts they had arranged—the alabaster clock with its statuette of Venus teaching Love to read, the crystal flambeaux, the tea table laid with a delicious white and gold Sèvres service.

At the foot of the canapé was a rose tree in bloom, its branches intertwined with white lilac, and bearing a card:

'Portrait of the mistress of this house.'

Madame de Lage, as she knew, was lucky to be alive. So many of those friends had perished on the guillotine or as victims of the increasing persecutions and atrocities and those who had emigrated were eking out a penurious existence all over the Continent. She herself had passed through many dangers but since many of them had been undergone in the service of her friends Stéphanie de Lage dismissed them as nothing.

At last her messenger returned and led her to her father. Madame de Lage entered into her initiation as an émigrée in England.

Most hideous of all the journeys made to this country was Chateaubriand's. After he left the army of Condé gangrene set in in the wound he had sustained at Valmy. Scarcely had he made some progress towards recovery than he caught smallpox. Barely alive he managed to take ship from Belgium to Jersey where he found refuge with an uncle under whose care his health was slowly restored and, when he was strong enough, he crossed to the mainland and came to London. Here he found friends who made him welcome and shared with him their miserable shelter.

The arrival of the rank and file of émigrés without family, friends or connections in England, was one of confusion and anxiety. First of all, as they stepped ashore, they had to run the gamut of curious eyes for groups of spectators always gathered on the quays, bombarding them with questions to which they were unable to make reply since few of them knew any English. This idle but good-natured curiosity added to their feeling of strangeness and apprehension for they could tell only by the faces of the crowd that they were well-intentioned.

From the coast of England too they had the bitter-sweet satisfaction of seeing still the forbidden shore of France, *tendebantque manus ripae ulterioris amore*. Added to that nostalgia for their country which, under their surface gaiety, was always an open wound, was their natural anxiety for the future. Inevitably experience had made them suspicious and they had learned that the welcoming hand could so easily turn into a closed fist.

Did England really offer them security? Would they be suffered to remain or would they once more have to take up their staffs and wander on and, if so, where? And, if they were allowed to stay, how would they live?

As they moved away from the landing-jetties these and many other questions clouded their minds.

V

Wilmot's Committee

'The fools here are opening subscriptions for the relief and support of the hordes of vagabond French, which I understand our own poor take amiss, and, in my judgment not without reason. I do not indeed see under what pretence all this charity is set forward,'

wrote Mr. Burges to Lord Auckland in September, 1792, following this letter a week later with yet another onslaught upon the émigrés.

'I know also that many of the better class have pretty much the same views, and I sincerely hope that some means may be found of getting rid of them before any bad consequences may come from their residence among us.'

Did Mr. Burges really believe that thousands of refugees, homeless and in want, could be left to starve to death or cast out to certain annihilation in their own country or in those countries of Europe being overrun by their compatriots now their enemies?

Happily for the French Mr. Burges's views were not shared by the majority of Englishmen and Lord Auckland as usual learned the opposite point of view from Lord Sheffield who reported with satisfaction that:

'The poor French have had upon the whole a very good reception, such as does credit to this country,'

and he hoped that there would be a good subscription throughout England. He was gratified to note a few weeks later that:

'The subscription in this country for the French refugees does us some credit but the backwardness of men in administration is passing strange, not one of them, except Lord Hawkesbury, has contributed.'

The spirit of the times as well as that of men like Lord Sheffield was in the émigrés' favour. Social conscience was rapidly developing and philanthropy becoming recognised as a fundamental virtue. The principles of humanitarianism were fast taking hold in the minds of men, ironically enough largely through the influence of the writings of Jean-Jacques Rousseau, to whose teaching the philosophers of the Revolution also owed much, and it is to the great credit of the English people at this time that they listened rather to the voice of conscience than to the ungenerous and inhumane sentiments of men like Burges (although it must be said in his favour that in his personal relations he was kindly and lavish, contributing a thousand pounds towards the payment of Pitt's debts).

For the ordinary Englishman it seemed preferable to run the risk of nurturing a few spies and agitators rather than pass the innocent by on the other side.

The precedent was there.

Although when the Huguenots landed in England in large numbers from 1685 onwards a small number of great families brought considerable sums, most of the fugitives came in a state of extreme destitution.

In spite of his sympathy with Louis XIV's persecution of the Protestants James II found himself obliged to authorise public collections for their benefit, while Parliament hastened to vote funds for their relief. In all some £200,000 sterling was collected. This fund, known as the Royal Bounty, was distributed to the indigent through the efforts of a lay committee, composed of the chiefs of the Huguenots, and a second committee of ecclesiastics, under the direction of the Archbishop of Canterbury, while James II secretly chafed at the necessity of extending his protection to those whom he regarded as his enemies.

The country found its liberality was not misplaced since the Huguenots, with their skills and habit of hard work, added to the prosperity of the country, earning from Parliament in 1709 the right of citizenship.

For those who were still unable to maintain themselves, a number constantly diminishing, Parliament generously continued to provide, its allocation being prolonged until at least the middle of the nineteenth century.

Now the eighteenth century brought a new test of the will and capacity of the English to relieve suffering. As before there were the few with the foresight or the opportunity of providing for their own support. As before there was the mass which depended on the goodwill of the country on whose charity it cast itself. Such is the unvarying pattern of mass emigration for political reasons.

Given the circumstances of the arrival of so many of the émigrés in England, particularly in 1792, and especially of the lower orders of the clergy, it was obvious that the majority would be dependent on whatever help was extended to them. Action was necessary if the émigrés were not to starve to death. But actions spring from men, 'dynamic individuals,' as Lord Beveridge has put it, 'possessed by the spirit of service. They call it forth in others; they create the societies and institutions through which it acts; they lead by their example.'

The hour found its man in John Eardley Wilmot. Now forty-two he was the son of the Lord Chief Justice, a Master in Chancery, who had been Member of Parliament for Tiverton from 1776 to 1784 and for Coventry from 1784 to 1796. Benjamin West's portrait of him* shows a man of fine features, the keen intelligence of his expression tempered by kindliness. The outstanding impression gained from a study of his face is of a character of great probity.

Wilmot was an extremely modest man like his father, who repeatedly refused the Lord Chancellorship and a peerage, so that, seeking nothing for himself, he is now one of those forgotten worthies who has left behind a few dusty volumes and a pious obituary, bare bones from which to reconstruct the story of his warm, human, practical sympathy for the sufferings of his fellows.

Wilmot was not inexperienced in dealing with distress. In 1783 he was appointed commissioner to enquire into the claims of the American loyalists to compensation for their losses incurred during the War of Independence, a task which he executed conscientiously and with kindness.

The continual scenes of distress which he daily witnessed in

* In the possession of Sir John Eardley-Wilmot to whom I am much indebted for showing it to me.

the streets of London, added to particular instances of misery which came under his own immediate observation, induced him alone, without previous communication with anyone, to advertise for a meeting in September, 1792, of the 'gentlemen then in town,' at the Freemasons Tavern in Bloomsbury, to 'take into consideration some means of affording relief to their Christian brethren.'

The meeting, according to the *Gentleman's Magazine*, was most numerous and respectable, among those present being the Duke of Portland, the Marquis of Buckingham, Earl Fitzwilliam, the Bishops of London and of Durham, the Lord Mayor of London, Edmund Burke, William Wilberforce, whose name was sure to be found in any humanitarian enterprise, the Earl of Radnor, Lord Onslow, Lord Sheffield and J. J. Angerstein.

Mr. Wilmot having been called to the chair and having stated his object in calling them together, subscriptions to a large amount were immediately entered into and a committee was constituted of 'Subscribers to a Fund for the Relief of the Suffering Clergy of France in the British Dominions.'

'No national prejudice, no difference of religious Persuasion, no political principles can suppress in the hearts of Englishmen the sense of Christian charity and beneficence',

ran the appeal which the Committee inserted in the newspapers. Local committees were constituted all over the country, one meeting at the Star Inn at Lewes being presided over by the indefatigable Lord Sheffield.

In London two societies were formed almost simultaneously with Wilmot's. The first, inaugurated by the Lord Mayor of London, John Hopkins, quickly amalgamated with his but the second, which met at the Marine Society Rooms in Bishopsgate, struggled on by itself, not without some brushes with the more influential body. Unlike Wilmot's Committee, which dealt originally only with the clergy, the Marine Society Committee met the claims of clergy and laity alike.

Wilmot immediately plunged into practical work. One of his first tasks was to insert a notice in the newspapers, stating that the number of French refugee clergy in and about London was twelve hundred, with the additional remark that:

'The Committee have published the above statement in order to shew the absurdity of an opinion attempted to be circulated by Ignorant or Malicious Persons that their numbers can have in raising the Price of Provisions.' [sic]

Obviously there was a current of opinion circulating against the émigrés at this time for which the newspapers must take some responsibility as is evident from the letter which Edmund Burke wrote to Wilmot on October 2nd, 1792:*

'I wish my stay in town would have permitted me to attend further in the committee to offer the little assistance I could give to forward their very laudable designs. I could do little more than to offer to the Gentlemen of the Committee, and to you, my best acknowledgments for the unwearied application, which all of you, and most particularly yourself, have shown to this charity, which, as long as it is conducted according to the ideas of the gentlemen of the committee, at once prudent and liberal, must redound infinitely to the honour of the national character. It is for that reason I beg leave most earnestly to recommend it to them, to consider only, what they themselves think proper to be done.'

And he continued in characteristic style:

'I know the sentiments of many of the most considerable subscribers and I can speak it with perfect certainty, that they repose the most unbounded confidence in the committee. I do not think them at all responsible to any other persons than to them, the subscribers, for any thing they may do. Above all they do not think themselves responsible to the anonymous scribblers of paragraphs in the newspapers. They wish that no man should give an account of his own free Bounty. If the contrary opinion of practice should prevail charity would be put under the direction of malevolence. We know of no *publick* to which we are accountable—because it is a vague name; and a sort of fictitious Tribunal before which we never can be acquitted. Above all, we do not submit to the Idea, that it should be represented by the newspapers.

* British Museum, Add. MSS 9828.

'Therefore, I for one, (and I am authorised to speak for more than one) entreat that nothing which can be said in them, should prevent you from giving that substantial and effectual relief to the objects of your Charity, which, respect to their persons, and, their comfortable subsistence, absolutely requires.'

More important than paying attention to 'anonymous scribblers' was to find suitable lodging for the priests, which was a matter of extreme urgency.

Wilmot wrote to Henry Dundas, the Home Secretary, asking that Government should lend a building for the purpose. His reply that it had already decided to put the castle at Winchester at the disposal of the emigrant clergy relieved the Committee of its most pressing anxiety but, as Burke wrote scornfully, this time to Lord Sheffield,

'What think you of ministry that gives the walls of an house at Winchester for hospitality, but suppose that to put beds in it would be a breach of neutrality and an act of hostile aggression about Citizen Pétion* and the sovereign assassins of France?'

For many weeks the Minutes of the hard-working Committee, which met two or three times a week, are full of discussion as to whose responsibility it was to provide bedding for the clergy and of resolutions taken for the investigation of the Castle and for its furnishing and victualling. Money was coming in now. By December, 1792, the subscriptions amounted to £19,303 16s. 11d., showing that Wilmot's confidence in the soundness of the British heart was not misplaced.

Contracts for feeding the priests were placed in Winchester and a ration scale drawn up. The allowance of food per day, including the servants, was to be:

Meat	1 lb.
Bread	1½ lb.
Vegetables	1½ lb.
Cheese	2 oz.
Beer	2 quarts (if wanting 1 pint more)

* Pétion was the commissioner appointed to bring Louis XVI back from Varennes and the first President of the Convention.

It was hoped to maintain the priests for six shillings a week at these prevailing prices:

Ox, beef, and mutton	3¾d. a lb.
Bread	½d. a lb.
Coals	£1. 11s. 6d. a chaldron
Turnips, carrots, potatoes, cabbages and onions	4.6d. a quarter

The washing contracts allowed each person a week:

2 shirts
2 pairs stockings
2 neck cloths
2 pocket handkerchiefs
1 towel
1 pair of sheets every three weeks

The cook received twenty-five pounds a year, his assistant eight pounds, the doorkeeper a shilling a day and the porter the same.

Not the smallest detail of household or institutional management escaped the Committee's vigilant eye and it was both prudent in its arrangements and as liberal, especially with regard to beer, as its means would allow. Ultimately some seven hundred clergy were housed in the castle.

Their first pre-occupation was to continue their ecclesiastical life as far as they could. They chose as their superior the worthy Vicar-General of Lisieux and instituted classes and discussions in moral and pastoral theology, but they did not otherwise remain idle.

The Marchioness of Buckingham organised a tapestry factory at the castle and she herself, with the aid of some émigré ladies, among them the Comtesse de Saisseval, undertook the sale of work done by the priests. In addition Lady Buckingham visited the castle daily, distributing money and kindness, particularly to the sick.

The Marquis of Buckingham has left an unsavoury political reputation, receiving little recognition from posterity for the astonishing philanthropic effort put out by himself and his wife.

In every humanitarian enterprise connected with the French émigrés one finds the Buckinghams' name, giving service even more than money.

If the worthy clergy of the emigration merit any reproach it is for their uncontrollable habit of bursting into bad verse to express their sentiments on every occasion, suitable or otherwise. Both Lord and Lady Buckingham were the victims of several laudatory odes and the priests caused an expression of their gratitude to George III to be engraved (in verse) on the walls of the chapel of Winchester Castle. In the dedicatory address attached to the poem they included 'the excellent British Senator, John Wilmot,' to which Wilmot suitably replied—in prose. They touchingly added that 'the fond record of these munificent acts will remain much longer on the tablet of our memories, than the record of them on the tablet of marble.' They forgot their mortality.

In housing the clergy aid was also given by Lord Bridgewater. With the eighteenth-century eye for landscape he considered that a final touch of picturesqueness would be added to his meticulously kept park at Ashridge if the monks to whom he gave hospitality should wear their robes and stroll about its shaven lawns reading their breviaries. Perhaps monks are less prone to versification than vicars-general and abbés for there is no record of odes addressed by them to Lord Bridgewater.

Not all the clergy, however, could be housed and employed at Winchester or Ashridge and there were not many Catholics in the position of Thomas Weld able to give them large enough residences. Relief was still needed, although whoever of the clergy could manage to support themselves did not make application for aid until his resources were exhausted.

But if the Fund continued to grow, though more slowly now, so did the demands on it. Costs continued to rise. The contractors at Winchester added another farthing to the pound of bread and another halfpenny to the pound of meat.

Not only the living had to be succoured. The dead, too, had their claims on charity for decent burial. Many of the priests were old and ailing and they were dying at the rate of some thirty a year. With undertakers' bills of six pounds seven shillings and threepence for a modest funeral the dead were often as heavy a charge on the Fund as the living.

The Committee were all too conscious of the problem, as Burke expressed it:

'I cannot bear the thought of their being (as I believe two hundred of them are) thrown like carcasses upon one another, two of them in a miserable little bed, and in some cases three—that some of them have been ten days without having their shirt washed. The inconvenience of nursing loathsome and often dangerous disease, with health—besides many other obvious inconveniences, which result from this mode of lodging, makes me most earnest that relief should be given against it. This inconvenient mode, I know had arisen originally from the number who crowded in at once and could not otherwise be disposed of—but it is continued, from the inefficiency of the limited allowance to answer all the purposes of Life in any manner whatsoever.'

It was not only housing that was difficult. Clothing, too, presented a difficulty.

'I confess I wish too, that attention may be had to their cloathing, which having been originally taken up as a disguise whilst they were hunted down in France here exposes them to the scorn and derision instead of the compassion of the populaces. Besides their dispersion renders it difficult for them to be kept under the inspection of their superiors; a bare necessity to their existence.'*

Since, after the first impetus, contributions slowed down, the rate of income being insufficient to keep pace with the expenditure, the Committee decided to issue a further appeal to the public, an appeal in which one may detect a note of panic.

'Let not then the lustre of a virtuous action be tarnished by its ineffectual performance, let us finish what we have begun, let not those whom we have hitherto upheld, whom our kindness has taught to look up to us with flattering hopes, be suffered to sink into Despair and perish under our Eyes for want of those [sic] which many of the wealthy inhabitants of this realm can spare from their abundance.'

* Op. cit.

Yet it was the wealthy inhabitants who seemed to be holding back, to the discontent of Lord Sheffield who again reported to Auckland:

'I have, however, the satisfaction of thinking that the prejudice in respect to the price of provisions and corn do not increase among the vulgar; yet a great part of those persons of liberal education, ideas, etc. say they do not choose to subscribe, because it would make the vulgar uneasy.'

Others had no such doubtful scruples. Subscriptions again poured in. The young gentlemen of Harrow School, 'having made a collection among them,' contributed forty pounds, no mean sum from the habitually empty pockets of schoolboys. Rugby School did the same. The Oxford Colleges sent their contributions and Cambridge University, through William Wilberforce, sent four hundred and nine pounds to the Fund.

'A respecter of conscience and an enemy to all Persecution' contributed three guineas; a gentleman with the motto, *homo sum humani a me nihil alienum puto* rated his common humanity at two guineas and so did 'Humanitas.'

If the wealthy held back the poor did not. It was the man in the street with his small donations, the poor person who sent a shilling, the workman who gave half a guinea, the soldier who squeezed two guineas out of his half-pay, who swelled the Fund. Often they gave anonymously, 'anxious to conceal the hand that administered to the wants of the émigrés, and hurt only by the reserve that hid them.'

Those who could not give in money gave in kind. A fishwife offered her fish for nothing, a greengrocer sold his goods cheap. One day a milkman pressed a coin into the hand of a priest walking in the street and rushed away that he might not be known.

Hannah More contributed to the Fund the profits on her two pamphlets, *An Elegant and Pathetic Address for the Ladies of Great Britain on behalf of the French Emigrants* and her *Remarks on the Speech of Monsieur Dupont* (who had shockingly avowed atheism to the Convention). This particular pamphlet was so appreciated that it brought in royalties of two hundred and forty pounds.

In the early months of the Committee's existence the trend of events led it to expect that the refugee clergy would be able to make a speedy return to France. As this hope faded schemes were set on foot to send the clergy to Holland, Brabant and even to Canada. Many of them did in fact go overseas but, when Belgium and Holland were taken by the French, there was a further influx and many who had gone were forced to return.

To administer the Fund among so many scattered over the whole country would have taxed severely even the zeal of the untiring workers of the Committee, reduced to an effective executive of John Wilmot, Colonel Thomas Glyn and the secretary, George Hughes. It was fortunate to find a tower of strength in the Bishop of St. Pol de Léon.

From the date of his arrival in England at the end of 1791, St. Pol de Léon had, on his own initiative and with the help of a pious Catholic lady, Mrs. Silburn, of whom history has left too brief a record, been acting as a one-man committee of assistance, doing everything he could to succour the poor ecclesiastics.

He lodged in Queen Street, Bloomsbury, a few doors from the Freemasons Tavern, at Mrs. Silburn's house, which soon became the Committee's office, giving himself wholly to the self-imposed task of charitable work on behalf of his fellows.

Danloux, the émigré painter, painted a striking portrait of the Bishop at work in his modest room which has come down to us in the engraving he had made at his own expense by William Skelton, giving the amount he received from the sale of copies as his contribution to the finances of the Committee.

Jean-François de La Marche, Bishop of St. Pol de Léon, now sixty-one, an Aramis with a difference, was a dragoon before he turned to the Church. His face shows the vigour of the soldier and the sweetness of the saint. The black, semi-ecclesiastical dress sits uncomfortably upon the burly figure of the man of action.

Beside him in the portrait a fire-screen shows a picture of Winchester Castle and on a writing-table are heaped prayers for assistance and list of subscribers to the Fund, clearly headed by the names of the Duke of Portland and John Wilmot. The Bishop is shown studying a petition.

Indefatigably he worked in the interests of the clergy, raising money on his own account to supplement the allowances made by the Committee. Its Letter Books during the years 1793 to 1796 are full of letters written by him, all pointing out how pathetically insufficient was the money available for assistance, not that St. Pol de Léon was grasping or ungrateful. His gratitude was almost embarrassing although happily it was expressed in prose.

In an epistle addressed to the French clergy in 1793, which was translated into English and might be had for sixpence, the Bishop called upon them to express their thanks to God and ever to be mindful of the benefits bestowed upon them by the British people, so outstanding in tolerance and beneficence.

In the days of French power and glory England had often disputed the field of battle, and her efforts were often enough crowned with success, in asserting her right to the dominion of both seas.

But she offered them a more glorious spectacle, a triumph of a higher nature. She had opened her ports to them, she considered them not as strangers; the English were not startled by their numbers; they thought the best use they could make of their great opulence was to afford succour to a greater number of persons in distress.

The Bishop concluded:

'The generosity of the English nation surpasses all the instances of benevolence recorded in the history of nations.

'May the God of mercies shower down his chosen blessings on a people who seem chosen by heaven to vindicate the violated laws of nature and humanity. May heaven, attentive to our prayers, grant peace and plenty to a country where we are so hospitably entertained . . . may England exhibit to all other nations the picture of perfect happiness, as she has held up to them the model of Christian benevolence.'

The language may to-day strike us as fulsome. Its sincerity is unquestionable.

Did Mr. Burges read this epistle? But then, in all fairness to him, it must be remembered that he had grudgingly allowed that 'the bishops and clergy are compassionated and respected.'

Striking evidence of this respect was shown by the solidly anti-Catholic University of Oxford, which had printed at its own expense and distributed gratis a Latin edition of two thousand copies of the Vulgate in octavo for the use of the French clergy refugees in England, and a little later, notwithstanding its prejudices, printed and distributed to the exiled priests the four parts of the Roman breviary.

This gesture immediately called forth a grateful response from St. Pol de Léon in the form of a Latin epistle to the 'meritissime Domine Vice Cancellarie' of the University.

But the source of private donations through the Committee's appeals was now practically exhausted and John Wilmot petitioned George III to allow a collection to be taken in churches on behalf of the emigrant clergy to which, in spite of his hatred of the Catholics and his frequent ill-humour with the émigrés, the King, James II in reverse, graciously acceded, writing to the Archbishop of Canterbury, ordering that this should be done.

The world was thus presented with the astonishing spectacle of Church of England Protestant clergy, headed by their Archbishop, preaching sermons in every parish of England with the aim of collecting funds for Roman Catholic priests.

This extraordinary effort raised over forty thousand pounds from the parishes of England for the Fund. It would have been hard indeed to resist an appeal such as was made by Samuel Horsley, Bishop of Rochester, in the sermon he preached to the House of Lords.

'None at this season,' he said, 'are more entitled to our offices of love than those with whom the difference is wide in doctrine, discipline and external rites, those venerable exiles endeared to us by the edifying example they exhibit of patient suffering for conscience' sake.'

Allocations for relief were running at over eight thousand pounds a month but funds were lagging behind. Private charity must one day dwindle to a useless trickle or have a complete stop.

Already Wilmot had had recourse to the Treasury for an advance on subscriptions and he and the Committee now felt the time had come to approach the Government for further aid for, when their own money was exhausted, then indeed those whom they had helped would run the risk of perishing under their eyes.

The time for an appeal to Government was not propitious and, if the elected representatives of England's tiny population of ten millions had felt it beyond their powers to do more and that the French émigrés must fend entirely for themselves, they could scarcely have been blamed. In fact, the response to Wilmot's pleas was a Parliamentary grant of over twenty-seven thousand pounds 'on account of French refugees.'

Charles Long, Secretary to the Treasury, warned Wilmot, however, that the arrangements for relief could only be temporary but, as so often happens in England, they became permanent, new classes of recipients being added as developments in the international situation brought fresh liabilities.*

When Government instituted its grants it requested Wilmot's Committee to concern itself with the laity as well as with the clergy, names of the laity in need being submitted to the Treasury. Not that the money granted was always forthcoming on time. St. Pol de Léon complained sadly of the bitter distress caused by the delay in payments. Many of the amounts voted by Parliament were 'to make good money spent on behalf of the suffering French clergy and laity.' But it is only remarkable that the money was found at all. When Pitt's own salary was in arrears when he died who else could complain at delay in payments?

To help the Committee with the distribution a French Committee was established of 'noblemen and gentlemen of the first respectability,' an arrangement which saved infinite trouble and expense, enabling Wilmot's Committee to exercise an overall supervision and decide on questions of policy while the French Committee actually handled the money. Funds were allocated with scrupulous equity by strict scale of rank.

The Bishop of St. Pol de Léon was charged with the clerical distribution. Bishops received ten guineas a month, all the lower orders of the clergy receiving thirty-five shillings a month, although even this amount had later to be reduced.

Distribution to the services was under the direction of high-ranking officers. General officers of the army and their wives received seven pounds ten shillings a month; senior officers of the navy ten guineas a month. The allocation to the magistrature varied between ten and four pounds a month.

The allowance to the émigrés who did not fall into any of these classes was a shilling a day, whatever their rank in society, but even then it was laid down by the Committee that this sum was to be given only to those in *absolute want* or as they became reduced

* See Appendix for details of Parliamentary grants.

to that situation, which was defined as being at their last guinea. And these small sums were given only upon the émigrés 'finding proper certificates of their being obliged to emigrate to this country in consequence of the rebellion in France.'

'What reserves can a man have who receives only a shilling a day?' mourned St. Pol de Léon, as he continually drew attention to the inadequacy of the allowances.

Compared, of course, with a weekly parish relief of fourteen to eighteen pence a shilling a day was princely but then those who received this amount had once lived as princes not as journeymen and labourers. If this amount might be stretched to provide bare necessities in health it could not do so in sickness and the émigrés were not less liable to the common ills than the rest of mankind. Indeed, they had passed through so many dangers and vicissitudes, so many reversals of fortune and so much anguish of heart, that they may have become even more prone to sickness of mind and of body.

Apothecaries were established by the Committee in several districts of London where the poorer émigrés huddled together and free medicines were distributed to the sick on prescriptions signed by doctors and surgeons known to and approved by the Committee.

Middlesex Hospital offered twenty-four beds for the use of the sick clergy and laity at the charge of the Committee. Devoted French nuns and priests took charge of this ward which was regularly visited by John Wilmot who reported that he found everything clean and in good order.

One practice which the Committee intervened to stop had caused great distress among the sick émigrés. This was the dissection of the bodies of those who died in the hospital, a process they described as 'bodies mutilated at the surgeon's pleasure, a practice so cruel to strangers.'

Many had lost their reason because of their sufferings and at one time Wilmot reported to the Treasury that 'there are so many in Bedlam there is difficulty in getting admission for more.'

Never flinching in what he held to be his duty Wilmot visited the private Hospital for Lunatics of Messrs. Miles and Kay where pressure on space was so great that the inmates had to sleep two in a bed. The thought of any hospital for lunatics in the eighteenth century causes a shudder but, if any glimmer of reason came back to these gently-nurtured people, the conditions must have been appalling to them. Perhaps in some cases the loss of mind *was* only temporary for at one moment there came a plaintive cry from the Middlesex Hospital, asking the Committee for increased funds, since 'convalescent lunaticks do have enormous appetites.'

The Committee continued with its self-imposed task with patience and perseverance as time slipped by. The members could have had little idea that an emergency measure for which the necessity seemed so brief would go on for upwards of twenty-two years.

VI

The Comte d' Artois

While in England the émigrés were slowly settling down and a
pattern of life was emerging for them, on the Continent many of
them were still without a permanent home. Bâle became a neutral
zone where revolutionaries and émigrés met in hotels and cafés,
often sitting at the same tables. There in the dark days they would
get news of the guillotining of wives and fathers and of other
disasters at home.

Artois himself was caught up in the general disorder after
Valmy. He reached Arlon, only to be forced on to Maestricht,
where he suffered a brief imprisonment for debt. At Aix-la-
Chapelle his carriages were seized but again he managed to escape
from his creditors. Finally, after three months' wandering, he
arrived in the middle of a snowstorm to join the Comte de
Provence in the uninviting little town of Hamm, which achieved
such fleeting fame during the last war. Here he was joined by his
sons and by Louise de Polastron.

In the little wooden house where hunger often stalked by day
the brilliant flame which had burned so brightly but so briefly
snuffed itself out. Artois succumbed to lassitude, finding consolation only in the tender presence of Louise. He played with the
idea of retiring with her to private life, renouncing a struggle
which had come to seem vain. His moral and material penury
left him powerless to help the émigrés whose star he had been and
who were now in even worse straits than he.

With the disintegration of their hopes of overcoming the
Revolution by force of arms, and the disappearance of their
focus at Coblentz, the émigrés fell into dissension among themselves. Divergence of views, personal resentments, rancours and
jealousies began to dominate minds left empty of their guiding
principle. They were no longer a corporate body and never

again would they agree among themselves as to the way of achieving their purpose.

The émigrés were shaken back, however briefly, into unity of sentiment by the news of the execution of their King. A cry for vengeance went up from the throats of all the French now scattered half over the world when, on January 21st, 1793, Louis XVI, King of France and Navarre, mounted the scaffold to join the roll of martyrs.

In England the September massacres had already materially reversed British friendly feeling towards the Revolution and the news of Louis' imprisonment had even acted more powerfully on men's minds, particularly on that of George III, threatening as it did the security of all kings. The English had almost become inured to the atrocities which succeeded each other so rapidly but Louis' execution was a shock that roused the whole nation to fury. As one-time regicides themselves they might have conceded to the French the right of beheading their King if they so wished but such was far from being the case.

Newspapers, bordered in black, fulminated against the King's murderers. The theatres closed for three days. Even as far north as Aberdeen handbills were circulated, requesting that the inhabitants appear in mourning during the course of the ensuing week, and it was very generally worn by all ranks all over the country.

Bishop Horsley's sermon in the House of Lords on Louis' death brought the whole congregation to its feet as a spontaneous tribute both to his eloquence and the victim.

Ten days after the King's execution France declared war on England. It had threatened for so long that, when it came, it was almost a relief and it seemed that Providence had offered a speedy opportunity for the punishment of the murderous French nation. George III was gratified by the declaration of war as the mode adopted seemed well calculated to

'rouse such a spirit in this country that I trust will curb the insolence of those despots, and be a means of restoring some degree of order to that unprincipled country, whose aim at present is to destroy the foundations of every civilised state.'

When Pitt, who had struggled painfully to maintain peace, saw, like Chamberlain a hundred and fifty years later, neutrality fall beyond his grasp he reconciled himself to the war as a form of shock treatment, which he hoped would ultimately heal the rivalry between England and France and establish that friendship which alone could ensure the lasting peace in Europe which was the foundation stone of his policy. The treatment took nearly twenty-five years to effect a cure, which Pitt did not live to see, but, so far as England and France are concerned, his diagnosis and prescription were correct.

His brother's death galvanised Artois into action and in February he journeyed to Russia to make a personal appeal to Catherine the Great. His charm and grace and prestige as a Bourbon prince subjugated that connoisseur of masculine attractiveness and for a short while he again basked in royal approval and in the luxury of palaces.

Catherine's advice was even more worth while; to go to the Royalist west of France and raise the partisans. In March, revolt in the Vendée, which was to prove the same running sore to the revolutionary governments as the war in the Peninsula to the Emperor Napoleon, flared up, but without Artois.

Catherine's praise and enthusiasm did fire him to try to go to England to enlist the help of Pitt but yet another humiliation awaited him here. He was, always under the pretext of the debts that bedevilled him, not even allowed to land at Hull and, after Catherine's reception, the English rebuff was too great a blow to his pride and consequence. All that remained of his visit to Russia was Catherine's good advice, on which he did not act, and a richly bejewelled sword, which he would not unsheathe, but which would one day assist him in his eternal financial embarrassments.

Once again on his unwelcome travels Artois fell a victim to total inaction and talked this time of putting an end to it all but there was always the thought of Louise to save him from any desperate action. It was also Louise, it was murmured, who prevented his taking that active part which the times demanded. . . . Gentle and fearsome, she could not bear to think of Charles-Philippe in danger or away from her, and in the shelter of her white arms he was caught up as inexorably as Laocoön by the sea-serpent.

In spite of the ambivalent attitude he displayed towards the

French Princes, Pitt's own feeling, to be constantly frustrated, was that the restoration of the monarchy in France would give Europe peace and he was confident that a restored monarch would be sufficiently happy to regain his throne without at the same time retaining the conquests of the Revolution against the will of Europe. His conviction that no revolutionary government was capable of maintaining peace was borne out by the instability of the successive régimes in France which kept in power only by means of violence and repression.

Many dutifully paid lip-service to Pitt's ideas of the war, the prevalent view being that it was a struggle to repel aggression, to defend the constitution, to preserve England's commercial interests, to restore order and tranquillity, and to establish the balance of Europe on a clear and solid basis. If, incidentally, the monarchy in France were restored it could never be held out as a motive for the war and the idea of its being undertaken for the interests of the Princes was not to be encouraged.

Lord Auckland expressed himself much more plainly:

'But surely it is to be wished that the war may be so directed as to effect a great and solid dismemberment of France, or at least a permanent impression, so far as the chain of fortresses is concerned.'

England's entry into the war, however, offered new hope to the émigrés and promised fresh opportunities of activity. Gouty though he was, the Comte de Provence left Hamm for Verona with the intention of pushing on to Toulon which had risen against the Revolution and was maintaining its position with the aid of the British fleet.

Lord Macartney, the British delegate, sent home a severe picture of Provence's court at Verona—the house barely furnished and with no comfort, the table served without elegance, the servants few and badly clothed, the barely disguised poverty—all that he recognised as the framework of exile and not without its own grandeur, but to him the real penury was the lack of intelligence in Provence's entourage, the sin against the spirit. In Macartney's view it was that which caused the monarchy to perish and it was that which condemned the emigration.

Artois remained in Germany. Even the heroic rising in the

Vendée failed to rouse him from lethargy and, although he promised repeatedly to join the partisans, he did not do so, beginning the long series of tergiversations and delays, of promises unfulfilled and projects entered into and abandoned which so discouraged the faithful adherents of the Bourbon cause in the Western provinces of France.

Sadly Lord Sheffield, ever a supporter of the under-dog, wrote to Lord Auckland:

'I find I am much more disturbed than you seem to be by the state of the poor miserable Vendée business. Affairs in Brittany seem to have failed and I fear for ever, by the tardiness of our efforts and succour. I never desponded so much as I do now in respect to a party rising in France. Insurrection has so universally failed, that even despair is not likely to make another attempt.'

But Lord Sheffield under-estimated the toughness and devotion of the Vendéens. They would be heard of again.

The year was once more darkened for all the émigrés by the news of Marie Antoinette's execution and Artois' grief and rage knew no bounds at the even more unpardonable crime of the guillotining of his saintly and blameless sister, Madame Elisabeth, which followed soon after.

His feeling was fully shared in England and it was for men and women of every class that Lord Sheffield spoke:

'The death of the Queen elevates me to such a pitch that I am equal to conflagration, murder, etc.'

Even the most ardent supporter of Oliver Cromwell felt that the French had gone too far while the moderates and liberals were shocked beyond measure.

William Windham, the Whig and friend of Burke, who had gone over to Pitt in 1792 with the Duke of Portland and his friends, exclaimed:

'The Queen, the fate of the poor Queen, for I now begin to justify all Mr. Burke's enthusiasm, saddens even our prospects of success, so much I wish that she might have lived to enjoy them. What others' intentions may be I know not; but my determination is to open steady war against the whole Jacobin faction, and junction for that purpose with whomsoever it may be necessary to join. . . . The sum of the opinion is, that I am a determined foe to the new system . . .'

The émigrés benefited by the current of sympathy which ran through the country and their hopes were quickened of a speedy return to France if their new allies should prove more successful in arms than they themselves had been.

The dissensions in the revolutionary government, the assassination of Marat, the risings in the Vendée, in Lyons and in Toulon, all suggested that the Revolution might be exhausted and about to immolate itself on the same scaffold as Louis XVI. The optimists were confident that a change in France was imminent. Even Lord Grenville, the Foreign Secretary, flattered himself that every fresh account from France brought decisive proofs that the system was drawing to its close and could no longer support itself.

It was, unfortunately, wishful thinking on Grenville's part. In December, 1793, Toulon was retaken by the French through the brilliant operations of a young and unknown artillery officer, Napoleon Bonaparte. And the fall of the city added to the number of émigrés to be cared for.

Writing to Lord Auckland from on board *Victory* in Toulon Bay, the British Commissioner, Sir Gilbert Elliot, told him that the two thousand five hundred refugees on board the British fleet seemed to fall peculiarly under his charge:

'So much joy for escaping the evils of yesterday, and so much despair and misery when they think of to-morrow, never perhaps were collected together as are now floating in this bay.'

But Toulon had graver consequences in the loss of an important bridgehead for English operations in France and Sir Gilbert went on to express his deep dismay:

'I am so entirely of your opinion, that the shortest and perhaps only good end to this war lies through France itself and that the best ally we can have against France is France, that I confess I have seen the disappointment of the views opened at Toulon with great concern.'

We catch a whisper whose echo was heard in 1940. The

Royalists believed that England did not want to preserve Toulon but simply desired to destroy the French fleet. It was precisely this suspicion of British treachery and of England's being actuated only by self-interest that was one of Pitt's major difficulties in dealing with the Bourbon Princes and their party. They could not reconcile this suspect conduct with their own firmly held belief, in spite of any evidence, that the British Government did put the restoration of the Bourbons in the forefront of their war aims because, in accordance with their own entrenched ideas, they confounded the interests of France, and consequently of Europe, with the interests of their dynasty.

Artois had a recrudescence of energy when unexpectedly he was invited to join the headquarters of the Duke of York's expeditionary force in Holland and this time he persisted in remaining in active participation in the war. He even professed himself firmly as willing to go to the Vendée but prudent counsellors prevailed on him not to expose himself to such danger. Louis XVI was dead, the little King a prisoner in the Temple, the Comte de Provence was childless and burdened with gout and obesity. Artois was the ultimate heir to the throne and the only able-bodied senior member of the family.

Sympathetic though George III was to Louis XVI and much as he deplored his fate he did not extend his friendly feelings to Louis' brothers. He grudgingly agreed that Artois might come to England to organise émigré corps to act for the restoration of the monarchy but he trusted that he would appear entirely incognito and, when his business was concluded, not think of prolonging his stay.

Artois himself had begun to doubt his standing with the European sovereigns and, while he approved and desired the plan of the French emigrants entering the levies to be raised by England and freely gave them permission to do so, he confessed himself as not knowing whether he would have any say in the formation of the corps and the nomination of its officers.

George III's fears this time proved groundless. Artois, on his way to England, was turned back at Rotterdam and again found himself a nomad. How far his wanderings took him and what depths of humiliation he touched is not known. He had to share the common table in the coffee-room of sordid inns like any lackey and this Prince of the Blood Royal must learn the ways of a mendicant friar. The Wandering Jew himself could have found pity for Charles-Philippe de France.

When the death of Louis XVII was learned in June, 1795, one more cup of wormwood to be drunk by the Bourbons, the Comte de Provence, who had called himself Regent, assumed the title of Louis XVIII and Artois in his turn became Monsieur, the simple designation borne by the King's eldest brother. From Verona the new King appointed Artois Lieutenant-General of the Kingdom, with the special responsibility of occupying himself with relations with the Western provinces of France, while Louis XVIII himself proposed to take care of relations with the rest of the world.

Europe, however, had little time for this King without a kingdom and without a treasury, whose sole supporters were a section of a ruined and exhausted nobility scattered across the Continent of Europe and hard to discipline or to unite.

However desirous Pitt might be of restoring the Bourbons, not in their own interest but in the cause of permanent peace, he realised as time went on how irrevocably they had committed themselves to the emigration which was anathema to the new France which regarded it as the unnatural survival of the *ancien régime* which had been overthrown. He likewise believed very strongly that the desire for a restoration must come from within France itself, unlikely though that might seem at the moment, for it was abundantly clear that, however difficult the revolutionary governments might find it to maintain themselves in power, the nation was by no means prepared to accept the restoration of their King by intervention from outside.

One hundred and fifty years later General de Gaulle showed how profoundly Pitt understood the temper of France when he, de Gaulle, insisted that France must take an active part in liberating herself, by action both within the country and outside, since it would be disastrous for her future as a great power if she owed her liberation solely to the efforts of her allies without any French participation.

This analogy may not ring true to the classic Republicans among the French who have finally rejected the monarchy and who continue, in the cold light of history, to condemn the emigration. But if we, as disinterested observers, substitute for the revolutionary government the government of Vichy, considering the Army of Condé and the French émigré regiments under British command as Fighting France, with the partisans in Normandy and the Vendée representing the Resistance movement within France, the whole picture can be mounted in a contemporary frame.

Auckland had no illusions about the power of the émigré chiefs to inspire a true resistance movement in France. He wrote to Pitt:

'As to the notion that there exists in Paris or in other parts of France a large party which will soon show itself in favour of the monarchy, I have ceased to "lay such flattering unction to my soul"; these speculations are, ought to be, utterly discarded.'

But the tenacity of the Western provinces in continuing their guerilla warfare still gave the British government hope that resistance to the revolution might spread. They poured money into the pockets of the chiefs of the movement. It fell to Windham, who became Secretary at War in Pitt's government in 1794 (an office he continued to hold until 1801), to disburse the subsidies from the secret funds. Sums as large as a thousand pounds a month went to Louis de Frotté in Normandy and at least one amount of fourteen thousand pounds to Puisaye in the Vendée. So occupied with the French did Windham become that he found it necessary to open his doors to them from morning until night.

Lord Grenville, together with Windham, clung to the idea of the improbability of any good settlement in France, except by civil war, aided by war from without.

But the war in France and the form its government should take in the future were far from being Pitt's only concern. In spite of the horror inspired by the Royal executions and the Terror in France the Radicals were still making headway and the writings of Mackintosh and Paine sold in their thousands. In 1794 the Government instituted a series of treason trials against the most prominent among the Radical leaders but their acquittal was a great blow to the Government and, so far from the revelations of their activities inspiring fresh enthusiasm for the war, the trials merely had the effect of increasing opposition to it. In the autumn

George III was mobbed on his way to open Parliament and the situation looked very ugly.

It was in general a period of distress, disturbance and economic difficulty even before the war had broken out, adding to the nation's burdens. Revolutionary propaganda in England brought the counter attack of repressive measures, including the suspension of the Habeas Corpus Act from 1794 to 1801.

The harvests of the years 1789 to 1802 were consistently bad, one of the worst being in 1792, when there was also an acute commercial and financial crisis, followed by another in 1793. In 1795 the price of the quartern loaf, which had been sixpence, had risen to a shilling. Wheat rose from a hundred and eight shillings a quarter in 1795 to a hundred and twenty shillings a quarter in 1799 and it was impossible to supplement the supply from other sources.

Rebellion in Ireland became a running sore. By 1797 the Budget showed a deficit of twenty-two millions and Consols fell to forty-eight. Naval mutinies in 1796 imperilled the conduct of the war. By 1799 Pitt found it necessary to introduce an income-tax.

As ever when the atmosphere is darkest the British showed in their brightest colours. Millions were poured out to sustain the prosecution of the war. In April, 1794, there was a subsidy of a million and a quarter sterling to Frederick William of Prussia and in 1795 a loan of four and a half millions to the Emperor. From 1793 to 1805 alone nearly nine million pounds was paid out in subsidies and loans to European allies. No one could level against Pitt's government the charge of 'too little and too late.'

This was still not the sum total of English self-imposed liabilities. Apart from the grants made to the émigrés and the funds handed over to the resistance chiefs in France there were the émigré regiments to be nourished and maintained. These had been recruited in England or from the remnants of the disbanded Army of the Princes; the regiments of Dresnay and d'Hervilly, formed from Bretons enrolled in the Republican armies and made prisoners of war; the regiment of Rothalier, formed from four hundred artillerymen escaped from Toulon, all of whose cadres were made up of former officers of the Royal armies; the regiment of Hector, of five hundred émigrés, nearly all former naval

officers, and the Loyal-Emigrant, regiment of the Duc de La
Châtre.

At the beginning of the war in 1793 it was thought necessary to
introduce an Alien Act, designed to keep subversive elements out
of the country. The threat of a fifth column was very real and the
Act no more than a common-sense measure of self-protection. It
was never invoked against the genuine political refugee.

An examination of its clauses shows that its provisions differ
very little from those governing the admission of aliens to this
country to-day. They had on arrival to declare their names and
places of previous residence and register with the magistrates
when they changed their address. Proper passports were required
and if they failed to comply with the regulations laid down they
were to be deported.

The Act proved useful not only as a means of dealing with spies
but also unwelcome visitors, among them the Duc de Chartres,
son of the regicide Philippe Egalité, *ci-devant* Duc d'Orléans,
and General Dumouriez, both of whom had fought with the
revolutionary armies and then turned their coats back again.
They were of a very different description from the émigrés who
were driven into England under pressure of misfortune before
war broke out and, recognised as such, were thrown out of the
country.

The war was not going well for England apart from victories
at sea. On land she had been unsuccessful and the Duke of York
was forced to withdraw from Holland. Auckland noted that the
country was very low-spirited as to Continental politics and very
inclined to leave the Continent to go to the devil in its own way.
In a defeatist mood he wrote at the end of 1794:

'There is a gloom over this country such as I cannot describe
to you; it is a mixture of rage at the triumphs of the Jacobins, of
mortification at our disgraces, of extreme indignation and
horror at the infatuated turpitude of some of the allied powers,
of grief and alarm at the ruin which is coming upon Holland
and upon the whole of the European continent; and with all
this a score of difficulties inextricable and a suspension between
two doubts—the doubt whether we can prosecute the war, and
the doubt whether it is possible to make any step toward peace.'

With the loss of Holland, and still believing in the possibility of an extension of the spirit of the Vendée to the rest of France, the Government doggedly pursued its hope of finding another bridgehead on the Continent. This time it mounted an expeditionary force, of mixed English and émigré troops, destined for Quiberon and a junction with the Vendéens. Pitt, too, relented towards Artois and in August, 1795, he was permitted to sail for Portsmouth, only to learn on his arrival of the disaster which had overtaken the Quiberon enterprise and of yet another crushing defeat for the Royalist army of partisans.

There was dissension among the leaders of the Vendéens and bitter disappointment that still no prince of the House of Bourbon had himself joined in the rising which was intended to lead to its restoration. Artois could not remain unconscious that, unless he now took some positive action, his honour and his probity would be seriously endangered.

Not without difficulty he succeeded in persuading the Government to mount another expedition to Brittany. Royal approval was graciously shown to his endeavour by the visit Artois received from the Prince of Wales, who spent two hours with him on board the frigate *Jason*, in which Monsieur was quartered. Then four thousand men, of whom a thousand were French, were reviewed by Artois at Portsmouth on August 15th, 1795, and with high hopes and great gaiety the fleet of sixty vessels sailed off to the shores of France. Everything demanded swift action but it was not until October 2nd that Artois' foot once again touched French soil at the Ile d'Yeu.

Misunderstandings and poor intelligence with the army of Charette, the Vendéen leader, contrary winds and an ill-equipped force, over-prudent counsels from his timorous entourage, all combined to force Artois yet once again into a position of inaction and failure.

On November 18th, 1795, six weeks after disembarking on the island, the fleet lifted anchor and sailed back to England.

Perhaps not much was hoped of this expedition by the English although the émigrés had once again presaged victory.

In December, 1795, Windham wrote darkly:

'All the gentleman-like spirit of the country being fled, it seems to me that a descent into Jacobinism, easy and gradual perhaps, but perfectly certain, is at this moment commenced . . . the management of civil affairs, depending, as they do, on the consent of others, liable to be thwarted at every step by their sordidness and folly, is the most thankless task of all.'

Certainly the unpopularity of the war grew and the nation's humiliation at the series of military failures increased the clamour for peace. Auckland, in a widely distributed pamphlet, demanded it and the pressure brought on Pitt to end the war was so great that he so far yielded as to send Lord Malmesbury to Paris to initiate peace talks. His overtures were rejected by the Directory, adding yet another humiliation, and the war dragged on. But the high-handed refusal of the French to discuss peace did re-kindle anti-French feelings and martial enthusiasm although England's part was now restricted to the war at sea and subsidising such of her European allies as continued to fight.

Artois' reputation suffered more from the abortive Vendée expedition than from anything else and to add to his discomfiture he was forced on his return to England to lie off Portsmouth in the *Jason*, unable to land for fear of arrest for the debts incurred for supplies to the Coblentz army. But he could not remain there indefinitely and at last the Government decided to smuggle him to Scotland where, in the Royal Palace of Holyroodhouse, he would be free from the menace of a debtor's prison.

VII

Auguste de La Ferronays

In their uneasy quest for somewhere to settle after the débâcle which overtook the Army of the Princes the émigrés found that, alone among the Rhenish states, Brunswick offered them asylum. Although the Duke had despised them as allies he yet gave a hospitable welcome to those who drifted into his territories and his wife, Augusta, sister of George III of England, showed great kindness to the ladies who found at her Court a pale shadow of Versailles. The little Duchy was calm and domestic and its friendly atmosphere brought some peace to those émigrés fortunate enough to be able to settle in Brunswick.

The Comte de Montsoreau and his family found a haven there. For three years, since he left Paris, his great brown travelling berline, its panels and doors outlined in gold arabesques, had lumbered across the pot-holed roads of Europe until in 1794 it came to rest at Brunswick. The Montsoreaus had left France with four small daughters but two of them had died in these nomadic years and it was only with Félicie and Albertine, who had spent their childhood in the shadow of the Court at the Tuileries but who had grown up in the brown berline, that they settled down. Their humble dwelling soon became a centre of attraction to the émigrés, for the Montsoreaus had a genius for home-making.

Among their guests were the Comte Eugène de La Ferronays and his slender young son of seventeen, Auguste, who had just left his school at Bellelay and was still under the shadow of grief at the loss of his adored mother who had died after being imprisoned for a year at Nantes. It was through Comte Eugène's brother, the Bishop of Lisieux, that the La Ferronays met the Montsoreau family and the young man found in their family circle something of the gaiety and charm that he had enjoyed in his own, and which was now lost to him for ever.

But Comte Eugène did not linger long in Brunswick. He would

not, like the Comte de Neuilly, who joined the army of Austria, found a new career under a foreign flag. He could not, like the Marquis de Falaiseau, withdraw from the struggle nor was he content, like so many of the émigrés, to wander on an aimless trail so long as there remained the smallest possibility of fighting for his King. For him there was no allegiance but to the white plume of Navarre and the lilies of France. Happily for La Ferronays there was still an opportunity of unsheathing his sword in their cause.

The Prince de Condé, unlike his cousin Artois, would neither accept defeat nor disband his corps. As the war progressed the tough old soldier joined whichever of the Allies would maintain his army, passing from the pay of England to that of Austria, to Russia and back again to England, marching, counter-marching, fighting and retreating, and spending dreary winters in cantonments.

It was in winter quarters at Willingen that his corps stood by their drums for a funeral service for Louis XVI when the old Prince mournfully uttered his valedictory oration,

> 'Long sorrow will never dry up the source of our tears and the depth of our woe, cruel to every sensitive soul, is to weep at the same time for the loss of our King and the crimes of our country.'

The situation in which Condé's army now found itself was pitiable. Distress was so atrocious in the winter bivouacs beneath the hoar-frosted trees of the Black Forest that the Prince exclaimed:

> 'If the devil himself offered me his purse I would accept it with pleasure for we are perishing for want of money.'

Yet it was to join Condé's army as the only honourable course remaining that Comte Eugène de La Ferronays and his son set out in the bitter winter of 1795.

Peace between France and Prussia had already been signed in April of that year and Austria was on the point of leaving the coalition. Who gave a thought to the handful of men calling themselves the Army of Condé?

If they were forgotten by the Powers and if their material situation was disastrous, wit and ardour took the place in their ranks of bread and fodder. When they were allowed to fight, these

A View in Perspective.

The Zenith of French Glory; _ The Pinnacle of Liberty.
Religion, Justice, Loyalty, & all the Bugbears of Unenlighten'd Minds, Farewell!

A contemporary cartoon

The first emigration, 1. Madame de Polignac, 2. the Comte d'Artois, 3. the Prince de Condé, 4. the Baron de Breteuil

Jean-François de La Marche, Bishop of St. Pol de Léon

The Chapel of the Annunciation in 1890 after the
water colour by T. Appleton

Comte Auguste de La Ferronays

Photo Giraudon

The Duc de Berri

Photo Giraudon

Louis XVIII

The Duchesse d'Angoulême

The Duc d'Angoulême

Charles-Philippe, Comte d'Artois

Louise, Comtesse de Polastron

gentlemen soldiers were lions in action but in the camp they cared neither for discipline nor anything else. At rest they shared the émigré propensity to write bad poetry:

> 'Rendre la France un jour son antique splendeur,
> Au peuple le repos, la gaîté, le bonheur;
> Relever, sous l'appui de deux augustes frères,
> Le trône de nos rois, les autels de nos pères.'

And they played. High play was their *péché mignon*. Members of their caste would always play high, wherever they might be, at Coblentz, in the winter bivouacs, in the prisons of the Terror, while waiting their call to the guillotine. But Condé's high-spirited young gentlemen would always drop everything, including their cards and their dice, to follow a hare or a pretty girl.

To Comte Eugène de La Ferronays any camp was home. For the young Auguste, shy and sensitive, the frivolities of the camp at Steinstadt, which was his initiation to the army, were a welcome change from the rigours of monastic Bellelay. Life on eight sous a day—when it was paid—was scarcely less austere than his school, but at least he had a uniform of iron-grey with a scarlet waistcoat and a white plume in his hat. If, under the waistcoat, there was only a shirt made of sacking, no one would know. But poor Auguste was obliged to spend a night at an inn in company with Monsieur de Belle-Isle and, although he used every artifice to delay the moment of undressing, his secret was at last revealed. Belle-Isle was touched by his poverty and his pride and Auguste came out of the incident with a fine new shirt which remained for long the only one he possessed.

Subsidies from England helped Condé to put his little army again on a war footing but still it trailed aimlessly up and down the banks of the Rhine for cold and dreary months.

Auguste's function in that army was a very minor one since he acted as a simple soldier in the second noble cavalry regiment. At Oberkamlach he received his baptism of fire but to small purpose for once again the French revolutionary army was victorious and once again the drums of Condé's army beat the retreat. Always the rain drove down on the troops, marching not only under the burden of their packs but also under the added weight of yet another defeat, sparing neither horses nor men and provoking a fever which took a greater toll than the enemy's guns. There was little they could do for the sick and dying whom they were forced to leave in the villages through which they struggled. They would be buried in foreign soil by alien hands.

After the failure of the Duke of York's expedition to the Netherlands Condé's army received the doubtful reinforcement of the younger son of the Comte d'Artois, the Duc de Berri, who had accompanied his father to York's headquarters.

Charles-Ferdinand was now approaching the age of twenty. He had inherited nothing of his father's grace and good looks and his neck was very short. His face was redeemed from ugliness only by an irresistible smile.

He had been dragged rather than brought up since when barely fourteen he had left Versailles with his father in 1789 and his subsequent behaviour disproved the Comte de La Ferronays' theory. His education had perforce been scanty like that of so many of the young men who had emigrated and he was not, like his brother, the Duc d'Angoulême, naturally studious. De Berri, however, was unconscious of any deficiency, unlike the Comte de Neuilly who apologises for his style in his Memoirs, saying rather sadly that it was that of a man whose education had been interrupted by the Revolution and who owed to himself alone what he had since been able to learn.

Charles-Ferdinand's barometric temperament had never found a level in his years of emigration and his tutors were unable to control the caprices of which he was so entirely the victim. From lethargy to impulsive action, from brusquerie to kindliness, his moods were unpredictable. While he showed great personal bravery and regarded himself as dedicated to a career of arms he was always at a disadvantage compared with his cousin, the charming and gallant young Duc d'Enghien, and there was persistent rivalry between them.

De Berri fought well at Oberkamlach but the stars in their courses were in combat against the Condéens and once more the little corps was threatened with annihilation. But even at this twelfth hour Condé would not accept the inevitable and in October, 1797, he persuaded the Czar to take his army into Russian service.

It was three months later, after a thousand-mile march, that in a grim December the Army of Condé, led by his grandson, the Duc d'Enghien, reached the river Bug on the frontier between Austrian Galicia and Russian Volhynia.

Before a hastily dressed altar, in the presence of Russian officers and a Greek Orthodox priest, the fine flower of the French aristocracy who had left France to save their King took the oath of allegiance to a foreign sovereign, to Czar Paul I of All the Russias. They tore from their hats the white cockade, symbol of their French allegiance and emblem of their devotion and fidelity. After so many years away from France this was the ultimate exile, the exile of the spirit.

Under grey skies the only prospect was of snow and ice. Across the Rhine they could see smoke rising from French chimneys. In this deserted and inhospitable marshland nothing recalled the scenes and skies of home. Their very Russian uniforms, vulgarly blatant in pale green reversed with black velvet and frogged with yellow, made them unfamiliar even to each other. The Condéens were exasperated by their enforced Russian service. Never were Voltaire and Diderot so much read in the camp as when Paul I put them on an index. Because the Emperor of All the Russias did not like waltzing everyone waltzed. The bitter cold and lack of every necessity intensified the misery and heartache.

In the miserable little town of Dubno, which constituted the winter quarters of the corps, Auguste de La Ferronays was lucky to find shelter in the oven of a bakery where he alternated between choking with smoke or being pierced by cold. One ray of sunshine irradiated for him the horrid gloom of the Polish winter. The Comte de Montsoreau and his family arrived in Dubno.

He might never have met them again for the Montsoreaus had seemed fixed at Brunswick but for the chance that the Comte was thought by the Comte d'Artois' advisers to be a salutary mentor for the Duc de Berri. To act as guardian to this turbulent and stubborn young Prince was no sinecure for Montsoreau but, where the service of the Royal family was concerned, for him there could be no alternative to acceptance. In addition to the problem of what to do with de Berri was his difficulty about what to do with his family. To separate in those times might mean a long and perhaps permanent parting. In the end the piano was strapped on the back of the old berline, so loaded with pots and pans that it made but slow progress, as Madame de Montsoreau with Félicie and Albertine followed him to Volhynia.

For once the all too familiar discomforts of the journey were mitigated by the kindly welcome they met in the châteaux of the Polish nobility. To be an émigré was a title to Polish regard for were they not expatriates in their own country and as much victims of persecution as the French?

In after years many of the émigrés must have looked back at Dubno as marking a turning-point. For Auguste de La Ferronays it brought a development which changed the whole course of his life.

The Duc de Berri took a violent and sudden liking to the poor little noble soldier. While the misfortunes which had so far made up Auguste's history had strengthened the native nobility of his character and deepened the qualities of a rare heart and mind, de Berri's haphazard life had served only to bring out his fundamental weaknesses. These two dissimilar characters were to remain close friends throughout the long years of their exile, though they were rarely in agreement, but the steadfastness of La Ferronays acted as a counterpoise to the volatility of de Berri. If, in later life, La Ferronays found de Berri's friendship as much a handicap as an advantage, there was no question but that de Berri benefited from his association with La Ferronays.

In the rigours of that awful winter both young men found a grateful warmth in the family circle of the Montsoreaus, dangling round the two young daughters. With the gentle and saintly Madame de Montsoreau, in whose face traces of great beauty survived the scars of smallpox, de Berri was at his best, finding in her the only maternal love he had ever known, and she was the only person who was able in any way to control him.

Félicie and Albertine saw no defects in the Prince's character. For them he personified all the virtues of the monarchy to which they were so whole-heartedly devoted and they were proud of being in the immediate entourage of a Prince whom they regarded as peculiarly their own.

To Condé, Monsieur and the Vendée were far away and he thought not at all of the vicissitudes then engulfing the allies in the West. He remained possessed by his fixed idea of defeating the French armies on the soil of central Europe and in 1799 it seemed that his undaunted hope might at last be justified. In that year the Russian columns started marching westwards under Suvarov, himself a portent of victory, and as they progressed towards Italy enthusiasm, unshaken by so many defeats and disappointments, ran wild.

'We went to that war as to a ball,' said Albertine de Montsoreau.

It was an enterprise to them as holy as any crusade and more joyful. Everywhere on the route of Condé's army balls and routs were organised in honour of the noble regiments. Princess Lubomirska came specially from Vienna to fabulous Lançut to welcome the French Princes at a ball.

Among all the dazzling uniforms Auguste de La Ferronays, with nothing to wear but his shabby private's dress, could find no one who would deign to dance with him. How happy Albertine would have been to dance had she not retired from the ball, over-come with its unaccustomed splendour. Her simple muslin gown, decorated only with a lavish display of cornflowers, would not have shamed Auguste's insignificance and, of far more moment, his happiness was becoming a matter of concern to her as was hers to him.

As the battle once more waxed and waned across Europe so the tender romance between Auguste and Albertine flowered word-lessly for neither had the courage even to address a word to the other and, although their world had tumbled in ruins about their ears, the strictest discipline was preserved among young people.

Suvarov had reconquered Italy. In France the Directory was dying and it seemed that a change of government might pave the way for a restoration of the monarchy. The marriage of the shadowy Duc d'Angoulême, now heir after his father to the throne, to Marie Thérèse, daughter of Louis XVI and Marie Antoinette, which took place in Mittau in Poland where Louis XVIII was now settled, seemed another happy omen for the émigrés.

Their burgeoning hopes were again doomed to frustration. Once more defeat, this time at Constance, so nearly within sight of France, drove the Army of Condé back across the Alps on the road to Bavaria. Here the silent lovers were re-united.

Auguste was no longer a gangly young boy but a young man of

grace and charm. He had, moreover, been appointed to the Duc de Berri's household which offered some prospects for the future which again for a brief moment looked brighter. Into the Montsoreaus' house Auguste burst one day with the news that General Bonaparte had overthrown the Directory. It seemed possible that he would be the new Monck who would restore the King, but Albertine had clearer sight than the others.

'Fortunate perhaps for France,' she said presciently, 'but not for us. France will no longer need a king since Bonaparte will give her peace.'

To de Berri Auguste confided his hopes of marrying Albertine and Charles-Ferdinand took the contagion, deciding that he too wished to marry, a sickness that became chronic with him and one that was to last for nearly twenty years, for de Berri, a penniless exile, was no *parti* for even the plainest and least dowered of princesses.

By the spring of 1800 England found herself as much embarrassed by the Army of Condé as Austria and Russia had found themselves. She decided to send the corps to Minorca but Bonaparte's victory at Marengo put an end to this plan. When the Peace of Lunéville in 1800 disarmed the coalition the English planned to send Condé's soldiers to Egypt but the French were unwilling to serve what were patently British interests since they served only their King's. The moment had irrevocably arrived for the final dissolution of the Army of Condé.

The émigrés who had for years known no other country but the camp, no home but their regiment, no family but their colours, came in a stream to take farewell of the Prince de Condé, their captain and their father.

As they saluted the Prince for the last time and turned away, their thoughts were of the future and what it might hold for them. It seemed, except to the few of indomitable faith, to hold nothing. All that remained to them was to carry to every corner of the earth regrets for the fanfares of battle and the refrains of love, sorrow for their beliefs and their illusions, eternal mourning for the France they cherished and seemed for ever to have lost.

The Montsoreaus were luckier. They at least were not parted from those they loved and did not suffer the ultimate deprivation of separation. With the spring came the thaw and the sinister

country turned into a radiant landscape which soon spread its
radiance over Albertine and Auguste.

The Montsoreaus still hung back. It was not fitting that
Albertine should marry before her elder sister, Félicie, and
although de Berri sighed after her the Comte de Montsoreau
would never have countenanced such a mésalliance for his Prince.
But he could not gainsay de Berri's plans for his faithful friend and
the Duc, who had returned to the army after a year spent with his
father at Holyroodhouse, decided to further Auguste's hopes.

The young La Ferronays had managed to scrape together a
possible yearly income of nine to ten thousand francs—very far
removed from what might have been his fortune if Comte Eugène
had not lost his estates in San Domingo—but a respectable com-
petence for an émigré.

Auguste did not, of course, address Albertine himself. Her
mother announced to her one day that a marriage had been
arranged for her with Monsieur de La Ferronays. Albertine
agreed submissively but perhaps the Comte de Montsoreau was
after all a little touched by the spirit of the times and he so far
disregarded tradition as to ask her if she was happy with the match.
Albertine, who had feared for one dreadful minute that Félicie
would be Auguste's choice, was able to assure her father that he
had secured her great happiness.

The marriage took place at Klagenfurth, everything regulated
scrupulously according to the usage of the Court of France, the
handful of guests dining and playing pharaoh after the ceremony.
For trousseau Albertine had three dozen chemises of coarse linen,
as many handkerchiefs and three dresses, but the marriage contract
listed in detail the diamonds and carriages which would have been
hers had she indeed married at Versailles.

Auguste de La Ferronays was twenty-five, Albertine de Montsoreau twenty. He had been an exile for twelve years, she for
eleven.

Almost immediately after the wedding Auguste was summoned
to his father's death-bed in Poland. For Comte Eugène there
would be no return to France. His exile was ended.

From that journey Auguste wrote to his young bride:

'Before I met you, my Alberte, I had a hungry heart and a head full of dreams. I felt the need to love but I did not know what it meant to love truly. O cara, idol' mio, what I feel for you is something stronger than love and even beyond it. I cannot guess what would happen to me if you ceased to love me.'

This was the first of many partings. Since the establishment of the Consulate the situation of the émigrés and the Princes in the German states had become insupportable, their cause the object of everyone's ridicule, themselves anachronisms. Even in Brunswick, to which the Montsoreaus returned, they found this carping spirit, but so long as they were not openly persecuted they had no choice but to remain.

De Berri, who had gone back to England to rejoin the Comte d'Artois, clamoured for Auguste's presence and loath though he was to leave Albertine he had no choice but to obey.

Perhaps in England he would find a friendlier atmosphere, though to Auguste no exile could be kind. There at least he would be nearer to France and thence indeed he looked longingly at its coasts, as he wrote to Albertine:

'There, then, is our country, there the unique object of all my desires. In a few hours I could be there . . . and yet what a distance, what a gulf separates us. O God, what sadness, what a life is that of poor exiles like ourselves and for how much longer yet? My heart is riven and no one will know what I have suffered because perhaps I shall never be able to show my unhappy country how much I loved her.'

VIII

England and the Emigrés

The England to which Auguste de La Ferronays came was one
where the émigrés had long been established and where they had
ceased to occasion any remark. No one now turned his head in
the street at the sight of a foreign face or unfamiliar dress and, if
Auguste himself found much to wonder at, his compatriots had
come to accept the different mode of life even if they had not
become wholly reconciled to it.

Some of them, of course, who knew England before the
Revolution were enthusiastic about it. They had taken away from
their visits to this country a tremendous admiration for everything
English and anglomania became the order of the day with the
French aristocracy. Louis XVI had felt impelled to reprove the
Comte d'Artois, who had fallen a victim to the prevailing craze, for
dressing in the English fashion and for organising horse races, an
aping of foreign customs which, in his opinion, accorded ill with
the dignity of a French prince.

While the superficial envied the free and easy lives of the
English and the absence of stifling etiquette the more thoughtful
among the French nobility admired most the active rôle which the
hereditary peers played in the political life of the country.

Until these recent unfortunate times in France it was unthink-
able that a noble should be in opposition to King and Court
unless he was prepared to receive a *lettre de cachet*, entailing a stay
in the Bastille or banishment to his estates. The system of
Louis XIV of attaching the nobility to his own person in his own
residence of Versailles, which he had passed down to his descendants, was as rigid as the regimentation of any Communist country
to-day.

In England the French found that it was not only possible but
even fashionable to be in opposition although, in absenting
themselves from the Court of George III and his ugly little Queen

Charlotte, the English nobility lost only dullness, austerity and respectability which contrasted disadvantageously with the effulgence the French would lose by their absence from the glittering splendours of Versailles.

They might console themselves that the English did not enjoy their own wealth of privilege, but they admitted that the freedom and breadth of English life, the wide interests of the aristocracy and the extent of their sphere of influence were far more precious than all the feudal rights they themselves possessed.

In their turn the English nobility, who had always been influenced by French manners, eagerly sought French salons where wit and grace shone to such advantage in contrast to the dominant English distractions of hard drinking, hard riding and high play. They copied French fashions and adopted everything that was elegant in the French way of life.

In most of the countries to which they went the privileged classes of the French emigration found themselves, by the automatic play of natural forces, in contact with their equals, to whom they were linked by the sympathy between class and class which overrides considerations of nationality, and by similarity of great wealth, great possessions and great rank.

It would be unrealistic to assume, however, that, because the English received the émigrés kindly and the French were grateful for that kindness, the mass regarded their enforced sojourn in this country cheerfully or that the English considered it as a long-desired happening. Both sides wisely decided to make the best of a necessary evil which, in the main, they succeeded in doing and which probably turned out better than either side expected.

One must distinguish here between the attitude of the man in the street to the émigrés and the relationship between the Government and the Royalist party as such with which the majority of the population and of the émigrés were not concerned.

There was between the mass of émigrés and the English people a certain degree of mutual suspicion and perhaps of mistrust. The French have never been distinguished as good travellers or good colonisers. Enjoying every benefit at home of climate and society they have by and large sought little change and have been happy to remain in France. Their parochial attitude induced them to regard all foreign cities as inferior to their own village and it is only since the end of the last war that the French have to any extent taken voluntarily to travel.

There was much that the émigrés actively disliked about England. First and foremost, like all visitors to this country, they showed an almost morbid pre-occupation with the climate. It was never really hot and never really cold. Heavy fog hung perpetually over London and the humidity was depressing. Vigée Le Brun, who stayed here for three years after 1802, claimed that her paintings would not dry unless she kept a fire burning in her studio and she had constantly to run home from parties to see that they did not get scorched!

The Comte de Montlosier, an amateur doctor, decided after a series of quasi-scientific researches that the English people were different from the rest of the world, an opinion which is not unique. To the climate he attributed the lack of animal vitality, so different from the hardiness of the Scandinavians or the vivacity and warmth of temperament typical of France and other Latin countries.

He even declared that, although the meat *looked* better and more succulent than elsewhere, it was in reality deficient in juice. The air, too, was lacking in substance which was why the English ate so many meals of such proportions and why they drank so much. His gloomy summing up of his impressions was to warn his compatriots that, as a result of all these adverse factors, the least to be expected on arrival in England was an attack of rheumatism!

More deadly, however, than rheumatism was the famous 'spleen,' a sort of boredom and melancholy combined which led to suicide, madness and stupidity of all kinds. One Frenchman went so far as to aver that the English lived on spleen and tea.

The French who had never been to England before found the social customs bewildering. Sunday, then as now, weighed heavily on them. The silence in the streets and the lack of any facilities on that day for amusement was both sinister and oppressive.

In general, too, they were disconcerted by the habit of silence among the English even on week-days. Montlosier, of course, attributed it to the endemic lack of vitality. The French were accustomed to express themselves with torrents of words and the freedom of gesture which characterises the Latin race but the English, they found, did not gesticulate and were sparing in their speech. Silence prevailed even at routs and assemblies and when the English did open their mouths it was not to indulge in what the French called conversation. Vicomte Walsh asserts that they suffered so much from boredom that they eagerly seized the opportunity of visiting French social gatherings and invited the émigrés to their own homes to marvel at a wit and vivacity so novel to them.

But when the émigrés dined in English houses they were scandalised by the men's habit of staying in the dining-room to drink port and talk politics rather than enjoy the conversation and social graces of the ladies, who also came in for their share of disapproval. When they did not buy the émigrés' articles of manufacture they were blamed for their want of taste and their bad style in dress.

Since the older émigrés continued to wear their hair powdered, which made them easily remarked in the streets, they were particularly bitter about the tax Pitt imposed on hair powder.

The pavements, then unknown in Paris, were an innocent cause of annoyance and, with their *esprit frondeur*, the French walked in the middle of the roads, disdaining the mud, to show their disapproval. And, as they walked, the characteristic Georgian architecture of terrace houses all of the same style with areas and area-steps struck them as particularly odd.

All of them arrived in England with a lively terror of highwaymen and footpads and at every halt on their journeys they were convinced that they were about to be robbed.

As the years went by and the émigrés became integrated into English life, or at least an accepted part of it, the mutual prejudices of the English and the French naturally softened and they learned to accept one another as they were. The English did not all the time regard the French as incurably frivolous while insensibly the French became accustomed to the English way of life, even to the coal fires.

They found the heaviness of the atmosphere, of which they all complained, was peculiar to London and in the summer, when they could afford it, they went out of the city to seek the purer air which reminded them a little of France. Hampstead village, a few miles out of town, was a favourite haunt, while the luckier ones were invited to the great country houses.

The greyness of the sky continued to oppress their spirits but they came to realise that their pre-occupation with the weather was shared by the inhabitants and there was nothing that anyone could do about it. And there were some times, as in July, 1793, when not a cloud was to be seen during ten days and the sun so hot that the strawberry beds and rose bushes were dying; or the beautiful November of 1794 when the sky was blue, the woods yellow and the lawns green . . .

Gradually the émigrés learned something of the language and even years later in France still larded their writing with English expressions while the letters written by Louis XVIII in the last years of his emigration here are so full of English phrases and quotations that it is hard to decide whether they were written primarily in English or in French.

They even became reconciled to the English Sunday so that on their return to Paris both Louis XVIII and the Comte d'Artois found Sunday observance there little to their liking and pressed for some more seemly practice on English lines. One cannot live, with however temporary an intention, in a country for fifteen years or more without adopting some of its habits and ways of thought.

Naturally each criticised the other and, as Auguste de Le Ferronays reveals in his letters, the French were not unaware of the unkind remarks sometimes made about them in English society. With his natural humility he found it chastening and useful to be reminded of his own shortcomings.

But on the whole the English sympathised with the difficulties of the émigrés and treated them with a rare amount of tact, being by nature unwilling to wound the susceptibilities of people in misfortune, at least to their faces.

Horace Walpole, of course, was not sparing of astringent comment on the émigrés. He was really quite glad to see his old friends and prepared to renew the former easy intercourse and pleasures of the Paris salons at Twickenham but he refused to make any new acquaintance among the French and limited himself but not his sarcasms to those whom he already knew.

For 'that scribbling trollop, Madame de Sillery (Madame de Genlis) and the viper that has cast his skin, the Bishop of Autun (Talleyrand)' he had no time. 'The woman and the serpent, I hope, will find few disposed to taste of their rotten apples.'

The attitude of the English and the émigrés towards one another was best summed up by the Comte de Las Cases, himself a former émigré, who looked back on his years in England from a far more rigorous exile with Napoleon on the island of St. Helena.

During that first sad winter of 1815 he was talking to Napoleon one day about the emigration and the Emperor was reflecting on what his chances would have been as an émigré. Las Cases told him firmly that at Coblentz he would have been kept to the place assigned to him by his rank in society, which was doubtful, and his rank in the army which was negligible. Napoleon, however, was very sure that he would have achieved celebrity under any circumstances in his chosen career of arms. Las Cases did not attempt to argue with him further for, after all, the Emperor could have been right, but tactfully went on to recount his own experiences.

The emigration, he said, did not like the English but there were few émigrés who were not attached to some English or other; the English did not like the emigration but there were few English families who had not adopted some Frenchman, a situation not without parallel in our contemporary experience of refugees.

It was the middle classes in particular, Las Cases added, who showed the greatest individual kindness towards the émigrés and it was they who influenced the Government to provide official aid.

George III offered a perfect example of Las Cases' thesis. Already in 1794 he was speaking of the émigrés with disapproval and five years later he had not changed his views. In August, 1799, the King was reported as making 'a curious sally against the emigrants and the French in general' and again in November of that year 'he had a very bad conversation at the levée about the emigrants.' Farington remarks that Benjamin West had said something fell from the King which caused him to think that His Majesty was very sick of all the French who were now in this country.

Yet one can dislike a body of people collectively and be perfectly amiable to individuals. Meeting Madame de Gontaut at Windsor with her twin daughters he was charming to the children and behaved to her with the greatest cordiality.

Learning that her husband was a nephew of Marshal de Biron

he told the children that the English nation owed him a debt of gratitude for having, during the American War of Independence, acted with great chivalry to Admiral Rodney.

The King then followed up this kind reception by requesting Parliament to grant a pension as a mark of national gratitude to the Marshal's great-nieces, a decision which was communicated to Madame de Gontaut by the Duke of Portland himself.

Perhaps out of his natural sense of opposition to his father, or because he genuinely felt sympathy with them, the Prince of Wales was much more friendly than George III to the émigrés. He may have been influenced by Mrs. Fitzherbert or possibly he experienced fellow-feelings for the Comte d'Artois whose equivocal domestic situation so greatly resembled his own.

Differences in customs and outlook did not diminish the real gratitude which the majority of the émigrés felt towards England but it is a very human characteristic to resent, if not to bite, the hands that feed one.

The émigrés did not go so far as this and many angrily refuted the insinuation that England was generous and hospitable only in her own interest while, beneath her benevolent façade, she harboured treachery and hatred. The same might have been said on the other side. Farington records that a French General, who dined with one of his friends, thought that the Directory ought to be impeached if it gave up Belgium, showing that 'an emigrant Frenchman loses nothing of the prevailing spirit of conquest.'

But far more representative of the typical émigré was Vicomte Walsh's indignant exclamation:

'Let those who received nothing from the British government cast stones. I, who drew the émigré's shilling a day, scorn to do so.'

It was inevitable that there should be wide differences of opinion among the émigrés for they were by no means all from the same *milieu* and faction tends to flourish among the dispossessed. Among them the party spirit raged for the emigration enshrined as many parties and divergences among its constituent members as existed in France, from the out-and-out reactionaries surrounding the Comte d'Artois to the constitutionalists and the republicans. They were united only by the common grievance of being expelled from their native country.

English feeling towards the émigrés moved uneasily against this chequerboard of opinion. Caution was necessary in assembling them together unless one were sure that they belonged to the same party. But the English could be charitable and understanding even about these differences of view. As Windham wrote in 1796:

'We abuse the emigrants for their hostility to one another. What sort of charity shall I feel for the Dukes of Bedford, the Plumbers, the Cokes and other large lists that I could name, when we meet in exile and beggary in some town on the Continent? My only consolation will be, that their wretchedness, from the greater indulgence which they have always required and enjoyed, will be something sharper than my own. . . .

'When England becomes too vile or too dangerous to live in and we meet in Siberia we shall at least have the satisfaction of thinking that we are not the authors of our own calamities.'

As was natural the émigrés of similar outlook and circumstances tended to congregate together. Although they scattered far and wide over the whole country many remained where they landed, lacking means or energy to go further. There was a particularly large concentration in Jersey and Guernsey, the Normans and Bretons finding in the Channel Islands not only the nearest point of refuge but also an atmosphere which resembled their own French homelands. The majority of the émigrés, however, and particularly those with ambitions to play a part in Royalist politics, were centred in London.

They settled in districts which had previously received an influx of French refugees and in tracing their homes one constantly comes upon evidence of previous inhabitants so that certain areas of London represent a palimpsest of foreign occupations.

The émigrés in easiest circumstances (one could not by any standards call them rich) lived on the fringe of the fashionable West End and the parish of St. Marylebone became their Faubourg St. Germain and the Marais. The families established here were those who had always lived in Paris and at Versailles and represented the *haut monde* of the exiles, those who were received on equal terms by the owners of the great mansions of Piccadilly and Grosvenor Square.

Nearly every house in a rough square bounded on the south by the Oxford Road, on the west by Portman Street, on the east by Harley Street and on the north by Marylebone Road was occupied by a French family. Those who could not afford whole houses for themselves took furnished rooms in the modest, three-storied Georgian buildings with their flat façades and narrow staircases with a pair of rooms on each floor. If these new homes lacked the elegance and richness of their châteaux and hôtels in France the young émigrés, who had never known the Court, might still learn there elegance of speech and manners.

From the congeries of little streets, most of which still exist though they have changed their names, French servants poured every morning into High Street, Marylebone, to make their modest purchases. They might pass that part of Marylebone Gardens, known as the French Gardens, because they had been cultivated by the Huguenots and it was their presence in the neighbourhood which is perpetuated by the name of a public house, the *Rose of Normandy*. In the High Street, too, was a French restaurant, the Véry's of the émigrés where, if one had the money, one could dine *à la carte* in the noblest, most numerous and most indigent company.

Many of the émigrés found a home in Soho, traditional haunt of foreigners, and on its fringes in Long Acre, Seven Dials and Tottenham Court Road where Chateaubriand said that he sucked sheets dipped in water to assuage his hunger. But Chateaubriand was the first of the Romantics and must be allowed his poetic licence.

Other émigrés were to be found in Thames Street, Aldgate, Cripplegate, Temple Bar, Bishopsgate, Shoreditch and Somers Town, which was particularly favoured because of the cheapness and availability of houses. Somers Town had been the site of much speculative building by one Jacob Leroux but on his death the project was discontinued and many houses were left empty at rentals as low as twenty pounds per annum, an inviting rent for the artisan class among the émigrés.

The Polygon in Clarendon Square was the centre of the area but few of the original houses remain as they were swept away first of all by the building of the railways and secondly by the blitz on London.

There was another reason for the émigrés' choice of Somers Town and that was the proximity of Old St. Pancras Church, over whose melancholy churchyard the Duchesse de Gontaut's room looked out.

The church and churchyard of St. Pancras were for many years noted as the burial place of such Roman Catholics as died in London and its vicinity. The reason assigned for this preference was that in a church in the South of France, dedicated to the same saint, masses were said for the souls of the deceased interred at St. Pancras in England. Some people averred that at St. Pancras Church mass had been sung since the Reformation. Others claimed unusual sanctity for a spot where a few Roman Catholics were supposed to have been burnt in the days of Queen Elizabeth I.

Whatever the reasons for its choice it was in Old St. Pancras Churchyard that the émigrés who died in London were buried. It is now a public garden. The bones were disinterred and reburied some years ago and the defaced tombstones are ranged round the walls of the garden where children play, unaware of the courage and the heartache, the fidelity and the misery that once lay under the grass.

Across the Thames at St. George's Fields in Southwark the face of the emigration was very different, sadder, more serious and more austere. This was not the world of the Court but of the provinces, less frivolous and less gay, a living mosaic of French provincial life, made up of the lesser nobility of the robe and of the sword. It was composed of elderly officers and magistrates, of dowagers and widows, of young girls and venerable priests. Some of the émigrés lived with their *femmes de chambre* and their menservants, of whom none received any wages but who still served their impoverished masters with devotion and affection.

In this unfashionable quarter lodgings were even cheaper than in Somers Town and away from the Court émigrés there were no social embarrassments to be feared, only the embarrassment of living. Sickness, misery and madness stalked the humble streets of St. George's Fields, where people were sustained by pride in lieu of bread. In their wretched garrets their days were given up to melancholy reflection as each day brought news of a France which seemed to bear no resemblance to the country of their birth and which was yet, in spite of all the horror it now inspired, so dear.

These were the elderly on whom the rigours of the emigration bore most hardly. For them there was nothing to do but to look back to the happy past and forward to the dark future. For the most part they had borne no part in the events which led up to the Revolution and were largely innocent victims of a progress they did not comprehend and whose future they could not foresee. They seemed to belong to a different species of the human race and hardest of all they, who had had the means and the desire to relieve distress in others, now found themselves unable to do so or to help themselves.

But they might count themselves fortunate in this at least that they had only their own thoughts and problems to contend with. Others were in far worse case. Here a lady, forced to flee from Holland immediately after a confinement, lost her reason, leaving five children, the eldest of whom was only seven, wholly destitute. Another aristocratic émigrée died of her privations, leaving uncared for a paralysed husband and three sick and ragged children. Yet another was in the last stages of consumption with a husband completely immobilised from wounds received in the Princes' service, unable to help herself or him and in want of every necessity.

Every house in St. George's Fields had a comparable tale to tell of stark misery within its walls.

In 1795 some English ladies, hearing these heart-rending stories, formed a special committee under the patronage of the Duchess of York for the relief of the 'female emigrants who were ill or *en couches*' and unable to provide for their own pressing needs.

They had not hesitated to go and see for themselves and verify that the reports that they had heard were true. Shocked and distressed by what they had seen they circulated a letter to their friends, detailing the truly pitiful stories and their appeal could not fail to touch any charitable heart.

'Heartsick as we were at the sight of these scenes of distress in which so many persons of the same sex and rank as ourselves have been so innocently involved, the ladies who were witnesses to them, together with several other persons of distinction, have determined to raise a subscription among the ladies of their acquaintance for the relief of the suffering of these unfortunates and to recommend them to the benevolence of those ladies living out of London in order to gain their support.

'In accordance with this resolution and in the conviction that such misery cannot fail to excite the sensibility of every true Englishwoman, your aid is solicited, in whichever way you see fit to give it, in order to supply at least, their indispensable needs.'

Ladies in London and out of it, particularly in Bath, Norwich, Chester and Wrexham, rallied to this appeal so that considerable gifts of linen, clothing, medicaments and money were made to the émigré ladies. Some of the émigrées *en couches* were admitted to the Lying-in Hospital in Brownlow Street but accommodation was still insufficient in other hospitals for the sick.

Having met with such success in their efforts on behalf of the indigent, the sick, the infirm and the aged of both sexes the ladies were fired to further efforts although they, like Wilmot's Committee, found that, so great were the demands, they had to limit their distributions.

They therefore sought the advice of the indispensable Bishop of St. Pol de Léon, who suggested that in future they should confine their charitable efforts to aiding their own sex. They decided to appeal for subscriptions. Since, however, needs were so pressing and money would take time to raise, the ladies of this committee rapidly collected a hundred and sixty-eight pounds among themselves.

In order not to prejudice the help given to the English poor a subscription of seven shillings a family was suggested and smaller subscriptions gratefully received. They calculated that their annual expenditure would be in the neighbourhood of two thousand five hundred pounds which they thought could be raised without difficulty among the ladies of Great Britain.

The particular classes of emigrant whom they took under their wing were the Quiberon widows, sole achievements of that abortive expedition, to whom an annual sum of ten pounds was allocated; and about a hundred and fifty girls, aged six to fourteen, whom they proposed to train to be useful members of society, costing, with what the Government gave to their support, about ten pounds a year each. The third class embraced the aged, the infirm, the ladies *en couches* and girls under the age of six.

St. Pol de Léon himself made great exertions on behalf of the Quiberon soldiers, many of them young men who had lost an arm or a leg or the use of their limbs through wounds received fighting in that expedition in a British uniform, the rags of which were all they had to clothe themselves with. Many, too, were suffering from double hernias from the unaccustomed weight of the packs they had to carry. For most of them, without his intervention, there could be no choice but between death by starvation and the most cruel mendicity.

Much more than six years of time lay between the *émigration joyeuse* and the heartbreak of St. George's Fields.

Outside London the emigration lived in easier conditions. The little group settled at Richmond enjoyed its purer air and the comfort and reinforcement of society.

Farther away still, at Mickleham in Surrey, a special order of émigrés congregated at Juniper Hall. They lived isolated from the other émigrés who looked askance at them. Their society might be the most amusing, their wit and talents of the highest order, but they were execrated by the *purs* for their political views.

Men like Talleyrand, Narbonne, Lally-Tollendal and women like Madame de Stael were the *constitutionnels* and *monarchiens* who had supported the concept of monarchy but so hedged round with limitations as to leave nothing of its traditional French character. True Lally-Tollendal had exerted himself greatly to save the King but that, in the estimation of the *purs*, availed him nothing. It was locking the stable-door after the horse had gone. It was from the misguided meddling of these liberals that they believed all their misery arose.

To Juniper Hall Fanny Burney came to be dazzled, enchanted and finally to wed her General d'Arblay, but she is an interested witness and could not enter into the feelings of the ultra-Royalist French.

It gave some of them malicious pleasure to know that the constitutionalists' betrayal of their caste had failed to save them from the common fate and that they had been tossed out to sink or swim with the devoted adherents of the *ancien régime*.

The Duc de La Châtre, who had lost everything in the campaigns of 1792 and 1793, arrived in England still wearing his uniform of Coblentz, which was all he had until a tailor obligingly lent him a suit of clothes.

Meeting the Comte de Narbonne, a leading member of the Juniper Hall set, he saluted him merrily with the words:

'You have ruined everything with your constitution. You are the primary cause of all our misfortunes. Well, there it is, and now let's all die of hunger gaily together.'

IX

How the Emigrés lived

The reasonably young and able-bodied had no intention of dying of hunger if their intelligence and industry could save them from it. To succumb to their misfortunes would gratify only the Jacobins who reputedly gloated over every disaster that befell the 'rebels and fugitives' and whom nothing would please more than that they become beggars and outcasts, but for those without family or friends in England survival was not easy.

To begin with the only money the émigrés had was obtained by the sale of such valuables as they managed to bring with them, although in the case of those who came from Holland and Belgium often little remained. Traders were soon quick to grasp the opportunities that offered of acquiring goods cheaply and they obligingly inserted advertisements in the newspapers, advising the foreign nobility that the highest possible prices would be paid on the spot for French diamonds and other jewels.

Calonne, who had given his liquid fortune to the Comte d'Artois, was fortunate in getting his fine collection of paintings out of France and he sold it advantageously in London.

But, although one bishop might boast that he had lived for five years more or less on his belongings, money, particularly to those unused to counting it, went with the swiftness of a song. There would seem to be enough for three months. With care it might be made to stretch for ten, but afterwards what?

Help might perhaps be had from more fortunate émigrés but it could only be a temporary measure and it did not consort with their pride to live on borrowed money as independence was to be valued above everything. Since the cause of their poverty was honourable they did not blush for it and they considered that, where all shared the same misfortune, it would be shameful to complain about their privations. The only humiliation they recognised apart from dependence was the refusal to bow courageously to necessity.

In their struggle for survival they were handicapped by their ignorance of daily life which was often total. Many of them had descended suddenly from opulence to indigence with no apprenticeship to poverty. They wanted to be careful but, having no knowledge of the value of money, allowed it to slip through their fingers.

Those whose servants accompanied them had some guides on whose experience they could rely but those who were alone found that they did not know how or where to buy the bare necessities of life. Their gallant efforts at self-sufficiency often ended in bathos. One lady tried the unaccustomed task of washing her linen but, having lost her soap in the process, did not know what to do. Another, having invited guests to dinner, ran to the market and bought up all the flowers, only to find that she had no money left to buy anything to eat.

They could not be blamed for their inexperience. In their previous lives bailiffs, intendants and servants had taken care of the material organisation of their households. Their function had been only to enjoy themselves and spend the money their stewards gathered in and, even with ample rent-rolls, they had often lived beyond their means. When the revolutionaries took over their estates they found at least half of them were mortgaged. It was not, therefore, to be expected that they could acquire habits of management and economy overnight. Nor had their way of living been unique. Wherever the émigrés found themselves they saw that their counterparts lived in the same way as they had done.

The past had to be put resolutely behind them. It was clear that if they were to survive and pride, more than any other consideration, demanded that they should, they must work to earn a living.

For the members of the Third Estate among the émigrés earning their livelihood, once they were established, was simple for they brought with them skills and crafts which were welcomed in England, which they enriched with their industry as she had been enriched by the Flemish weavers of the sixteenth century and the Huguenot silk-looms of the seventeenth.

For the nobility it was different, yet they found a thousand things to do of which they had never dreamed themselves capable and their ingenuity in finding occupations inspired admiration in the English as well as their determination to be independent.

'Instead of breaking their hearts as Englishmen would do, from being counts they turn cobblers or anything for a livelihood.'*

Perhaps no one actually became a cobbler but they taught French and dancing and chess and fencing. They opened boarding schools and restaurants. One sold coke and another became a tailor. The Comte de Caumont learned bookbinding and his work is highly considered to-day among bibliophiles. Another nobleman became a cataloguer.

Many of the men, of course, remained on the Continent with the Army of Condé or served in the émigré regiments raised in England. Others spent their days haunting the government offices in an effort to get employment and there were those who did not scorn to work as agents for the British like the Comte d'Antraigues, who consequently lived in affluence, keeping his carriage, or the Comte de Puisaye, who had been appointed by Artois to command the Royalist armies in Brittany and became disgusted with the vacillations and delays of his Royal masters. Ultimately he took British nationality and died as a British subject in this country.

Some émigrés, lower down no doubt in the social scale, were employed by the Police Office to go to and from France to collect information. Apparently, however, the British placed little reliance on them for it was only by comparing their accounts that 'they collect something like the truth from these fellows,' remarked Farington. 'They are searched at Dover, even to taking off their buttons, every time they go or return.'

Since all had to work, great tolerance was shown by the *doyens* of the émigrés towards the choice of employment, but there were some methods of earning a living which they felt unable to countenance.

When a certain chevalier of the Order of St. Louis became a servant it was felt that the indignity was too great to be permitted, in spite of his heart-rending plea of bitter poverty.

A court-martial was duly constituted by a group of senior officers who first heard mass, then proceeded to promulgate its

* Farington: Diary.

judgment: that the state of servitude into which this gentleman had entered did not accord with the dignities of the Royal and Military Order of St. Louis and he was solemnly destituted of the title and distinctions he bore. This judgment was inserted in the newspapers to give the English people an idea of the esteem in which the Order was held and the honour attaching to its possession.

It was the women who were largely the most successful in earning a living for they were able to put to practical use the accomplishments they had learned in their convents. With their natural taste and elegance they soon excelled in making articles of ornament and fashion. Their work was made easier by the new rage for simplicity. Gone were the elaborate wigs, the monstrous hats, the huge panniers with which these amateur seamstresses could not have coped. The vogue for plain dresses with big straw hats and a natural style of hairdressing suited both their own present way of life and their skills. No doubt, too, they benefited by the advice and help of Rose Bertin, Marie Antoinette's *marchande de modes*, who had followed some of her customers to London.

More than a revolution would be needed to quench a Frenchwoman's innate interest in fashion. The Comtesse de Neuilly, who kept a *magasin de modes* in Hamburg, was deeply troubled in both heart and mind, anxious for her son who was fighting with the Austrian Army and distressed about the fate of her country, but she wrote regularly to her daughter about changes in fashion and was particularly concerned that she should manage the new short style of hairdressing successfully. It was so useful for repairing the damage done to hair by the use of wigs.

Madame de Gontaut had anticipated the day when her funds would run out. During her winter in Rotterdam she took lessons in painting and now, in London in her little house in Somers Town overlooking St. Pancras churchyard, she worked away, painting such trifles as *Love Conquering Lions*, or *Tigers* or *Nymphs*.

Her husband, too, painted amusing nonsenses and her mother made little frivolities. These ornaments sold well in the bazaar organised for the purpose where all, without giving their names, might take work to be sold and fix the price themselves.

English society ladies discreetly aided the émigrés by arranging lotteries of French porcelain and millinery at a guinea a ticket—

and no blanks—one of the prizes being a *bonnet aristocrat*, stamped with fleur-de-lis and *Vive le Roi!*—the émigrés' retort to the *bonnet rouge*.

At Richmond the Marquise de la Tour du Pin who would not, out of regard for her English family, draw the Government's shilling a day, aided some neighbours in marking linen. This little group of workers had a good angel in a French neighbour who once a week, and sometimes oftener, went on foot to London to carry out commissions entrusted to him by the émigrés who lacked the money to make the journey by coach.

Madame de Saisseval, whose arrival in England was so terrifying, started making straw hats, a favourite article of manufacture among the émigrés. They found great favour in America but she fell a victim to an unscrupulous agent who appropriated her invention.

Next she turned to embroidering the white dresses which were so fashionable, selling them at a guinea apiece and, with the aid of a charitable and ingenious abbé who helped her to package them elegantly, they sold very well.

Madame de Saisseval had no husband in the background to supplement her earnings for, as a result of wounds received during his service with the Army of Condé, the Comte de Saisseval had lost his reason and, in addition to supporting herself, her mother and her daughters, she had to pay for his keep in a madhouse. Later she received an allowance for her family from the Committee of seven pounds seventeen shillings and sixpence a month but even so when her husband died in 1798 she and her daughters had to pawn their coloured dresses to buy mourning.

The working day was long and her mother, Madame de Lastic, who had been lady-in-waiting to the daughters of Louis XV, was able to give Madame de Saisseval very little help. When she was in London, Madame de Lage, her cousin, worked with them but her hands were made to flirt a fan, not ply a needle, and she found bending over her sewing all day arduous and tiring. Sometimes when she had more orders than she and her mother could manage by themselves Madame de Saisseval invited their friends in need to come and assist them. Their pay was twopence an hour—when they didn't talk too much!

Working together in large rooms, which the émigrés dignified by the name of *ateliers*, was popular because in company and conversation the hours of unaccustomed manual labour passed more quickly. In many of these work-rooms they plaited a particular type of straw hat which took three days to make but which sold for twenty-five shillings.

The younger people, who spoke better English than their elders, were entrusted with the task of selling the hats, which they did not find wholly congenial, for they lacked the assurance of professional salesmen, although the hardest part of all was to return to their work-mates and confess that they had sold nothing.

These were the times when, the day's work done and the work tables cleared away, they did not dance in the evenings. For a long time after the Quiberon expedition they did not dance at all, for too many of their number were in mourning for lost members of their families, with material distress to embitter their sorrow further.

At other times, when the poor tallow candles were lit (and it was a graceful gesture made by a young man to his hostess to bring a candle which he placed lighted on the mantelpiece), they would dress in their best and assemble to talk and dance and become so gay that the English were amazed that they could be so apparently carefree in their misery, not understanding that, by laying aside their anxieties, however briefly, they drew fresh courage for the next day's tasks.

'The men that you bought fruit off in Market Street, the hairdressers and fencing-masters and French teachers, they turn back by candlelight to what they used to be at home, and you catch their real names. There wasn't much room in the washhouse, so I sat on top of the copper and played 'em the tunes they called for—'Si le Roi m'avait donné,' and such nursery stuff. They cried sometimes,'*

said Pharaoh Lee of the émigrés in Philadelphia but it was much the same in London, although it was rarely that they allowed themselves this last indulgence, at least in public.

As time went by and the émigrés made friends among the English they were welcomed in their houses and the great ladies among the French still tried to keep something of a salon. Even

* Rudyard Kipling: '*A Priest in Spite of Himself.*'

work-and-careworn Madame de Saisseval received her friends in the evening and large numbers of them were drawn to her by her charm and distinction and talent for singing and reading aloud.

If one belonged to her circle, one called on the Duchesse de FitzJames—who had managed to get to England—was invited to dinner and, on leaving, discreetly dropped three shillings in a vase placed for that purpose on the mantelpiece.

When they could afford it the émigrés dined out in restaurants where they could eat French food at very modest prices. At the French House in Lisle Street, Leicester Square, there was a *table d'hôte* in the style of Paris. Dinner at four o'clock was three shillings, supper at ten o'clock two shillings, but rare were the evenings when the mass of émigrés could afford even these small sums.

They might go and eat ices at the café of the Comtesse de Guéry who discovered in herself an unsuspected talent for making them. Her ices were soon considered the best to be obtained in London and her café was patronised by the Prince of Wales and the Royal Dukes.

On days when articles sold well there might be outings to Vauxhall or Bagnigge Wells, and the émigrés were always happy to accept the offer of tickets for the Opera made to them by their English friends. Then they could hear again the operas of Gluck, which Marie Antoinette had made so popular in France, or of Cherubini and marvel at the great singers, Banti and Mara, and later Grassini and Catalani.

The early arrivals might have gone to see the 'pantomimes of the horrors of the Bastille' whose sanguinary tableaux so disgusted Horace Walpole. Later, when she brought her cero-plastic museum to the Lyceum in the Strand the émigrés flocked to shudder at Madame Tussaud's realistic models, some of them carried out at the foot of the scaffold.

Society was necessary to them for their spirits would not bear solitude. There was too much to remember and too little to which they might comfortably look forward. Their social contacts with the English often resulted in marriages, for emigration had not diminished the natural gallantry of the French men nor the *espièglerie* of the women. While they were in no position to seek wealthy brides it did often happen that marriage was a solution of their financial problems. One can see the poor Grub Street clerk positively sucking his quill pen with excitement as he wrote an entry for the *Annual Register* of 1804, under the heading,

Marriages—

> 'In Buckinghamshire, Louis Montgaillard, Esq., a French emigrant, to Miss Arabella Norman, a young lady of exquisite beauty, with a fortune of 30,000*l.*'

Those Frogs had all the luck!

Even their work and the bounty of the Government did not bring affluence to the émigrés and not all of them were able to find a livelihood. Happily an unexceptionable way of making money was within the compass of a number of people for whom the carrying on of a regular trade was an impossibility. The years of the emigration saw dozens of French publications of all kinds pouring off the presses to be sold by French booksellers like De Boffe and Dulau, a firm which survived until the blitz of 1941 when unhappily all its invaluable records were lost.

The easiest books to write and those sure of an immediate sale were accounts of their own recent experiences. The *Journal of the Occurrences at the Temple during the Confinement of Louis XVI, King of France*, by Monsieur Cléry, the King's *valet de chambre*, received a favourable notice in the *Anti-Jacobin* in 1799, which also noted that a German edition was printing in London, which gave the reviewer an opportunity to fulminate against the Emperor and the King of Prussia who had the base pusillanimity to comply with the request (or rather the mandate) of the French Directory, that it might not be printed in their dominions.

> 'How long will the Sovereigns of Europe thus continue to favour the views of their implacable enemies, by degrading themselves in the eyes of their subjects?'

The Marquis de Bouillé, who so unsuccessfully organised the King's flight which ended at Varennes, published his memoirs and so did the Chevalier du Haussey, literal *nom de guerre* of Madame de Bennes who had fought side by side with her husband until Quiberon. In accordance with custom she sold the book herself at her house, 22, Maddox Street, Soho.

Many of the books written at this time—and it seemed almost that anyone who could hold a pen wrote something or other with it—have left nothing but their titles, *L'Emigré à Londres*, *L'Emigré en 1794*, *Le Valet Reconnaissant* and a play, *Les Emigrés Français à Londres ou Le Préjugé Vaincu*. Was it ever performed?

Polemists, pamphleteers and journalists abounded, like Mallet du Pan whose work had already had some influence on the Revolution and who, like several other émigrés, was in closer relation with the British Government than with the French Royalists.

Jean Peltier, a professional journalist, edited a series of periodicals from 1793 onwards, including the famous *Actes des Apôtres*, and there were many ephemeral publications which lasted for a short time only.

Among those destined to find in London her vocation as a writer was Madame de Flahaut, the illicit relationships of whose family are so confusing. By Talleyrand she had a son, Charles de Flahaut, who became in his turn father of an illegitimate son by Hortense de Beauharnais, Queen of Holland, the Duc de Morny, who was the half-brother (though there were some who would have said the full brother) of the Emperor Napoleon III.

Madame de Flahaut was lucky enough to emigrate direct from Paris to London with enough money to travel comfortably post, being much impressed by the cleanliness and politeness she met at inns on the way but, of course, in dire apprehension of highwaymen. When her money began to run out she began to make the ubiquitous straw hats but she soon wearied of this work and the want of the kind of society to which she was accustomed in Paris. At last Talleyrand showed awareness of her presence in England and she rushed off to join the witty company at Juniper Hall, rejoicing in the companionship of old friends and a Parisian atmosphere.

She had begun a novel in Paris, *Adèle de Senange*, which she now took up again, acting herself as copyist, for she could not afford to employ one. The routine work, however, allowed her no time for reflection on the precariousness of her position. She launched a subscription, the book was published, reviewed, met with much success and netted her forty thousand francs. Madame de Flahaut was successfully embarked on her career as a novelist and during the years of her emigration she wrote many more, drawing on her experiences as an émigrée for copy.

Most prolific writers were the clergy. They wrote and published books of devotion, translations of the scriptures, works of piety, including Christian thoughts for every day of the year, sermons, treatises on dogma and theology, sermons and their funeral orations for the great and famous. Of course they published their poems, generally of a sacred nature, and advice to the faithful priests on the part they should play on their return to France. They wrote histories of the persecution of the clergy and chronological tables of universal history. Their subjects ranged from theses on the theory of the universe to histories of French literature and treatises on French grammar and even on the teaching of English which were adopted in English schools.

Many of these works have vanished for ever. One, and the most important for a student of the period, has happily survived, the *Journal Historique et Réligieux de l'Émigration et Déportation du Clergé de France en Angleterre*, by Monsieur l'Abbé de Lubersac, Vicar-General of Narbonne, Abbé de Noirlac and Royal Prior of St. Martin de Brive, who adds proudly to his overloaded title-page, *Emigré Français*.

The work was printed by Cox, Son and Baylis of 75, Great Queen Street, Lincoln's Inn Fields, and might be bought from numerous booksellers and from the author himself at 24, Queen Anne Street East. The copy in the King's Library at the British Museum bears the binder's label of the Comte de Caumont.*

Charles François de Lubersac de Livron was born in 1730. He had witnessed the outrageous insults poured upon the King and Queen at the Tuileries in June, 1792, which so filled him with horror that he wrote an account of that day, appending a parallel of the sufferings experienced by Jesus Christ before his death, a prophetic narration.

Warned by Madame Elisabeth that his name was on the list of proscribed, the Abbé left Paris and joined the emigrants at Trèves and later at Luxembourg where he indulged further his taste for writing, composing this time, after Holy Writ and the Psalms, four holy interviews such as he imagined Louis XVI addressed to God in his oratory some days before his death. These interviews he had

* The author's copy has the same binding.

printed and distributed to a large number of émigré families living in Luxembourg. With bitterness the Abbé chided the French people for not remaining in holy attachment to their good King and his family. What, he asked, had these generous masters done to them that they so cruelly massacred them on altars dressed by their regicide hands?

The date of de Lubersac's arrival in England is not known but he remained here until his death in 1804. Much of his time must have been given to writing his *Journal* which was published in 1802 and, although devoted primarily to the clergy in England, also includes much information about the laity.

The Abbé gave full measure to the purchasers of his book for to his narrative he added his funeral oration on the pious Madame Elisabeth, with a most moving account of her death and deportment on the guillotine, and a full list of bishops and archbishops who emigrated to England, together with the funeral orations for those who died here.

As if this were not enough he appended a dissertation on the grandeur, force and majesty of holy religion and the French monarchy united, an apologia for the powers spiritual and temporal, dedicated to the Most Christian King, Louis XVIII, King of France and Navarre, Elder Son of the Roman Church, with a dedicatory verse beneath an idealised portrait of Louis, surrounded by a wreath of lilies broken in the middle.

De Lubersac was one of the worst offenders among the clergy in rushing into bad verse, of which this is a typical example:

> Son Trône est usurpé, mais sa vertu lui reste:
> La mort, O ma patrie! à toi seule est funeste.
> Descendant des BOURBONS il tient moins sa grandeur,
> De l'éclat de son nom, que de son noble cœur.
> Non, ce n'est point des Rois la pompe et la puissance,
> Qui manquent à LOUIS, mais LOUIS à la France.

The whole book is dedicated (by gracious permission) to George III in grandiloquent terms and the Abbé de Lubersac could not resist the innocent temptation of translating the national anthem into French and Latin nor of composing an additional verse:

Que le Ciel favorise,
L'immortelle entreprise,
De Georges III!
L'on verra les François,
Alliés aux Anglois,
Chanter comme autrefois,
Vive le Roi!

The real poet among the émigrés was the Abbé Delille who represented the apotheosis of contemporary French poetry but to-day his work reads arid, cold and formal. Delille was far from being one of the saintly clergy of whom de Lubersac so justly writes with great respect. He had acquired a 'niece', whom he subsequently married, from a café where, as a singer, she earned some thirty sous a day and a bottle of cider. She treated him with great severity, forcing him to write thirty lines of verse before breakfast because a bookseller paid her a premium for them, ensuring that he accomplished his task by hiding his breeches until he had finished.

Danloux painted the Abbé Delille, declaiming his verse while the idealised 'niece' sits by with a pad in her hand. The Abbé seems to have been completely under her thumb and his only retort when one day she threw a large quarto book at him was to remark plaintively:

'Wouldn't an octavo have been enough?'

Probably the domestic indignities to which he was submitted were not known in the elegant English circles where Delille's readings were very popular. One of his great admirers was the Duchess of Devonshire and no doubt he found some balm to his spirit in the aristocratic atmosphere of Devonshire House.

Reading aloud from their writing was a cheap and pleasant form of entertainment for the émigrés. Chateaubriand received a large company in his rooms on Saturday evenings at which punch was served while he read pages of his *Génie du Christianisme*. No doubt the punch was paid for from the proceeds of his *Essai sur les Révolutions Anciennes et Modernes* which was published in England and not by the money he had earned teaching French in Suffolk.

Inevitably the writers and the intellectuals were attracted to each other's society and formed a homogeneous circle. One of their number was the Comte de Montlosier who, having studied anatomy in France as a hobby, had some intentions of qualifying as a doctor in England. Since, however, his whole fortune consisted of a hundred louis and he knew no English he had to abandon this project.

He decided, therefore, to practice magnetism, which was very much in vogue at the end of the eighteenth century and at which he was adept. In doing so he fell foul of a jealous husband, for Montlosier was much given to amorous adventures, and risked being thrown out of the country, but was saved through the intervention of an influential friend.

After this narrow escape Montlosier cast about for some more innocent occupation and some unexpected funds allowed him to found a journal, the *Journal de France et d'Angleterre*.

Newspapers were of great importance to the émigrés eager to learn about events on the Continent and so tap the barometer by which their hopes rose and fell. As few of them at the outset spoke English they were fortunate to find in existence in England a French newspaper.

This paper had a curious history. It was founded in 1776 as the *Courrier de l'Europe* by a Frenchman named Serres de La Tour, the proprietor being a Scot named Samuel Swinton. Swinton was a cadet of the ancient Scottish family, the Swintons of that Ilk, and had served in the Royal Navy. Between the time of his quitting that service and buying the *Courrier de l'Europe* Swinton, who was something of a soldier of fortune, had become very rich and he had interests in several English newspapers, including the *Morning Post*.

The paper went through several changes of name and by the middle of the seventeen nineties had become the *Courrier de Londres*. For a short period of its early life, Brissot, the *conventionnel* and leader of the Girondists, was associated with Swinton in the editorship, but they fell out and Brissot returned to France, where he died on the guillotine in 1793. The paper had many editors, among them the Abbé de Calonne, brother of the Minister, who excelled in translating the debates in the House of Commons.

In 1797 Montlosier joined his paper to the *Courrier de Londres* and assisted the Abbé de Calonne in editing it. By this time

Samuel Swinton was dead and the paper belonged to his widow, Félicité, born Lefebvre, who became the ancestress of several distinguished British families.

When the Abbé de Calonne went to Canada Montlosier remained as sole editor and became co-proprietor with Mrs. Swinton. After his return to France the paper continued with yet another change of title and was published until 1826. Montlosier never completed that part of his memoirs dealing with his later association with the *Courrier de Londres* and its further history seems lost for ever as there are no records of it in the Swinton family.

It was, however, evidently a newspaper which enjoyed great prestige, although Montlosier's opinions were not always viewed with favour either by the Comte d'Artois or by the British Government, but it was too useful to suppress.

Another newspaper of importance was the *Courrier d'Angleterre* which published all the acts of the British Government translated from the *London Gazette*. It seems to have run from 1805 to 1814.

That ambivalent character, Fauche-Borel, who acted as an agent for the British Government, suggested to Lord Grenville, the Foreign Secretary, that he should distribute copies on the Continent as counter-propaganda to the French papers flooding Germany, an early instance of political warfare. Although it was a costly enterprise and the Treasury showed no more munificence then than it does now Lord Grenville secured its assent or perhaps its distribution was paid for from the secret funds.

If their sole need had been literature the émigrés were certainly well provided for but there were other gaps in their lives remaining to be filled. Although the Committee, the Government and their own efforts combined to keep them from material want their spiritual needs could be met by themselves alone.

X

Self-Help

Only the chapels attached to the embassies of Catholic powers, the Sardinian in Lincoln's Inn Fields and the Spanish in Manchester Square, were accessible to the earliest French arrivals in London. Neither, however, was large enough nor conveniently situated to accommodate the growing numbers of émigrés, especially when the clergy who came *en masse* in 1792 naturally wished to celebrate their rites according to their own usage.

The problem was complicated still further when, as a consequence of the renewal of the Alien Act in 1796, the émigrés were removed inland from the coastal districts and the Channel Islands and more of them crowded into the capital. Since the arrival of most of the émigrés war had broken out between England and France and they were in a somewhat equivocal position. Their removal from areas of possible invasion showed that, however benevolent the Government might be to them, it was not unaware of the possible danger they constituted. It was not, however, considered necessary, as in 1939, to send them into mass internment. Although John Wilmot thought that, in spite of its good provisions, the Alien Act did not go far enough, it did in fact prove adequate to deal with any possible threats from this body of foreigners within a country at war.

The invasion scare and the requirements of the war brought fresh work to the Committee. When, in 1797, the Castle at Winchester was needed for a barracks the seven hundred priests who were then living in it had to be re-housed in other parts of the country, notably at Reading and at Thame.

Those who had to leave their former places of residence proved a fresh charge on the Committee's funds. Among them were sixteen clergy from Lewes. Their spokesman reported to the Committee for re-imbursement of their travel expenses, stating that he and five other ecclesiastics had come on foot, a distance of over fifty miles, nine others came outside the coach at a cost of ninepence each, and one, who was afraid to ride outside, came within at a charge of one shilling and sixpence.

The Committee had now perfected a machinery to deal with developments of this nature. It was not expected nor did it intend to deal with the spiritual requirements of those it aided materially.

When the Abbé de Lubersac wrote that the most august favour that George III deigned to grant to 'this numerous tribe of French pastors' was to allow them to raise the sacred altars of their faith in the cities of his kingdom he allowed his sense of indebtedness to run away with historical accuracy. It was the unwearying efforts of the champions of Catholic emancipation which forced the King, in spite of his pronounced antipathy to Roman Catholics, to yield his reluctant consent to the Catholic Relief Act of 1791 which eased the penal laws against them. The émigrés speedily took advantage of the clause which permitted the erection of Catholic places of worship, provided that they had neither bells nor steeple.

Under the aegis of the English Vicar Apostolic, John Douglass, the French began to build their own chapels, choosing quiet and unobtrusive sites, actuated in their choice as much by lack of funds as by the desire not to wound the susceptibilities of the dominant creed.

First of the chapels to be built, with the support of Mrs. Silburn, was that of St. Cross, established in 1795 in Dudley Court, Soho Square, followed in rapid succession by others in St. George's Fields, in Somers Town, in Tottenham and in St. Marylebone.

The chapel in St. Marylebone, founded by the Abbé Bourret of St. Sulpice in Paris, was originally housed in a cellar on the corner of Dorset Mews and Paddington Street, leading out of Baker Street. It stayed here for a year but the Abbé Bourret, considering this an unworthy place in which to celebrate mass, managed to obtain a site from the Portman family in the mews of Little George Street, now Carton Street, at the angle of King Street.

Here the clergy helped with their own hands to build the new chapel and the clergy house attached to it, money for the building raised among the émigrés themselves and English sympathisers. Great ladies of the neighbourhood, like the Comtesses de

Vaudreuil and de Saisseval, took under their charge the decoration
of the altar, the maintenance of the vestments and the furnishings
of the chapel which was dedicated in 1799 to the Annunciation by
Monseigneur de Boisgelin, Archbishop of Aix.

The curious can still see the Chapel of the Annunciation,
although it has long since ceased to be called by that name. From
the mews in Carton Street one steps into what is scarcely more
than a large room, whitewashed and lit by a skylight in the roof.
Above the entrance passage a gallery is supported on slender
pillars. On one side of the gallery a corkscrew staircase leads up
three flights, each with a small room where lived the ministering
clergy.

This very modest building quickly took the ascendant, both as a
spiritual centre and as the parish church of the distinguished
residents of the borough, soon doubling the functions of the
Royal Chapel at St. Denis, traditional burial place of the French
kings, and of Notre-Dame in Paris. Here all too many funeral
orations were pronounced by the prelates who lived in the neighbourhood; orations for the Duc d'Enghien, for the Abbé
Edgeworth, who accompanied Louis XVI to the scaffold, for
Louis XVIII's Queen and for those Princes of the Church who
died in exile in London.

Arthur Dillon, Archbishop and Primate of Narbonne, preaching
the funeral sermon for Madame Adelaïde, daughter of Louis XV,
reminded his congregation of the gratitude that they owed to
England that they were thus publicly able to render the last
honours to the aunt of their King, extolling the virtues of that
nation

'so honourably and magnificently hospitable which has received
us in its bosom and which, almost alone in Europe, offers us an
asylum inaccessible to the persistent furies of the usurpers and
tyrants of our country.

'Let us therefore proclaim to the universe; that to be in
distress, to be faithful to one's God and to one's King, are the
most powerful titles to the regard, to the sensibility and to
the beneficence of this generous Nation.'

On great occasions like this the benches of the little Chapel were
filled to overflowing with the greatest names in France, spiritual

and temporal, and, when the service was ended and they streamed into Baker Street in their robes with the ribbons and crosses of their Orders, the passers-by stared until, with the passage of time, it became a familiar sight. Certainly many of them were drawn by curiosity and attracted by the pomp to attend some of the services.

By no means all the émigrés were devout, for in France their caste was distinguished rather for its outward conformity than for its inward piety, but even the least orthodox among them were drawn to the chapels as being something more than religious centres where they married and baptised their children and had masses said for their martyred dead. The humble buildings became a focus for their society and their sense of strangeness and isolation was lessened by knowing that in them they could recapture some spirit from the old life and in their familiar atmosphere revert to the persons that they had been. The clergy who ministered in these chapels were not unaware of the opportunity offered to them of bringing back the sceptics to religion and their perseverance, their eloquence and their own piety very often achieved this result.

One outstanding pastor, who inspired as much by works as by faith, was the Abbé Carron. Born at Rennes in 1760, Guy-Toussaint-Julien-Carron de la Carrière became a member of the Order of St. Vincent de Paul. In 1792 he was imprisoned and deported with a convoy of two hundred and fifty other priests, landing with them in Jersey where he immediately resumed the work for which he had become distinguished in Rennes, beginning by founding a chapel and a school for orphan children.

When he had to leave Jersey in 1796 the Abbé Carron came to London, settling first in Fitzroy Square, where he founded another chapel and a seminary for aspirants to Holy Orders. He also organised religious instruction for the children in the neighbourhood.

Leaving these foundations to other hands to carry on, the Abbé Carron moved to Somers Town, where there was already a small chapel and where he found ample scope for his religious and charitable zeal, earning the gratitude of the émigrés for his selfless devotion to their interests and the admiration of the English, many of whom associated themselves with his work.

'The Abbé Carron is a gentleman who does his native country honour . . . he has been of incalculable service to his distressed fellow-sufferers who are enthusiastic in his praise,'*

wrote J. T. Malcolm, the London historian.

His energy, equalled only by his enterprise, makes it difficult to enumerate all that he undertook to ameliorate the lot of the émigrés, particularly the sick and aged.

He opened a *Chambre de la Providence*, a repository to which people were invited to bring such articles of linen and clothing as they could spare for those more unfortunate than themselves. He established a bathing house for the émigrés and a library for the priests, never mindful of the care of the spirit to the exclusion of the body. Next he rented two houses in the Polygon at Somers Town as a hospice for forty aged and infirm clergy, who were maintained by the Government at the rate of thirty-five shillings a month, but whose care was the responsibility of the Abbé Carron. The chanting of the old men night and morning of *Domine salvum fac regem nostrum Georgium* must have disturbed their neighbour, Mary Wollstonecraft.

Since the demand for hospital beds was greater than could be met by those set aside by the Middlesex and Lying-in Hospitals, the Abbé supplied the deficiency by organising a hospital for female emigrants, staffed by pious émigré ladies. And he replaced the small existing chapel with one that still survives in its original state as a Catholic place of worship.

The Church of St. Aloysius in Phoenix Street, Somers Town, is a plain and simple building, barely furnished, but larger than the Chapel of the Annunciation. Within its walls are commemorated its founder and that other outstanding leader of the emigration, the Bishop of St. Pol de Léon.

The tablet dedicated to the memory of Jean-François de La Marche, Bishop of St. Pol de Léon, is now hidden behind the altar and a bust of him is in the sacristy but in the church itself there is a bust and an inscription commemorating the life and works of its founder, the Abbé Carron.

In truth no one more than he merited the words carved upon that marble slab, 'father of the poor, protector of the widow,

* *Gentleman's Magazine*, 1813.

supporter and cherisher of the orphan, guardian of the aged and infirm, friend of the destitute and unfortunate, comforter of the afflicted.'

The Abbé Carron's vision was large. His church was open not only to the French but to the whole population of Somers Town, and sermons were preached there in English as well as in French.

If humanity demanded that every effort must be made for the relief of suffering among the sick and aged it was the welfare of the children, the hope for the future, which offered a more reward-ing outlet for the Abbé's zeal. He set up schools for them in Somers Town, one for boys on the lines of the best *collèges* in Paris, and one for girls modelled on the convent of Penthémont and the Royal establishment at St. Cyr, founded by Madame de Maintenon.

The Abbé Carron's were not the only schools in London. One had been established in Hammersmith with the aid of the Marchioness of Buckingham where thirty young girls were instructed in grammar, in English, geography, drawing, music and sewing and embroidery with the object of making them virtuous Christians and useful and educated wives. Later, for reasons of economy, this school was amalgamated with the one in Somers Town.

There were also fee-paying schools like the one conducted by the Abbé de Broglie, son of the Marshal-Duke de Broglie, at Kensington, where the price of the pension was fifty guineas, a sum far beyond the reach of most émigrés, and where the pupils rejoiced in a uniform consisting of a blue tunic of fine cloth with gilded buttons and a white waistcoat. And there were the schools, like Stonyhurst, formerly conducted by monks and nuns in France and Belgium, which were re-established in England.

One notable institution was founded on the initiative of Edmund Burke at Tyler's Green House at Penn, not far from his own home. Burke himself laid down the principles on which this academy should be conducted and he drew up the curriculum with the aid of the Bishop of St. Pol de Léon. Sixty boys were educated here at the expense of the British Government, all sons of French officers or magistrates, most of whom had perished at Quiberon or in other naval and military engagements.

Burke, who had recently suffered the death of his own son, took a fatherly interest in the boys and was rewarded by the filial devotion of the young émigrés who even addressed him as father on his daily visits to the school.

Higher education was not neglected, as far as lay within the émigrés' power. In 1799 a school to train young men for the magistrature was set up through the efforts of Monsieur de Barentin, formerly Garde des Sceaux. Among those who there studied Roman law and the principles of French law was Vicomte Walsh de Serrant when he left Stonyhurst. It was hoped to attract the young to replace the losses which death was daily bringing to the ranks of the magistrates among the émigrés who had little expectation of being able to take over the legal system instituted by the revolutionary governments when ultimately they should return to France.

The Lord Chancellor had given his blessing to this law school. In fact no public institution for the benefit of French émigrés was founded without the approval of the British Government and often with the aid of its funds. But if the Government paid, and they paid no more than the current rate of relief for the émigrés, the inspiration for and the conduct of all these institutions was in the hands of the French themselves.

Although they had to bow to the necessity of accepting the bounty of Government and private persons the French were both too proud and too independent to rely solely upon charity if there were any way in which they could help themselves. They no doubt knew that the Huguenots, actuated by the same spirit, were the originators of the friendly societies which were, in the first instance, associations for mutual aid and thrift.

It was the Abbé Bourret, of the Chapel of the Annunciation, who conceived the idea of raising subscriptions among the French themselves in each of their chapels to supply the deficiencies in organised charity which did not always reach out to those whose pride or inability to reach its source often left in acute distress.

The Archbishop of Aix inaugurated the subscriptions in a sermon in which he drew attention to the fact that foreigners in distress have fewer connections in and fewer rights than the native inhabitants of a country, but he added:

'One has to put a term to charity. In England it has taxed itself perhaps beyond what a wise administration envisaged but yet how much remains to be done. We know how greatly those among us who have not lost their all have shared what they have with family, relations and friends, but some of those in need are unused to ask for charity and conceal from other eyes the extent of their misfortunes.'

An upper limit of five guineas a year was fixed for subscriptions and lesser contributions were welcome but no one might give more. The money thus collected was administered by a committee, presided over by a bishop, and used for the special relief, particularly nursing, of those sick who did not receive public help or whose illnesses were of such a nature that the fixed allowance was insufficient.

And, as the Archbishop said, they helped each other in other ways, showing great care not to wound each other's susceptibilities.

The Archbishop of Narbonne had six bishops from the Languedoc at his table in George Street. Talma, cousin of the great actor, who practised as a dentist in London, looked after the émigrés' teeth for nothing.

When Madame de Lastic sought Madame de Polastron's intervention in obtaining an increase in the allowance she and her daughter received from the Government, Louise de Polastron sent her fifteen louis, saying that Madame de Lage had charged her to remit this sum, a delicate attention which did not deceive Madame de Lastic but which touched her greatly.

Whatever the émigrés could organise for themselves they did. The Abbé Carron, like the Bishop of St. Pol de Léon, was always in need of money to carry on his indefatigable work of mercy but happily he had the priceless gift of attracting others to help him and he even persuaded the grasping Catalani to give a concert in aid of his charities.

Another concert promoted by the French in aid of their poorer compatriots was attended by the Prince of Wales, the Duke of York and all the French Princes. The soloist was the Vicomte de Marin, one of the most accomplished harpists of the day who, after performing a repertoire of classical items, began playing as an encore the songs of old France so dear to his audience, *O Richard, ô mon roi* and *Vive Henri IV*. There was not a dry eye in the hall and the applause was deafening but reached the peak of enthusiasm when the Prince of Wales turned to shake the hands of the French Princes. More important for the object in view, the presence of Royalty had necessitated the taking of a larger concert hall to accommodate all those members of high society who wished to attend so that the charity benefited substantially.

There were, of course, those who were not in a position to help their fellows although they could help themselves. Repeatedly the clergy returned to Wilmot's Committee, when they found themselves able to do so, moneys that they had received, nor would the émigrés always accept the allowance offered to them.

The Comte de Narbonne wrote to Wilmot:

'Please inform the Lords Commissioners for me that the asylum and protection that I have found in England during my thirteen years' residence here have secured to the country, to the Nation and to the Government eternal rights to my gratitude; but that asylum and that Protection are the only benefit which up till now I have expected from them.'

The desire to relieve distress was by no means parochial. Charity stretched out its hands far beyond the limits of Somers Town or St. George's Fields extending even as far as Guiana. Many of the clergy had been deported thither from France together with some of the laity and their acute material distress was learned from letters which somehow arrived in England.

From their meagre allowance, which barely sufficed for their own needs, the clergy managed to raise the sum of twelve hundred pounds which was taken by a devoted young officer to Guiana for the sufferers.

In England itself another problem arose for the priests and one of peculiar delicacy. In the prisons of Portsmouth, Bristol, Norman Cross and in the hulks at Chatham and Plymouth some thirty thousand French prisoners-of-war were languishing and in great need of succour. No fear and no consideration of opposed political views entered into the minds of the clergy when there was distress and misery to alleviate.

St. Pol de Léon took upon himself the finding of missionary

priests to work among the prisoners in the hulks and prisons with the permission of the Government department concerned with prisoners-of-war.

The first task was to relieve the physical distress of the prisoners, living in a squalor which only intensified their ferocity and antagonism to the émigrés. Most of them were in rags, the fault no doubt of the Republican Government which failed to provide for them.

Always practical, the missionary priests set themselves to collect worn clothing and they were successful in obtaining among themselves two thousand five hundred pounds weight of it. The next task was to raise a subscription to pay for the packing and despatch of parcels of clothes to the various centres and to provide the prisoners with some of the necessities of life. How much could have been left of the priests' shilling a day?

It was not until they had made some progress in alleviating their physical misery that the clergy turned their attention to bringing them spiritual comfort. They used in this part of their task so much tact and delicacy, addressing themselves in the first instance to those who seemed the least unreasonable, that they did meet with some success in softening the hearts of the prisoners towards religion.

It could not have been without shame that these men of the Revolution saw those whom they had vilified and chased from their homes act towards them only in a spirit of love and perhaps in their hearts they regretted the excesses which had deprived their country of sons so outstanding in the virtues of piety and humanity.

Artois in England

In Edinburgh the Comte d'Artois was again in a palace, if Holyroodhouse with its grim, forbidding walls and its half-dismantled interior, really merited that name. Although its architecture was in the French style it must have reminded Charles-Philippe rather of the Bastille than of Marly, St. Cloud or Versailles, but he was learning to count himself fortunate to have a roof over his head with some prospect of stability.

For three long years of Scotch mist and austerity he lived at Holyrood. Never during these years nor at any other time did any expression of regret for the amenities and luxuries of the vanished past cross his lips. He learned to accommodate himself to his circumstances and years later, when King of France, preserved the habit of having his cuffs turned, the collars of his coats renewed and his boots re-soled.

If he had failed, and continued to fail, in the part that should have been his as a leader of the resistance movements in France, in his relations with the mass of émigrés in Great Britain he was a brilliant success, his essential qualities of generosity and kindliness developed by adversity.

If he was constantly disillusioning the Vendéens he never disappointed the émigrés who were not personally concerned in the plots and attempted risings. Each one of them with whom he came into personal contact had some story to tell of his affability. For them he was again Galaor, the princely paladin, and they felt their vicissitudes less, knowing that they were shared by their Royal house. Limited though his means were he never refused an appeal from the poor émigrés, and most of what he did have was applied to assisting them.

Because of the constant threat of arrest for debt his days had to be spent in the sanctuary of Holyroodhouse and he was able to leave it only in the evening, since the King's writ did not run from dusk to dawn. When evening fell he went out for his nightly game of whist to the house near by which Louise de Polastron shared with her friends for propriety's sake in strait-laced Scotland.

Far away in Turin and then in Klagenfurth the Comtesse d'Artois languished forgotten. She was not allowed to attend the wedding of her son, the Duc d'Angoulême, but de Berri at least did go and visit her. It is doubtful if her husband ever gave her a thought. He was entirely given over to Louise.

If she and Artois did not share the same roof they shared everything else in the way of joys and sorrows. Carrying the burden of his confidences and suffering with him all the hopes and fears of their varying fortunes proved almost too much for a woman so sensitive and delicate, while her heart was continually wrung by requests for help and by the misery brought to her attention.

'If you knew,' she wrote to Madame de Lage, on one of her many lengthy absences on the Continent, 'how hard I try to be an ignoble miser, you would be surprised, for it is not my nature.

'For very good reasons we all have to practise the strictest economy, no carriage and only two courses at *his* table, fewer servants, etc. I have drawn up a budget of so much for this and so much for that, and that so much is so very little.'

Whist and reading relieved the monotony of days which slipped by with nothing to distinguish one from another. Sunday's gloom, when Artois was free to leave the Palace during the day-time, was at least lightened by paying visits to the neighbouring nobility and, in a country which had not forgotten Charles-Edward Stuart, this other Royal exile was made welcome for the Young Pretender's sake as much as for his own.

The little circle round the Comte d'Artois was small, made up of his oldest friends. They attended mass in the Palace on Sundays conducted by the Abbé Latil who had been sent to Edinburgh at Artois' request. He particularly asked for someone without pretensions who would not wish to eat his meals with the Royal party, and Latil, who was of humble origin, admirably fulfilled the requirements demanded.

The arrival in Edinburgh of the Comte de Vaudreuil enlarged the Royal entourage and, if he brought one more mouth to feed, his presence added wit and charm to their lives and one more reminder of the old happy times at Versailles.

After the Duchesse de Polignac's death Vaudreuil, who had been her most faithful and devoted lover, fell in love with and married in 1795 a young cousin, thirty years his junior. He was at that time living at 36, Great Pulteney Street in Soho, but the imposing signatures on the marriage contract would not have disgraced Versailles.

It was Court usage to obtain the consent of the Royal family to one's marriage and the absence of a Prince from England was a source of distress to many French émigré families, who felt their marriages invalid without the Royal *imprimatur*. In Vaudreuil's case the Duc de Bourbon, son of the old Prince de Condé, stood sponsor and signed the contract, which did not, like the La Ferronays', list an inventory of hypothetical jewels and carriages. More realistic, Article 9 read:

> 'Given the uncertainty of events and the inability of the contracting parties to verify their real and personal estate, they are obliged to refer in this respect to the declarations they have respectively made.'

In the sad light of reality their material possessions were painfully few. In Edinburgh Vaudreuil managed to find a house for a pound a week out of the total of ten pounds a month he possessed for everything. Monsieur sent two courses for their dinner from the Palace. Vaudreuil had hoped for something more substantial, although he was well aware that Monsieur could not reasonably do more since he had so much difficulty in meeting his own household expenses.

Some linen and pots and pans were essential and these might be had second-hand from French dealers. Vaudreuil felt unable any longer to endure slovenly meals without table napkins or refinements of any sort. The bread of exile is not only bitter—it tends to be very coarse.

In gratitude for his efforts to help them the Comte d'Artois' friends did what lay in their power to enliven the sad sameness of their dreary life in Edinburgh.

When the Duc de Berri was paying his long visit to his father in 1798 they produced a play which was an exceptional indulgence, but even then they were afraid that rumour would turn this innocent distraction into a sybaritic orgy, so hard did Artois' early reputation die. They had all been so fond of acting at Versailles where Marie Antoinette herself had taken to the boards and the young and giddy Artois learnt to walk a tight rope to astonish them all. Now he sat soberly and watched his friends perform, while servants constituted the remainder of the audience.

Such interludes were few. While waiting for the possibility of a loan which he thought might be obtained from Lord Moira, one of the Prince of Wales's friends, Vaudreuil had to sell his piano, the last possession he had to sacrifice and a real one, for it meant that the mournful evenings could no longer be brightened with music, with the nostalgic songs of their childhood which made home seem less far away.

They talked, of course, in their evening gatherings, of the past and of the future, but Vaudreuil at least realised that all talk of the France they had known was illusion. He knew that she was finished for them and if, when, they returned, they would find only the bloodied skeleton of the country they had lived in, and that skeleton inspired him with horror.

Sometimes there were visitors at Holyroodhouse, messengers from the Vendée, emissaries from Louis XVIII far away in Poland. There were projects for new landings in the West which constantly asked for a Prince, for money, for arms and for unity.

It is almost impossible to unravel the complexities of these comings and goings, to elucidate these plans of high hopes and these missions of failure. As far as Artois was concerned they ended in one thing. He stayed at Holyrood.

Perhaps his excuse was that he could not leave Scotland without running the risk of being apprehended for debt, or perhaps at this time the Government gave him no encouragement. It was certainly unwilling to mount another British expedition. But by 1799 Artois managed to make an accommodation with his creditors and he bade good-bye to Edinburgh with few regrets and, as he thought, for ever.

When he arrived in London he found that the émigrés had settled down into well-defined groups, each having a distinctive life of its own. They had their own institutions, their own places of worship and they had more or less accommodated themselves to the strangeness of England. Artois was welcomed into their midst with enthusiasm and their whole society took on fresher colours from his presence.

Artois settled down in Baker Street while his entourage disposed itself around him in the neighbourhood. Baker Street was comparatively new, having been built arrow-straight to link the new Portman and Manchester Squares with the Marylebone Road, where it ended. Beyond lay the meadows and farms of Marylebone Park Fields, now Regent's Park, and then a favourite place for outdoor meetings.

Although the houses in Baker Street could not rival the gilded and coffered elegance of the mansions in Portman Square, which were far beyond Artois' means, they were genteel enough, comprising a large drawing-room on the first floor and three or four master bedrooms. The rental was a hundred and ten pounds a year, and the rates nineteen pounds five shillings. Holyroodhouse might have cost Artois nothing in rent but at least in Baker Street the sun sometimes shone.

Madame de Polastron was installed at 18, Thayer Street, with her faithful friend, Madame de Poulpry, as chaperon and with French neighbours all around her. Her house, which practically backed on to Manchester House where the Spanish Ambassador dispensed magnificent hospitality, was more modest than Artois', costing only seventy pounds a year with rates of twelve pounds five shillings. It was probably rented furnished. Although Artois' house has been swallowed up in a block of offices, Louise de Polastron's still exists only its Georgian windows have been inappropriately replaced with leaded lights.

At 39, George Street, the Duc de Berri was installed and doing his best to earn the sobriquet of *vert galant* which had been his father's. Two doors away lived the Archbishop of Narbonne whose life provided no edifying example to the young Prince. Now at the age of eighty his sole concern with the things of the flesh was to take electricity treatment near by for his deafness, for which purpose he left his house every morning before de Berri was up.

In Orchard Street the Duc de Bourbon had a house and would soon embark on his adventure with Sophie Dawes which would have such disastrous consequences for him. His father, the Prince de Condé, when he finally gave up the struggle on the Continent and retired to England, settled at Wanstead with his mistress, the Princesse de Monaco, whom he afterwards married.

Heir of the Bourbon-Condés and all their aspirations, the young and gallant Duc d'Enghien was living quietly at Baden whence he would be called by treachery on to French territory, to be arrested and shot as an example to Bourbon conspirators, his execution a tragic blot on Napoleon's scutcheon.

In London the Comte d'Artois quickly re-established his familiar routine but with something of a return to the formal etiquette which had previously governed his life. Once again, as in Coblentz, the ultra-Royalists grouped themselves round him, feeding him with rash and unjustified hopes instead of with plans for positive action. Its place was taken by a set pattern of regulating the disposal of his time for, although he was only forty-two and still handsome and youthful in appearance, Artois led the life of a much older man, the strict adherence to his cherished habits masking the real emptiness of his days.

Every day at noon the captain of his non-existent guards bowed him into his carriage (it was never paid for and Howard, the coachmaker, ultimately went bankrupt) which was to take him down Baker Street to Louise's house.

Any passer-by who stared at the royal arms of France on the carriage-door might be assured of a graceful bow from the man whom he vaguely knew as His Highness MOUNSIER. The Royal York Street Marylebone Volunteers, a most respectable body composed principally of master tradesmen but officered by gentlemen under the command of Colonel the Viscount Duncannon, received a special salute as they swung up the street in their handsome scarlet jackets, trimmed with gold lace, and blue pantaloons, to go through their drill on the greensward where on other days the Marylebone Cricket Club lobbed their full tosses in what is now Dorset Square. (The Volunteers are remembered in the public house called 'The Volunteer' which faces the entrance to Regent's Park at Clarence Gate.)

Mr. Pitt, who during his brief period out of office lived at York Place, the upper end of Baker Street, might be glimpsed by the Comte d'Artois who could see the former Prime Minister's house from his own windows.

After his call on Madame de Polastron, Monsieur returned to his own house to dine, often accompanied by the ladies, and nearly always by his son, the Duc de Berri, who showed his dutifulness by giving his father rather than his *chère amie* his company at dinner. Of course it cost him nothing to eat at his father's table, while gallantry surely demanded that he paid for his mistress's dinner. How very far away were the reckless extravagances of Versailles! The French people could now have nothing of which to complain of the style in which their royal family lived.

After dinner, Monsieur returned to Thayer Street for his invariable game of whist, while the ladies worked and talked in a corner of the modest salon.

Once a week he received the gentlemen who had belonged to the Court, the Ducs d'Uzès, de Maillé, de FitzJames, de Lorges, de Duras, de Choiseul, de Castries, de Sérent . . . although the drawing-room at Baker Street was of handsome proportions it was scarcely large enough to hold the great names of France.

Three times a year only the Comte d'Artois gave formal dinners, on New Year's Day, on the feast day of St. Louis and on his own name-day, St. Charles. Any larger hospitality was impossible on account of the absence of the Comtesse d'Artois, his official hostess, and the slenderness of his purse.

However little consideration the Bourbon Princes and their schemes might receive from George III he could not permit them to earn their bread or line up at the offices of the Committee for a dole. In fact the British Government made allowances to them all. In addition to the loan of Holyroodhouse the Comte d'Artois received five hundred pounds a month and the Duc de Berri three hundred. When Louis XVIII came to England he was given six hundred pounds a month while the Duc d'Angoulême received the same amount as his brother. Since the larger part of these allowances went to the maintenance of their circle of attendants and in donations to charitable causes and the poorer émigrés there was nothing for luxury or display.

The Government showed scrupulous fairness in its assistance to the French royal family, even the children of the regicide Duc d'Orléans receiving a grant of four hundred pounds a month, although he had earned the detestation of the English by his betrayal of his family and his caste.

The Duc spent much time in England before the Revolution where, in spite of his popularity with the radical elements and the freemasons, of whose order he was a high-ranking member, he was also friendly with the Prince of Wales. The Prince had, in fact, commissioned Sir Joshua Reynolds to paint a portrait of Orléans which hung in a prominent place at Carlton House.

When news reached London of his shameful conduct, the Prince ordered the removal of the portrait and also had Orléans expelled from the *Je ne sais quoi* Club which met at the Star and Garter in Pall Mall. His expulsion was attended by the added indignity of having his name scratched off the list of members by a mere waiter.

His son, the Duc de Chartres, had started off in his father's footsteps but later recanted and together with his brothers made his submission to the Comte d'Artois. With great magnanimity, if not great warmth, Artois received those sons of Philippe Egalité, who had voted for his brother's death, but not before they had repudiated the tricolour and sworn to defend legitimacy against all comers.

Vicomte Walsh de Serrant recalls seeing Louis-Philippe, now after his father's execution Duc d'Orléans, beating his breast at the mass at the words *Domine non dignus sum* and nothing could have been more edifying than their apparent repentance. How superficial it was Artois would learn in years to come.

Now he bade his entourage call on the Orléans Princes to pay their respects, a command most unwillingly obeyed for, in spite of the act of submission they had performed, the émigrés, lacking the Royal generosity of mind, gave them no general absolution. The Orléans saw that they were little liked and in their turn disliked the other émigrés, attending no fêtes or large gatherings and consorting with their father's former friends, which did not add either to their popularity or to the consideration in which they were held.

When the young Duc d'Orléans went abroad to find a more congenial atmosphere and a younger brother, the Comte de Beaujolais died, the Government with admirable impartiality re-distributed the allowances they had been receiving, increasing those of the Ducs d'Angoulême and de Berri by fifty pounds a month each.

Artois' arrival in London re-kindled hopes of his taking a more active part in French affairs and he expressed his willingness to go to the Continent to join in yet another Vendéen expedition. William Windham was much occupied with this proposition and spent a great deal of time with Artois and his advisers. It all seemed settled when an announcement in the Press stated that the Comte d'Artois had succumbed to an unfortunately timed or diplomatic attack of haemorrhoids. Whichever was the case he did not go and never again was there talk of his going to the Continent.

It is certainly true that he did suffer from this complaint. When Lady Atkyns—the dedicated woman who spent her fortune first on trying to liberate Louis XVI and Marie Antoinette, whose friendship she had been privileged to enjoy, and after their execution in attempting to free the young Louis XVII from the Temple—wished to call on Artois to invoke his assistance she was told he was ill and unable to put on any clothes other than a pair of trousers, in which unsuitable costume he could not receive her.

Lady Atkyns pursued her chosen course alone, full of suspicion at the lack of support she received from the Bourbon Princes in her unremitting search for what she believed was the true Louis XVII, spirited away from the Temple while another boy died in his place.

Artois turned his mind to more immediate matters. In London he had a part to play as a Royal Prince. He took an immediate interest in the schools and all the other charitable organisations set up by the French. He made an early visit to the Abbé Carron's institutions at Somers Town and sent him a hundred guineas as a donation towards their maintenance. So pleased was he with the hospice for aged clergy and the female hospital that he returned on several occasions.

At the schools he was received with particular enthusiasm and he, in turn, was touched by the loyalty and warmth of the welcome he met, recapturing some of the adulation of the Coblentz days.

These occasions followed the course of all such royal visits, with speeches from the children and hand-made gifts for Artois which he accepted with his habitual grace.

As was customary the children submitted to public examination about their studies. In the course of her dissertation about the history of France one young girl, remarking on the enmity which had for so long persisted between her country and England, asked the examiner whether he thought these unfriendly feelings would persist in the future.

His answer was:

'No, Mademoiselle. There is no Frenchman in London who does not give thanks to the generous hospitality with which he has been received and always treated here.

'The obligations which a regenerated France has contracted to Great Britain during its long and painful distress are of a nature never to be forgotten.

'France may indeed once more become the rival of England in many spheres, but an eternal gratitude will never in any future century allow the return of a jealous hatred in a French heart.'

It is always unwise to prophesy but in this case the speaker was justified. In the hundred and fifty years since he made this speech France and England have sometimes been rivals but they have never ceased to be friends.

XII

The First Returns

All through the last years of the eighteenth century John Wilmot and his Committee continued their unremitting industry on behalf of the French émigrés. Although after the entry of the Treasury into its affairs it continued for some time on a voluntary basis, inevitably its procedure became more official and subject to control. Burke's wish that no man should give an account of his own free bounty could no longer be fulfilled.

The Lords Commissioners of the Treasury bombarded the Committee with letters, always with the unvarying instruction:

'that they trusted it would use its best endeavours to reduce the heavy expenses sustained by the Government for this service.'

and the Committee loyally tried to carry out their wishes.

General revision of the lists went on continually. In the year 1796, when there were nearly six hundred servants receiving a guinea a month, it was found on investigation that many of them were not necessary to the families for whom they worked and that they were able to get their own livelihoods. A reform therefore took place in this, as well as in other classes of French emigrants, in consequence of which the number of servants was reduced by about a hundred. By 1801 the number still remaining on the lists was two hundred and nine.

An examination of the roll of names of those receiving relief from the Committee brings to light the fact that a very large number of them were without titles or the *particule* and consequently belonged to the Third Estate. Less of them, of course, would be in direct contact with the Princes and therefore in receipt of money from them.

In 1799 the lists of the Committee were closed, it having been decided in principle that, except under special circumstances, no émigrés who had arrived in this country after 1797 could be admitted to its books. Only when a vacancy occurred in the lists by death or departure from the country could admissions be made to them. It was not until the absence of the Comtesse de Menou, widow of a General, that the Comte de Caumont, as the most senior general officer carried on Louis XVIII's list, was appointed by the Comte d'Artois to receive relief. Perhaps book-binding was not so lucrative after all?

When application for instatement on the lists was made, either to the Treasury, to some patron or to the Committee itself, the cases were referred for investigation and, unless the reasons given were irreproachable, the applications were refused. The same procedure applied to requests for augmentation of the set allowance.

Thus, when the Baron de La Ferronays, an uncle of Auguste de La Ferronays, sought or had sought for him an increase in his allowance, the Committee reported to the Treasury that, as the Baron was on the list of French general officers and his lady also, having been urgently admitted thereto by the late Duc d'Harcourt, and their joint allocation was therefore seventeen pounds ten shillings per month of thirty days,

'We submit our opinion to their lordships that there does not appear to us to be any reason to grant a further increase in this case which might not apply to others on that list.'

All these claims and resolutions the Committee faithfully noted in its books, since it flattered itself, and rightly, that its returns were correctly taken and that it devoted much time and attention to this business.

It noted, too, that the Abbé Carron had been prescribed medicinal baths, of which he had taken ninety in all, for which he ultimately requested re-imbursement. The money was freely granted and handed over with the soft chiding that,

'he be desired not to let the charge for such bathing as may in future be necessary for him to run on so long.'

The Committee did not restrict its vigilance to its domestic affairs alone. As a Member of Parliament, as well as executive chairman of the Committee, John Wilmot had his eyes open to

everything that concerned the French émigrés. He wrote uneasily
to Charles Long, Secretary to the Treasury, that,

'Observing so many apprehensions and alarms inculcated in the
newspapers concerning the numbers and ill designs of the
French emigrants in this country it has occurred to me that it
would be desirable and not difficult to get at the birth of these
reports.'

Apparently, although by now the émigrés were accepted by the
British, they could not entirely rid themselves of their native
suspicion towards the French.

Still later the Committee noted with concern:

'Upon the report in the Public Papers that some French
Emigrants have been taken upon charges of imposing upon
the Public by pretended magical exhibitions, it is ordered that
the Secretary make Enquiry of the Public Office as to the circumstances of the case and report the same at the next meeting.'

Unfortunately no such report figures in the Minutes and now
one will never know the nature of those 'magical exhibitions.'

A keen eye was kept by the Committee, or perhaps by the
Treasury, on the trend of events, hoping always that a lessening
of tension in France might induce some of the émigrés to return.
There had always been a trickle of people who risked going back
either to France itself or to some safe Continental place like
Hamburg, but these few departures did not greatly affect the
burden of relief carried by the Government.

While Nelson's resounding victory at the Nile in 1798 brought
new confidence to the British, Bonaparte's escape from Egypt to
France and the *coup d'état* of the 18th Brumaire strengthened
French resistance to renewed attempts by Pitt to negotiate peace.

Although in 1799 Lord Grenville could still write to Talleyrand, now Foreign Minister in France, that:

'The best and most natural pledge of the reality and permanence
of peace would be the restoration of that line of princes which
for so many centuries maintained the French nation in prosperity
at home and in consideration and respect abroad'

he no longer had much hope.

In that same year Heriot, proprietor of *The True Briton*, assured Farington that a restoration of the monarchy would be the result of 'these strange-fangled schemes,' which is what he called the Consulate, but Albertine de Montsoreau, far away in Austria, saw more clearly when she said that with Bonaparte to give her stability France would no longer want her kings.

It was from this point that the British Government ceased to take into account the possibility of any concerted rising in France on behalf of the Bourbons. Inevitably they bowed to the fact that, however tired the French might be of the excesses of the Revolution, they were not yet ready, if now they ever would be, to recall the Bourbons.

It now also became clear to the Englishman in the street that, with the Consulate and Napoleon Bonaparte giving the French stable government and a renewed sense of national glory, his own freedom lay in his will and ability to resist the military threat represented by the First Consul, whose advent had entirely changed the character of the struggle. If Napoleon fought for the greater glory of France Pitt and his successors must fight for the survival of England. Almost without exception the men who had given a general support to the Revolution, and who had opposed war with the Republic, rallied to the Government.

Nevertheless the short-lived peace of 1802 was deliriously welcomed, the ordinary Londoner showing his joy in a way that Lord Sheffield, not without justification, considered as extravagant.

'I feel much annoyed,' he wrote, 'by the senseless levity of the public expression, so ridiculously and extravagantly in favour of peace . . . the rejoicing, however, is so general, as to be a proof of how completely the nation was tired of the war, and for peace on any terms.

'Were you not ashamed of our *bêtes*, *badauds*, and blackguards in changing themselves into coach-horses, to drag the carriage of Bonaparte's aide-de-camp, General Lauriston?'

Since Sheffield knew, but the people did not, that General Lauriston was a descendant of that John Law whose South Sea Bubble had ruined so many English people, he naturally considered their enthusiasm even more ill-advised. But what really roused him to fury was a report in the *Morning Post* that at the house in Portman Square opposite to Citizen Otto, the French Ambassador, there was a transparency of the

'ingenuous, good and benevolent Bonaparte, with an inscription, "the saviour of the universe." Here, also the language was appropriate; anything short of blasphemy would have been a platitude.'

Lord Sheffield had apprehensions also about the durability of the peace and about the stability of the new régime in France.

'I hope we shall maintain somewhat of the principles on which all nations act. If the Jacobins should again prevail in France, they will endeavour to inoculate or introduce their principles, and we may not then be able to revive the Alien Act without risking another war with France.'

When the Consulate was established in France the possibility of a return for the émigrés seemed more hopeful, although they were still subject to the same penal decrees. The Concordat between the Pope and Bonaparte, concluded in 1801, which re-established the Roman Catholic church in France, opened the way for some of the clergy to return. Many of them did so, encouraged by the appeal of their former parishioners.

The clergy's example heartened the moderates who were not deeply committed to the Bourbons. They were worn down with years of poverty and tired of eating the bread of charity—and they were getting older. But returning to France was not easy. Passports were required and they had to obtain false certificates, proving that they had never left their country and never ceased to exercise their rights as French citizens.

Then, on the other side of the medal, was their regret at abandoning their cause, of losing the prizes to be won on the glorious day when the Bourbons would be restored, and they feared the scorn of the *purs* at their weakness.

There was apprehension, too, as to the fate that awaited them in France. They heard of denunciations, of imprisonments, and of executions. They were anxious to know how they would live in France with their property confiscated. Their refrain was:

'Where shall I go to hide my poverty?'

Fortunes had changed masters. Even those who had remained at home and managed to survive had done so only in indigence.

But the young people, like the Comte de Neuilly, were agog with excitement. They had cherished a dream of a France they had left almost as children and was now half-forgotten. They had found no other loyalties, no other attachments. After a life of wandering and vagabondage France offered them once more the prospect of a home and a fatherland. Only in France would they find a cure for that *mal du pays* which had intensified rather than lessened with the years. They consoled themselves with the thought that they need not be less Royalist in France, only more prudent in expressing their feelings.

The Comte de Neuilly's mother in Hamburg viewed the return severely:

'Every day the émigrés are leaving in groups of twenty, thirty or more, why one does not know exactly because, except in particular or exceptional cases, they do not recover their goods and chattels. The young men are seized for the army, the young women are obliged to continue to work as they did during their emigration. The old men and old women die of hunger. But it is an epidemic. Most of them do not know why they left and know still less why they are going back.'

The Comte de Vaudreuil addressed a wise memorandum to Louis XVIII on the subject of the return of the émigrés. Vaudreuil may have been a courtier to his finger-tips but it did not prevent his being at the same time a man of considerable political acumen and his advice to his friend, the Comte d'Artois, was always sound and sensible.

Vaudreuil argued that since, in the main, it was impossible to prevent the émigrés going back, it would be impolitic to show dissatisfaction, especially as so many of them were almost forced to do so in view of the insecurity of their position.

England and a few places on the Continent were their sole refuges but, in view of Bonaparte's growing military ascendancy, there was always the hazard that he would successfully invade this country.

Essentially the émigrés were faithful to the cause for which they had suffered for so long and it would be statesmanlike on the part

of Louis XVIII not to condemn their action but rather, by showing confidence in them, to encourage them to constitute a Royalist
party within France which might in time prove extremely useful.

Louis XVIII had, during his years of exile even more humiliating than his brother's for after all he was the King, not ill spent his
time. His political sagacity had grown and matured and perhaps,
left to himself, he might always have acted with prudence and
intelligence, but he was, like Artois, surrounded by the old guard
of the émigrés and it was difficult in his circumstances wholly to
shake them off. But Louis listened to Vaudreuil's advice and
allowed it to be known that he did not disapprove of the return.

So the émigrés began to go back to France either in the hope of
recovering their property or at least of living there quietly again
until better times came, but they did not go without the blessing of
their Princes.

The young Vicomte Walsh and his cousin went to a reception
at the Comte d'Artois' to ask for his authorisation for their return
to France.

With his customary grace and kindliness Monsieur said to them:

'Go . . . and when France has many Frenchmen like you in her
bosom she will recall us. The King, my brother, did well in
inscribing on the colours of the Irish Brigade, *semper et ubique
fideles.*

'You have been faithful to the Stuarts, faithful to us, faithful
everywhere and always. Go then, talk about us to your friends
and tell them that we cherish the hope that one day we shall
find ourselves amongst them.'

All the French emigrant laity who applied for money to return
to the Continent were required to attend the English Committee
(as distinct from the French Committee from which they normally
received their allowances) before their requests could be complied
with and an inquiry made into their situations. Then, if the
Committee was satisfied and they renounced further relief, they
were given six months' allowance in advance to defray the cost of
their journey which, before the Peace of Amiens, had to be made
via Hamburg and Emden and was both long and costly. Among
those who renounced her allowance and went back to France with

147

her two daughters and a domestic was the Comtesse de Saisseval, worn out with the struggle to maintain herself in England.

The immediate effect of these returns on the remaining émigrés was an increase in their monthly allowance. When in 1801 the clergy began to go back in large numbers the general allowance was augmented from one pound eleven shillings and sixpence to two pounds a month.

But many who went back found the most cruel of deceptions and often they returned to what had for so long been their home and which now showed a face more familiar than this new France.

This tendency the Committee noticed in a letter to the Treasury, dated December, 1801.

'We cannot help observing that the emigrants, particularly the clergy, appear to be less eager than they were in their desire of returning a few weeks ago and state the difficulties that their brethren who have already taken that measure have met with in France.'

Yet some fifteen hundred émigrés left in the course of the year and the numbers at this date receiving relief from the London Committee were three thousand and sixty clergy and fourteen hundred laity.

When first the Peace of Lunéville and then the Peace of Amiens in 1802 brought an end, although it was to prove no end but the shortest of lulls, to the eternal war, more of the French decided to take the risk of returning, although they were by now fully aware of the hazards. Many of them met the fate that would have been theirs had they stayed in France in 1792, an adjournment of sentence which now proved to have availed them nothing. Others were swallowed up into obscurity, while yet others bowed to the inevitable and rallied to the First Consul. They would ultimately form a part of that *fusion*, the amalgamation of the old with the new nobility he would create for his Empire, which would be a cornerstone of his social policy.

The Treasury was concerned not at all with the fate of the émigrés once they returned to France. All that it worried about was the most prudent expenditure of public moneys. Austerely the Secretary wrote to the Committee:

'It appears to us that since the Peace an alteration has taken place in the grounds or principle of granting or continuing relief to the French emigrants.

'During the war they were on account of their political principles either driven here by necessity or being here, they were in general not able to return to France; but those who have returned either before or since the Peace do not seem to be under the same necessity of repairing to England a second time —there is not the same reason for re-admitting them on the Relief List.'

But not even the Treasury in any way abrogated the principle of political asylum by interfering with or withholding relief from those emigrants who did not wish to return to France or using any pressure to make them return.

While continuing to adjure the Committee to cut down its expenditure the Treasury raised no objection to certain acts of generosity in which it now found itself able to indulge.

The Committee received this instruction:

'The case of the Abbé Comte de Lubersac having been under the consideration of the Lords Commissioners of His Majesty's Treasury, I have received their Lordships' command to desire that in consideration of the Abbé being of a Superior Order, of a very advanced age and a man of literature, you will cause a further allowance of four pounds per month to be made to him to commence from the first of this month.'

At last the Abbé had his wish and was distinguished from the general ruck of the clergy, for he had allowed himself a little asperity when recording in his *Journal* the fact that all orders of the clergy below the rank of bishop received the same allowance. We hope that he was gratified by the appellation, 'a man of literature,' and we hope his last days were eased by this extra indulgence. He enjoyed it only for a year before his death, and the later years of the emigration have no equally devoted chronicler.

As often happens, Mrs. Silburn had exhausted her means in helping others but the Committee appreciated her devoted service and particularly the use they had been able to make of her house as a meeting place throughout the long years and when she, too, was obliged to apply for some relief in her expenses it was happy to agree.

The Treasurer of the French Committee, who had handled all the sums devoted to the French laity, received a hundred pounds as a gratuity when he applied for a grant to enable him to return to France to settle some of his affairs.

The numbers of émigrés in the country continued to shrink, so that by 1802 the persons remaining to be aided, exclusive of the Corsicans or those paid under special orders, totalled only one thousand seven hundred and twenty-nine persons.

'As little disposition appears among them at present to leave this country, we are not able to make any reduction in the estimate,' reported the Committee to the Lords Commissioners, but some economies were effected by removing from the relief lists young men who had attained the age of sixteen.

Peace was welcomed in England not only for its own sake but because the Continent was once again open to the English for travel. They now crossed the Channel in their thousands, flocking especially to Paris for a close-up view of the formidable General Bonaparte. They noticed many significant changes, not only the dominant martial spirit but the great alteration in manners since they last visited Paris in the dying days of the *ancien régime*. The young men and women were sour and rude in their address, while the gaiety for which the French were habitually distinguished seemed to have disappeared with their former civility. Regretfully the English must have compared them with their own French émigrés, most of whom were now fast vanishing from England.

While the English were wining and dining in Paris and admiring the spoils of war that Bonaparte had brought back from the palaces and galleries of Italy the peace was abruptly broken and those who lingered too long found themselves interned for a period of nearly eleven years, for this new war was of a different order. It would be fought to a finish and in a spirit of dogged determination.

As Lady Auckland wrote to her brother in August, 1803:

'You never saw so military a country as this. Nothing but fighting is talked of. The zeal throughout the country, from the highest to the lowest, is wonderful; and I am convinced that should an invasion be tried, that you would see all the ladies letting their nails grow, that they might scratch at the enemy.'

The war brought no change now in the life of the émigrés. They no longer counted for France, who saw in them no menace. The handful that remained in England no longer counted for the Government except as recipients of their charity. The Princes might have a nuisance value but they in no way entered into the Government's schemes.

As the renewal of war brought fresh liabilities to the Government a new enquiry was ordered in 1803 into the circumstances of the émigrés to see whether they really needed the *bienfaisance de la Nation*. (The Committee had been in contact for so long with the French that they sometimes seemed to find difficulty in choosing the right English word. They habitually use the word *secours* in their reports instead of 'aid' and a good many other Gallicisms have crept in. Although the Secretary of the English Committee did his counterpart on the French Committee the courtesy of addressing him in French, it was good Anglo-French with none of the felicities of style that the French themselves managed to instil into their letters of business.)

As the émigrés returned to France and schools and chapels closed the need for help grew less but it never wholly ceased. The orphan children, with no homes to which to return, had perforce to remain and still had to be cared for. Many of the aged were too infirm to attempt a return to France and they still had to be maintained. There was as much for the Abbé Carron to do as there had been.

By 1807 the numbers of émigrés on the Committee's books were reduced to fourteen hundred and sixty-one, made up of fifteen bishops, five hundred and thirteen inferior clergy, three hundred and twenty-five nuns and eight hundred and eight of the first and second classes of the laity, including children. These figures do not, of course, represent the total numbers of émigrés in the country as they exclude those who were not in receipt of official aid.

This was the hard core which altered little, except when it was reduced by death, until the Restoration, and even after 1814 some of this band remained in England either because they were unable,

by reason of age or infirmity, to attempt the journey or because
they had lost all their relatives and means of support in France,
so that the Committee's work ultimately continued until 1823.

If the problem of succouring the émigrés remained unchanged
although reduced in scope the Committee was changing too. It was
now no longer known as the 'Committee of Subscribers for the
Relief of the Suffering French Clergy and Laity' but as the
'Emigrant Office,' with the status of a para-governmental
department.

In 1806 Jean-François de La Marche, Bishop of St. Pol de Léon,
died, worn out with fifteen years of exertion on behalf of
suffering humanity. He was laid to rest with his peers in the
churchyard at St. Pancras but, after the Restoration, his bones
were disinterred and taken to his see of St. Pol de Léon on the
Breton coast. As the seven spires of the town are a landmark to
shipping, so the tomb of Jean-François de La Marche should be a
guide and an inspiration to the weak and suffering. There has
been more than one Good Samaritan.

In the year of St. Pol de Léon's death John Wilmot suddenly
resigned from the Committee and the émigrés lost at one time,
but did not forget, their two chief practical sympathisers. From
1792 until 1806 Wilmot had devoted himself to the business of
the Committee, attending meetings once or twice a week, getting
through a vast amount of paper work, as well as visiting hospitals
and other institutions.

It appears that from 1797 he and Colonel Glyn, his co-
Committee member, received an honorarium of three hundred
pounds a year each and the Secretary of the Committee two
hundred pounds. Wilmot was a comparatively rich man and this
amount could have sufficed only to pay his expenses. One wonders
why he took the money, but the Minutes yield no clue. In any
event for five years he had given his services without reward but,
when he resigned, he received neither honours nor official thanks.

The circumstances of his resignation are puzzling. In 1805 there
was a sharp series of letters from the Audit Office, querying the
accounts of the Committee. There is neither evidence nor sugges-
tion of peculation, only a bald entry in the Minutes chronicling
the resignation of the chairman, John Wilmot. Perhaps he was
tired and glad to be relieved of his task. Perhaps the years of

Treasury goads and pricks had enervated him. History does not say.

Wilmot retired to his home, Bruce Castle, in Tottenham, where he died in 1815. His successors at the Committee did not stay long in office, but theirs was now a purely routine task. None of them has the credit of having conceived, initiated and carried through a great humanitarian enterprise.

That credit belongs to John Eardley Wilmot and his achievement cannot be better described than in the words of his obituary:

'Mr. Wilmot dispensed under Government (and even before its intervention) the national bounty, a task well suited to that universal benevolence and kindness of heart which so eminently distinguished him and in which he had few equals and none superior.'

XIII

Louise de Polastron

The year Auguste de La Ferronays spent with the Duc de Berri
in England in 1803 was not entirely happy. He would much have
preferred to be the witness of de Berri's military exploits, in which
he would so willingly have participated, rather than of his
amatory adventures in which he would not, his heart and thoughts
were with Albertine in Brunswick.

De Berri's temper was always uncertain but, as Auguste
shrewdly remarked in a letter to Albertine, it was always worse
when he was displeased with himself, and he had good cause for
his dissatisfaction. His brother, Angoulême, was far away in
Poland with Louis XVIII and the hopes of the West, frustrated
in Artois, turned to de Berri, who proved as great a disappointment to them as had his father.

In justice to de Berri it must be said that he was not always
unwilling—he, too, had fought bravely with Condé's army—to
join the partisans but either his father's advisers or the British
Government or some other daunting circumstance invariably
prevented his so doing.

Neither by nature nor by education was Auguste de La
Ferronays inclined to engage passively in some occupation to
ensure his livelihood until chance or the passage of time brought
alterations to the circumstances of the émigrés. It was, indeed,
against his will that he was forced, by his attendance on the Duc
de Berri, to spend much of his time in ante-chambers, idly
dawdling and obliged to listen to the futile and dangerous gossip
of the ultra-Royalist clique.

By instinct and training he was a soldier and his ardent desire
was to serve his cause on the battlefield. His sword was always
half-way out of its scabbard as for years he rushed round Europe
at the charge, seeking to justify his family motto, *In hoc ferro vinces*.

His character was too independent to make him a successful

courtier and it was probably a disadvantage to him to be in such close proximity to the Princes because he was able to see all too clearly their weaknesses and failings.

Repeatedly but in vain La Ferronays tried to make his masters understand that invocations to the white plume of Henry of Navarre and to the God of St. Louis were drowned in the noise of the cannonades thundering across Europe. The sound of his still small voice was lost in the buzz of conversation. Bitterly he noted that, when action was required, they sought it in distractions, when silence was needed they chattered then, when all was lost, they mourned over the fate of their friends.

After a year of frustration Auguste could no longer bear the inaction and returned to Brunswick for a joyful reunion with Albertine while de Berri set out on yet another of the matrimonial quests which occupied so much of his time in these years but which always ended in failure.

Even in Brunswick Auguste could not rest and soon he set out on his travels again, often in disguise, always in difficulty, seldom with sufficient means, living sometimes for economy's sake on milk and hard-boiled eggs, and always with his eyes and ears open for French spies on his trail.

When, after the Restoration, La Ferronays met Fouché, the Minister of Police who turned his coat more often even than the Vicar of Bray, he asked why, throughout these years, he was so consistently pursued in his journeys by French spies and informers.

In reply Fouché offered to show Auguste his dossier, which contained details of his participation in every kind of conspiracy, real or imagined. Nothing could have been more out of character. Every enterprise in which Auguste de La Ferronays was engaged took place in full daylight and he scorned to do anything which was not in accordance with his delicate sense of honour, for no one more than he possessed that 'sensibility of principle, that chastity of honour, which felt a stain like a wound.'

Now he undertook a mission to the Duchesse d'Angoulême in Warsaw, returning to Brunswick only to be forced to leave immediately as he was believed to be in danger. The very day of his departure his son, Charles, was born. This time he went to seek assistance from the Princess Sapiéha who had formerly shown kindness to him and to his father but she failed him. Next he tried to offer his sword to the Czar of Russia who politely declined it.

It seemed, however, that there was hope of action nearer home. Georges Cadoudal, the Royalist partisan, had obtained the co-operation of the British Government in an anti-Bonaparte plot. If all turned out well and he succeeded in raising an insurrection de Berri would land in France but, to Auguste's despair, the capture of Cadoudal and his friends and their subsequent execution not only put a summary end to the plan but ensured that there would not be another such.

Instead of the heady adventure of landing in France, Auguste was obliged to return to England in pursuance of his duty, which was merely to dance attendance on the Duc de Berri. He found the Royal circle in shadow. Louise de Polastron was dying.

Her health was always delicate and the privations and exertions during the years in which she had followed Artois in his painful wanderings on the Continent accelerated the progress of consumption of which she must for a long time have been carrying the seeds and which the inclement climate of Edinburgh had done nothing to stay. Her house in Thayer Street, too, was damp, and in the congested little streets round about no pure air.

Louise had long been aware of the state of sin in which she lived and it was not without much inner struggle that her passion for her lover gained the victory over her remorse for her way of life. Latterly her grief about the irregularity of her union with Artois had made great inroads into her consciousness and her spiritual struggles weakened still more her fragile body.

In the portrait painted about this time by Vigée Le Brun the ravages that illness had caused in Louise's appearance can be seen plainly. The delicacy of the beauty is still there but the face is strongly marked by pain. Of this decline Artois noticed nothing and his friends were unwilling to draw his attention to it. He was so wedded to his immutable habits that, once installed in the evening at Thayer Street with his whist and his partners, he took everything else for granted, and Louise exerted herself to conceal from him her growing lassitude and her persistent cough. Only in his absence did she allow herself the luxury of relaxing with pain.

The Duchesse de Gontaut, however, became alarmed at the state of Louise's health and called in her doctor, the Père Elisée. A strange and somewhat sinister figure, Elisée became indispensable as a masseur to gouty and obese Louis XVIII but many people considered him a charlatan. Madame de Gontaut found his diagnosis unsatisfactory and, in spite of Louise's urgent pleas that nothing should be done to alarm or disturb Artois, insisted on her consulting Sir Henry Halford, the Royal physician.

Sir Henry, who was no respecter of persons and who did not in any case recognise in the quiet gentleman awaiting his verdict the brother of the King of France, roundly told Artois that Louise was in the last stages of consumption and advised her being sent immediately to live in a stable, which was the accepted treatment for tuberculosis.

Brompton Grove, now Ovington Square, lying on the edge of London and considered an extremely healthy spot with pure air, was chosen but medical science, such as it was, could do nothing for Louise de Polastron. Her life was ebbing away and she knew that, in the short time left to her, she had one more service only to render her lover—to save her immortal soul and, in so doing, to save his.

Her regrets at leaving this world were few, except for the pain it would cause to those she loved and above all to Charles-Philippe. All this she wrote to her friend, Blimonette, who, immediately on receipt of Louise's letter, set off for England, where she arrived after a terrible journey lasting six weeks on January 21st, the anniversary of the execution of Louis XVI, a day of fatal significance to the émigrés.

What the two friends said to each other when they met again Madame de Lage was too shattered to record. They must have talked of their happy childhood at Penthémont, of the days of awakening and merriment at Versailles and of the tribulations of the long years of exile which were ending now for Louise.

Artois, refusing to recognise the inevitable and clutching at straws, hoped much from Madame de Lage's arrival, but she brought only the comfort of her presence.

To Madame de Gontaut she was less welcome. The two ladies patently did not like each other but, in spite of Madame de Gontaut's carping nature, it was not the moment for personal antagonisms and in the face of Louise's agony all feelings of jealousy were suppressed.

Louise was resigned to her end and she had the courage to make the one sacrifice which to her was greater than the leaving of this world. She consented not to see Artois again while she lived, causing him for the first time in their joint lives to suffer through her. She begged for one final indulgence only—to be allowed to see him once before she died.

The man who influenced Louise to consent to this sacrifice was the little Abbé Latil who had been growing in moral stature since the days when he was chosen because of his insignificance to go to Edinburgh as the Comte d'Artois' chaplain.

Latil now took complete command and by his piety and eloquence even succeeded in overcoming Artois' bitter opposition and wrested from him his submission to the separation which he had devised to ensure Louise's salvation and that of her lover.

When the hope offered by Brompton Grove proved illusory and Louise was brought back to Thayer Street to die, her only earthly thought, now that she had made her peace with God, was for Artois' welfare. She entreated that he should be spared as much suffering as possible and that no interference should be made with his settled habits. Madame de Lage was urged to see that he took his usual outings and to protect him in every way from the grief which possessed him.

All Louise's fortune had long since been given to Artois. From her few remaining material possessions she divided up among her friends some reminders of their steadfast friendship.

Time was now very short for Louise. Her son, Louis, who held only second place in her heart, was brought from the Abbé de Broglie's school in Kensington to say farewell to his mother. In the adjoining room Artois paced up and down.

When Louise's death agony began Latil allowed him to step on to the threshold of her room but with an imperious gesture stopped his approaching the bed.

With a great effort Louise fixed the cherished face with her failing blue eyes for the last time and gasped,

'Before I die, Monseigneur, I beg one last thing from you. Belong henceforward to God.'

'I swear it,' answered Artois.

'Only to God,' Louise added painfully, 'to God only.'

And with these words Louise de Lussan d'Esparbès, Comtesse

de Polastron, died on March 27th, 1804, at the age of forty, in exile but at peace. Her hand was still in that of her friend, Stéphanie de Lage, and round her bed were her son and her childhood friends, Madame de Poulpry and Madame de Gontaut, and near now in spirit as well as in body Charles-Philippe, Comte d'Artois, who for twenty years had been all her life.

They buried her in old St. Pancras Churchyard but the heart which for so long had beaten only for Charles-Philippe, and which was removed from her body, was never found.

So ended an association blessed in everything but by the rites of religion. Never in the years they spent together did either of them have cause to add a line of correction to the words written by the Comte d'Artois to Madame de Lage in the first days of their love:

'Je puis vous confier une partie de mon bonheur. Ah! Madame, qu'il est pur, qu'il est ravissant! Grands dieux, il est si vrai que dans l'univers entier je n'existe que pour elle seule! Jamais, non jamais, le ciel ne se plut à former deux cœurs, deux êtres mieux faits l'un pour l'autre; je le crois, j'ose même en être sûr et vous n'avez pas l'idée combien cette pensée me donne d'orgueil.

'Mais si je suis digne de votre amie, si mon cœur est digne de rendre le sien heureux, c'est à elle seule que je le dois. Ce sont ses conseils et plus encore les sentiments qu'elle m'a fait connaître qui ont épuré, relevé mon âme; et jugez ce que je lui dois, si elle m'a mis en état de faire mon bonheur.'

In the following year the Comtesse d'Artois died forgotten in her refuge on the Continent but her marriage to Charles-Philippe had never been more than an alliance of state. It was not for the sake of Marie Thérèse de Savoie that he remained a widower but for his devotion to the memory of Louise de Polastron, the charming, gentle creature who sought neither riches nor honour and who counted the world well lost for love. Never did Charles-Philippe forget her and never did he break his promise to her.

'Love sanctifies marriage; marriage does not sanctify love.'

Not all the world saw Louise in a favourable light.

The young Duc d'Enghien wrote to his grandfather, the Prince de Condé:

'The death of Madame de Polastron, although it must grievously affect her friend, may be a cause of good fortune for him; for I have heard it said that she often held him back from exposing himself to danger as she feared that she would die of grief. If I had such a mistress, I should quickly have left her.'

Enghien was himself too young to know the depths of a great passion which matures with time and he never would know because, shortly after writing this letter, he was caught in Bonaparte's trap and shot, casting the emigration everywhere into mourning for a gallant and chivalrous Prince. It is, perhaps, ironic that the woman he loved, and some say married, the Princess Charlotte de Rohan, should have mourned for him and been as faithful to his memory as Charles-Philippe to Louise.

To Artois from Mittau came kind and sympathetic letters of condolence from his brother, Louis XVIII, creating a far friendlier feeling between them than there had been for a long time.

The two brothers had not seen each other for ten years, during which time their policies had often been in conflict. Now, in October, 1804, at Louis' invitation they met again in Sweden, the King burdened by gout and fat, Artois still graceful and good-looking but bowed under the weight of his inconsolable grief.

Gustave IV of Sweden, who made the Bourbon cause his own, now offered the Duc de Berri a command in his army. Having overcome the British Government's disapproval of the plan, de Berri set out full of enthusiasm but Auguste, who accompanied him, mistrusted the Government's change of heart, believing, as it turned out rightly, that they had been permitted to leave England only because their mission was unlikely to succeed. Nevertheless, he felt that any action was preferable to wallowing in idleness.

The Swedes gave de Berri and La Ferronays a charming welcome and Louis XVIII, whose family feelings were strong, was happy to see his nephew again, but Auguste was disillusioned by his meeting with the King's entourage. He asked himself how the English, with their well-developed political sense, would judge these men who sought only in the past the solution of the prob-

lems of the future. It was a question to which he found no
answer.

Auguste's obsession with the need for action drove him constantly to rage at the lack of real energy shown by his fellow-
émigrés in Royal circles. Always convinced of the justice of his
cause he deplored the effect that the lethargy of the ultra-Royalists
must have on public opinion, lending credence to the belief that
they were merely lukewarm in their protestations of undying
devotion to their principles. His travels and contact with people
of all shades of opinion were broadening and deepening his own
outlook and he saw more clearly into the future than those
émigrés who lived in the restricted atmosphere of Royal purdah.

'How sad to see so many people behaving like madmen, finding
it unjust that the world has not taken up arms on their behalf
when for fifteen years they haven't even seen a match burn in
battle and have remained in the most deplorable state of
inaction. . . . The principles of justice are with us. If we have
not shown signs of energy, let us at least show some patience.
We ought to have dominated the course of events, instead of
weeping about them from the shelter of a safe place. We might
now be dead but we would be safe from scorn.'

But it was only Albertine who read these letters and, such was
her devotion to Auguste, that if he had turned Republican it
would have remained unaltered and unalterable.

Auguste, of course, was right about their participation in the
Swedish war. The whole project came to nothing and de Berri
and he returned to England to resume their aimless life.

In London de Berri, frustrated by this abortive expedition and
humiliated too by his other fruitless journeys in search of a wife,
threw himself into English society, whither La Ferronays would
not accompany him. While de Berri was paying calls Auguste
slipped away to near-by Manchester Square and watched the
children playing on the grass, thinking of his own little Charles,
far away in Brunswick. When no one was looking he would
ardently embrace the children in the brief illusion that it was
Charles whom he was caressing.

De Berri, who was not wholly lacking in talent or in virtues, had
two most attractive traits. He was strongly drawn to the arts and

was a keen collector of paintings. Of necessity he was able to buy only those that cost little, but Vigée Le Brun praised his sure taste and some of the pictures he bought in London, such as a Wouwermans, were good enough for him to hang later on in the Elysée.

He was also passionately devoted to music. He played the flute and he liked to go to the Opera when kind friends presented him with tickets, as he found it an expensive outing for an émigré prince.

It was probably at the Opera that he first saw the beautiful Amy Brown, with whom he formed a liaison, and by whom he had two daughters.

Rumour for the last hundred and fifty years has played with the idea of a marriage between de Berri and Amy Brown but no trace has ever been found of a marriage certificate, although the baptisms of the two little girls were duly registered at the Chapel of the Annunciation. The importance of proving a marriage rests on the fact that Mrs. Brown also had a son. Her partisans contend that he was also the child of the Duc de Berri and was born in wedlock. If this were so then de Berri's second marriage, contracted after the Restoration, was bigamous and the succession to the throne of France would be upset. Other protagonists of Mrs. Brown agree that there was a marriage but that, before he married in France, de Berri obtained an annulment of it from the Pope.

Although a tremendous amount of ink has been spilled on the subject of this putative marriage it seems unlikely that it ever took place nor is there any reason why, if the son were de Berri's, he should not have been baptised in the Chapel of the Annunciation as were the girls.

In spite of the fascination that the married state seemed to have for him, de Berri was too much of a prince to forget what he owed to his House by marrying a Protestant commoner of doubtful reputation.

In settling down in a state of domestic bliss with Amy Brown without benefit of clergy (which she had apparently not missed before she met him) he was only following his father's example, and his liaison with her did save him from some of his previous excesses. De Berri had inherited the temperament of his famous ancestor, Henri IV, and, although the story of his having left twenty-two posthumous children when he died may be apocryphal, he certainly owned to a number of authenticated illegitimate offspring. The two daughters he had by Amy Brown he acknowledged on his death-bed and they were legitimised and titled by his uncle, Louis XVIII.

De Berri's behaviour in London was by no means monkish and when, early in 1806, he fell ill with gout which also affected his sight, La Ferronays attributed it to the life he led.

Auguste now had to play the part of sick-nurse which led him to fulminate to Albertine that he and de Berri would never understand each other, that de Berri's soul was completely sterile and that he, Auguste, served him from gratitude alone. Auguste expressed himself like this only when he was particularly exasperated. They could not have lived in such intimacy for so many years without mutual esteem. In fact, he was most attached to de Berri.

'He is very impetuous, I know, but nobody really understands his heart. They think it only good; it is excellent. He also has wit. Why does he so rarely use his fine and noble qualities?'

was Auguste's real opinion when he had come out of his ill humour.

Writing to Albertine was all very well but it could not recompense Auguste for his separation from his wife and child which bore on him most hardly. There was little for him to do in England and, in spite of the dangers and difficulties of a journey through Europe once more in the throes of war, and the slenderness of his purse, he again risked going back to Brunswick to see his family.

The Royal circle he left behind was changing. After Louise de Polastron's death Artois moved away from Baker Street, whose associations were perhaps too painful, and settled at South Audley Street, but he spent the hunting and shooting seasons in the country where, as Auguste remarked, and one can almost see the curl of his lip, 'his shots unfortunately find no echo in the world at large.'

It was true that the cannonades in Europe crashed to greater purpose. Nothing seemed able to arrest Bonaparte in his meteoric course and France was intoxicated with the glory he brought her.

Only at sea did he suffer checks but, although after Trafalgar in 1805 the Volunteers still drilled conscientiously and Britain was no longer menaced by invasion, there was still no point at which the British land forces could meet the French in combat and, until they did so, Napoleon's hegemony in Europe could never be absolute.

When the Prince of Wales was celebrating the victory of Trafalgar with a banquet at Carlton House the name of the Comte d'Artois figured on the lists but the Prince crossed it through, saying,

'He is too French to come and I am too much a man of good taste to make him do so.'

Where no political considerations were involved Artois was now going out into Society. He still played his nightly game of whist at the Duchesse de Coigny's or Lady Salisbury's, for there was no Louise to keep him by her side. Every evening he and de Berri were at *ton* parties, at the Duchess of Devonshire's or the Duchess of Gordon's, and once at a superb entertainment given by the Duke and Duchess of York at Oatlands.

The French Princes seemed reconciled to their new rôle of lions in British Society.

XIV

The La Ferronays

Pandemonium reigned in Hamburg. Its status as a free Hanseatic city was threatened by the French in Holland and by the British fleet cruising up and down at the mouth of the Elbe. Down by the waterfront the tortuous streets, lined with medieval houses, offered perfect hiding places for the swarm of spies, malefactors and refugees who constituted an equal danger within the city wall. The city was crammed with French émigrés and equal numbers of representatives of the French Government who lived uneasily side by side.

At Altona in Danish territory across the river the stray Englishman who had lingered too long on the Continent after the Peace of Amiens had been broken in 1803 might still take ship for England if he could avoid the hazards of French troops and secret agents along his route.

It was for this purpose that the young Lord Kinnaird, who had been wintering in Brunswick, arrived in Hamburg in February, 1806. Fond of foreign travel and residing much abroad, his lordship, with characteristic English phlegm, disdained the dangers of a Europe in turmoil, finding ample compensation in the facility with which he could purchase works of art dispersed by the Napoleonic Wars for the collection he was forming at his new home in Scotland. His taste in art was refined, his appreciation of the eighteenth-century masters particularly keen. He seemed to show the same discrimination in the choice of a travelling companion for, during his stay in Brunswick, he had also acquired a personable secretary of about thirty, by name Phillips.

At the inns along the roads he travelled it was noticed that, although he behaved with the customary hauteur of an English nobleman, he treated his secretary with kindly condescension, sharing with him all the comforts procured by the lavish use of an overflowing purse. Phillips in turn showed a proper gratitude for all Lord Kinnaird's amiability, but once they parted for the night and retired to their respective rooms the submissive Phillips disappeared, and throwing himself at a table he would write far into the night—but his writing had little to do with Lord Kinnaird's affairs. In page after page he fulminated against the necessity for Lord Kinnaird's protection, which wounded his susceptibilities, and the benefits he was forced to accept but to which he was unable to contribute.

'Ah, how much I envy the lot of those who have a country, who are not like us, penniless and without support. If only I could become wholly French again. Happy are those whose spirit knows how to resign itself to humiliations, to pity and to disdain! My misfortune is to feel too keenly. I cannot bring myself down to the level of my position. Unhappy vagabond that I am, reduced to hiding even my name.'

The name he hid was that of Auguste de La Ferronays, making yet another of his hazardous journeys to England after a brief reunion with Albertine in Brunswick, to rejoin his exigent master, the Duc de Berri, in London.

On this occasion he was in even graver danger, for Fouché suspected him of having had some hand in a recent attempt on the life of Napoleon. His thin disguise had soon been penetrated and a warrant issued for his arrest.

At the inn where he was staying, a mysterious stranger sought him out, saying:

'If you are the Comte de La Ferronays get out of here as soon as possible. In an hour it will be too late.'

While suspicious of the man's bona fides La Ferronays nevertheless thought it advisable to leave the inn and with great resource went out in his slippers under the pretext of going to the bath, puffing out clouds of smoke from an enormous pipe to hide his face. He reached Altona without incident but only just in time, to find that the man who had warned him was an English sea-captain who had got wind of an attempt to arrest him. Together with Lord Kinnaird he embarked safely for England.

Not everyone travelled under such particular suspicion as La Ferronays but also not everyone had the protection of an English peer. If he chafed at that protection it was partly because he delighted in the difficulties of the journey. Obstacles were important to him only because they could be overcome. Frustrated of proving himself in battle, Auguste's consolation lay in pitting himself against the hazards of journeys across a Continent almost permanently in the grip of war.

In October, 1806, war again broke out between Prussia and France. The Montsoreaus drew up the roots they had struck in their years of residence in Brunswick, which was now threatened by the French, and made for the North German coast, with the intention of going on to England. Auguste had left in advance to prepare a home in the hope that they would follow but at the last moment the old Comte de Montsoreau seemed reluctant to do so. He feared that in England he would have no means of subsistence since the little amount of money he had came from France through the Duchesse de Tourzel, who had returned there with many of the other émigrés. The pension the Comte had been receiving from the Duke of Brunswick was obviously at an end since the Duke was blinded in battle and himself forced to flee.

At last, in spite of Montsoreau's hesitations, and urged by Auguste, who had returned to Germany to fetch them, the Montsoreaus with Albertine (overjoyed at the prospect of being permanently re-united with Auguste) and little Charles embarked at Husum for England. Out of their five years of married life Auguste and Albertine had spent but two together.

Before the Montsoreaus left Brunswick Auguste wrote to his wife, counselling her to have a riding habit made of amazon blue cloth and also one for Félicie de Montsoreau. He urged her to see that they were well cut, having presumably noticed, in spite of his inattention to mundane matters, that English women excelled in this style of dress. He also desired her to bring some sheets, since these were indispensable and an unavoidable expense.

He had hoped to be given a house but the failure of a pension de Berri was receiving from the Spanish Court frustrated this plan, so Auguste bestirred himself and was fortunate in finding a suitable dwelling, part furnished, and a few steps away from the Prince, at 36, Manchester Street, the cheapest of its kind to be had in London. A cook would be unnecessary because their life would be extremely simple, a soup and a main dish constituting their meals. No more was served at the best émigré tables.

With Auguste beside her Albertine managed very well on her first journey in a big ship, but at Customs at Harwich they were surprisingly badly treated, due no doubt to the fact that they travelled with a number of merchants and were probably suspected of carrying contraband. As it was, their jewellery was confiscated (though later it was returned through the intervention of the Princess of Wales).

The first night in England was spent in the stage but on arriving in London at eight o'clock in the morning they were met by the Comte d'Artois' carriage. To have it always available for his friends and dependents Monsieur did not keep his own horses but hired them when the occasion arose so that he could always lend the carriage to any of his circle who wanted to go to a ball or to pay a formal visit. Madame de La Ferronays calls this carriage the hackney of the emigration.

Albertine found the three-storied house charming, although she would have liked a stable if Auguste was with her. On their arrival the Duc de Berri rushed to see them again and all the émigrés came to call. To add to their happiness at being reunited Auguste was nominated first gentleman of the chamber, in succession to the Duc d'Harcourt.

They quickly established their routine. Every morning the family went to mass at ten o'clock. While Auguste lunched with de Berri the family had lunch by themselves. When Auguste returned to the house he visited Madame de Montsoreau and Félicie on the first floor while Albertine awaited him below on the ground floor. His visits were much appreciated by his mother- and sister-in-law but Albertine, awaiting him impatiently, found them very long. Finally he would come downstairs to draw and to paint under Albertine's admiring eyes.

Every afternoon at four o'clock de Berri called, renewing the old habits of far-away Dubno, and stayed while the Montsoreaus had their dinner at five. After dining with his father de Berri returned to Manchester Street to spend the rest of the evening with the family.

Madame de Montsoreau sat at her eternal tapestry which, like Penelope, she never finished. Albertine was at the piano, sometimes accompanying de Berri on the flute, while in a corner sat Félicie, silent and withdrawn. The Comte de Montsoreau, who did not care for music but resigned himself to the Prince's wishes, marched up and down the room. The Comte liked still less the comedies they sometimes played although he disciplined himself so far as to put up the screens they used for wings and to light the candles, but it was a sacrifice. Like his son-in-law he would rather have served his Prince in a more noble way than as stage-manager.

Their life was calm but monotonous. They went out very little. For émigré society they did not care, finding it a hotbed of gossip and intrigue. English society was too costly for them to frequent. Artois' carriage was not always available and it was impossible to go far afield without one, but even to hire a conveyance once a month was beyond their means.

As usual Auguste's gaiety and ingenuity found a solution to this problem. If invited some distance away they set out on foot, hailing a hackney on their way. When they left they had to squeeze through the press of carriages, stopping the way in all directions. Auguste would call as he went,

'James, James, . . .'

No doubt many a James answered the call but it was never their coachman for the very good reason that they did not have one. Once out of sight they walked gaily away, happy to have escaped the humiliation of being recognised as people who did not keep their carriage, a situation which accorded with their income but not with their pride.

But these occasions were rare for Madame de La Ferronays was too timid to venture out much and, after the quiet life she had led for so long, she could not accustom herself to English social usage. Once at a rout, to which this time they had been driven in Monsieur's carriage, she lost Auguste in the crowd and, knowing no one, she stood alone, put out of countenance by the well-bred stares of the *haut ton* and ready to weep with vexation. Happily she caught sight of Lady Kinnaird who took her under her protection for the rest of the evening. Albertine shared all Auguste's sensitivity and thought that people stared at her because she was an émigrée and an outlaw, not realising that she had been regarded with passing curiosity or mere indifference.

It is to Lord Kinnaird's credit that he kept friendly with the La Ferronays for the early impression Auguste had of him as a generous man seems to have been unjustified or perhaps Lord Kinnaird had changed for a contemporary lampoon treats him unkindly:

> Here's a Park without Deer,
> A Cellar with Beer,
> A Kitchen without Cheer,
> Lord K lives here.

And later Farington mentions his avaricious disposition although he praised his fine taste in works of art, while Sir Charles Bagot wrote that he was 'hand in glove with all the Jacobins in all the worst holes and corners of the Continent.'

But the Kinnairds did invite the La Ferronays to dinner and this time the Duc de Berri drove them to the house. They arrived only to find that Lord Kinnaird had gone to ride in the Park and it was half an hour before Lady Kinnaird finally rushed into the drawing-room, still pulling on her long gloves. Never again would the La Ferronays arrive punctually in an English house and to add to their mortification they had to leave on foot, which may have scandalised the lackeys but which certainly distressed Auguste and Albertine.

They were happier in the society of the Duchess of Brunswick, their old friend, who renewed in London the kindness she had shown them in her own palace, and that of her daughter, the Princess of Wales. They were frequently invited to dinner with her and with the Duchess either in London or in Blackheath but the Duchess always sent her carriage for them.

The old lady thought of nothing but her death. The doors of her room at Blackheath were very narrow and she showed them to Madame de Montsoreau and Albertine, remarking,

'I'm afraid they will have great difficulty in getting my coffin through—I don't know how they'll manage.'

Then she rallied.

'Oh, well, it's their business, not mine.'

There were some English families with whom the La Ferronays were on cordial visiting terms, the Sheldons, Mrs. Elliot, whose husband was governor of Madras, with a delightful salon, and Lady Perceval who was absolutely devoted to the Princes and a sincere friend of La Ferronays.

Albertine's time for sociability was limited. In the seven years she spent in England she had six children who did not all live to grow up. Félicie died at birth. Little Adèle fell ill and she, too, was sent to the more salubrious air of Kensington where Madame de La Ferronays, although she was expecting another child, visited her every day, perforce making the journey on foot. But it was all in vain.

To Auguste fell the sad task of burying Adèle beside her sister. He adored his children and wept that they had known of life nothing but suffering but more even than losing them he felt the pain of leaving them one day behind in foreign soil. And what would be the fate of the others, of little Pauline and of her brothers? Perhaps they would one day envy their sisters' repose in the grave. He hoped that his children would be faithful to their principles and would not hesitate to lay down their lives for their Princes and their unhappy country if despair, poverty and unhappiness had not ended their days before they could serve the cause.

'I thought losing them was the worst possible thing that could happen. Perhaps it is as hard to wonder how they are going to survive. It may be that a few months hence all Europe and England too will be in flames. What will happen to us then, wretched creatures, withdrawn from the numbers of the living, without a country, without a home, rejected and cast out everywhere.'

In his grief Auguste was being somewhat unjust to the English as well as extremely pessimistic about the war. It was not in his usual vein but then he wrote under the influence of strong emotion.

He himself knew full well that, even if they could not at the moment give the émigrés back their country, the English were putting every effort into the war, seeking ceaselessly to find a foothold on the Continent. He also knew that the English were doing their best for the émigrés in their exile. Out of the fifteen pounds a month on which the La Ferronays lived ten pounds a month represented the amount which Auguste received from the Duc de Berri but five pounds a month was his allowance from the British Government.

This allocation must have been carried on the special list as Auguste arrived in England after the Committee's lists were closed and there is no mention in the Minutes of any application made on his behalf.

The Montsoreaus, too, were the beneficiaries of the Committee although they did not receive the special relief for which the Princess of Wales very strongly recommended them. It was noted that the Comte de Montsoreau had been in receipt of an allowance from the late Duke of Brunswick, the Princess's father, but that, as he was receiving ten pounds a month as a former officer of the Army of Condé, he was not entitled to any additional sum.

In the interests of general fairness the Committee did not hesitate to refuse the requests even of the Princess of Wales. They did, however, allow a guinea a week to the Comte de Nantouillet, a relative of Madame de Montsoreau's, since he was not receiving any other relief.

If Auguste's pessimism about the war was in the event not justified it did indeed seem as the nineteenth century grew older that the Princes of the House of Bourbon and their faithful adherents in England, now reduced to a couple of thousand persons, were struck off the rolls of the living and would drag out their ghostly time until they died in a forgotten exile.

The French victories at Austerlitz, Jena, Eylau and Friedland, enhancing still further the prestige of him who now called himself Emperor of France, determined Louis XVIII to leave the Continent, which seemed to hold no place for him, and go to England.

Since he neglected to inform the British Government of his projected arrival it is scarcely surprising that Louis XVIII, or rather the Comte de Lille, for he was refused his rightful title, was not allowed to land and the ship in which he travelled was forced to drop anchor in Yarmouth Roads.

After protracted negotiations the Royal party was allowed by the Government to disembark and proceed to Gosfield Hall in Essex, which the Marquis of Buckingham, adding yet one more to his benefactions to the émigrés, had put at Louis' disposal. The Government, however, would not allow the King to come to London.

The change which Louis XVIII's arrival brought to Auguste de La Ferronays was that he had now to divide his time between his peaceful domesticity at Manchester Street and dreary sojourns at Gosfield Hall where his presence was frequently necessary in attendance on de Berri.

Gosfield weighed heavily on him. He could not stand the flatterers and he was unpopular with the place seekers. Why, he asked, had fate thrown him like an impotent fly into this spider's web?

'Remote from my thoughts is the impossible dream of equality,' he wrote to Albertine. 'The human race needs masters. It is by being useful to these masters, and through them to my country, that I wish to serve them and prove my devotion.

'As for the titles and the appointments which link us directly to them I must confess to you, my Alberte, that either because of proper pride or improper vain-glory I am convinced I was not born to the position which fundamentally reduces us to the useless and humiliating status of super-lackeys.

'How mad those people seem to me who spend their time in unworthy occupations or in sacrificing their repose to win a mere look from one of those whose merits consist rather in his birth than in his worth.'

Dangerously revolutionary utterances, with their echo of Beaumarchais' 'because you are a *grand seigneur*, you think you're a great genius. You took the trouble to be born and that's all,' from anyone but Auguste de La Ferronays whose genuine devotion to the Royalist cause was unshakeable. He might have returned to France, as others did, and led an active life serving the glory of his country with the Imperial forces but he chose the life of a poor exile because, whatever his feelings about the men who represented that cause, his attachment to it in hardship, disappointment and even disillusion never faltered.

He found relief in repairing the deficiencies in his education left by the good fathers at Bellelay. When his service was finished at night he retired to his garret at Gosfield, and later at Hartwell, spending long hours in study where he could forget the unhappy present by burying himself in the historic past.

He re-studied the languages he had acquired in his years spent in exile in many countries, translating his ideas into those he knew. He read Young's *Night Thoughts* and read and re-read

Chateaubriand's *Génie du Christianisme* in search of the faith he had lost somewhere along the road that led from France.

All this intellectual activity was looked at askance by the King's entourage whose pre-occupation with the pettiness of arid etiquette, so misplaced in their comparatively humble circumstances, sickened him. One thing alone pleased him in this empty and monotonous life and that was the rapprochement between the Comte d'Artois and Louis XVIII.

XV

Hartwell House and Manchester Street

The Duc de Berri's life in London was fully occupied. He spent much of his time with the two little daughters whom he adored and with their mother, Amy Brown. Then there were his social activities, his visits to his uncle, Louis XVIII, now installed at Hartwell House in Buckinghamshire, and the hours he passed at Manchester Street with the La Ferronays.

Apart from practising the flute de Berri found time to paint some charming aquarelles of himself in various carriages, on the panels of which were painted the Arms of France with the collars of the Royal orders and the Crown surrounded by fleur-de-lys. Always in these little paintings he is attended by coachmen and footmen in liveries of the Royal colours, green coat laced with gold and crimson facings and breeches.

Either the pensions he received from foreign Courts as well as his allowance from the British Government were large enough to pay for these extravagances or else de Berri was indulging his imagination and painting himself as he would like to have been.

Such distractions were not in La Ferronays' vein since, in spite of his devotion to his family, he found a purely domestic and social life hollow and he continued to hope that the Princes would show some energy and some initiative which would lead to positive action although he recognised, in view of Napoleon's stranglehold on the Continent, that the field for activity was very restricted.

At last his patience was rewarded and an opportunity for using his sword again came to Auguste.

More persistent in his devotion to the Bourbon cause than they appeared to be themselves, Gustave IV of Sweden once again entered the lists against France and Auguste immediately determined to join him. This time Artois did not disapprove and even seemed inclined to smooth his path but de Berri ridiculed his Don

Quichotterie, saying it was absurd for a married man with children to risk his life as a volunteer. Secretly Auguste agreed that it was imprudent but would not allow so unworthy a thought to influence his firm decision to go to Sweden.

They had reached an impasse when Angoulême stepped in and invited Auguste to attend him on his journey to Sweden where he was going to fetch his Duchesse. De Berri could not refuse his elder brother's request for Auguste's company and together they set out on board the *Prince of Wales*, to arrive eleven days later in Gothenburg, where the English fleet was assembled round the *Victory*, with an expeditionary force under Sir John Moore on board.

Angoulême's intervention was fortunate for Auguste and one would like to know more of the impulse which prompted it but Artois' elder son remains a shadowy figure with whom history has concerned itself but slightly. Studious and pious he differed almost as much as is possible from his flamboyant brother, de Berri, on whom all the limelight played.

Angoulême was content to spend his years of emigration submissively at his uncle's side and to obey his commands to marry Madame Royale, his first cousin. The marriage, perhaps to no one's surprise, was without issue.

If Angoulême can be reproached with anything in what seems to have been a blameless life it is for being too self-effacing but he seems to have been amiable and was perhaps more popular than his brother.

This year of 1808 was to prove the pivot on which the fortunes of Napoleon would turn. It was the year of the outbreak of the Spanish insurrection. No one at this point could foretell that the Spanish adventure, apparently no different from any other of his enterprises, would eat into his great empire until there was nothing left but the little island of Elba, and then only an alien rock far away in the South Atlantic Ocean.

Still, the revolt of the Spaniards and the despatch of a British expeditionary force under Sir Arthur Wellesley quickened a general excitement and roused even de Berri to determine to join the insurrectionists, news which caused La Ferronays' heart to lift.

He was less pleased when de Berri wrote ordering him peremptorily to return to England to make preparations for Spain. The

King of Sweden had finally granted Auguste a commission in the Swedish army and he was in honour bound to stay in it. To yield to the Prince's importunities and relinquish the commission so lately accepted was not in accordance with his code of behaviour. Inevitably, of course, de Berri reproached him but now he scarcely cared.

At last he was smelling powder again and for a time he was happy. In war everything enchanted him. He no longer needed to reason, only to march and to fight, but even so his sensitive skin prickled with the consciousness of his circumstances, aware that at this time an émigré was regarded as some strange kind of monster whose nature no one understood and still less the impulse which guided him.

It now, however, became increasingly clear that Gustave of Sweden was no longer in full possession of his faculties and Sir John Moore, seeing that he could be of no service to a man going out of his mind, re-embarked his troops and sailed for home.

Auguste, after a great mental and moral struggle, persuaded Gustave to release him and he eagerly set his hopes on joining the army in Spain, but once again the British Government stepped in, as it had done so often in the past, and would not allow de Berri to leave England while on their side, an even greater humiliation, the Spaniards refused to take any exiled Bourbon into their forces.

La Ferronays perforce started back for England, bitterly disappointed at the continual frustration of his efforts to do something worthwhile, although at the moment he was pre-occupied with a minor worry. For some unexplained reason Angoulême had taken his best coat and Auguste wrote urgently to Albertine, telling her to get the tailor to make him a new one in blue cloth, as cheaply as possible naturally, and to have it ready for his arrival. So often in the life of the émigrés the high endeavour ended in trivialities. But the coat was the only new thing in his life which resumed its normal dreary course, alternating between London and Hartwell, the emptiness of its routine more sharply underlined by its contrast with the life of action from which he had so lately come.

At Hartwell the shadow King Louis XVIII had settled down to the life of a country gentleman, closely watching events in

Parliament and on the Continent, but perhaps more happily occupied with the success of his camellias or concerned that the frosts had ruined the espaliers. The lease of Hartwell would soon run out and he inspected Warwick Castle as a possible residence, only to find that it was not to let. He seemed to have laid aside all thought of taking up lodgings in the Tuileries.

Louis bore with kingly fortitude the death of his Queen who, more fortunate than her sister, the Comtesse d'Artois, had remained with her husband and who had always had his respect and attention if not his heart. That had belonged first to Madame de Balbi, who had so far forgotten what she owed to her Royal protector as to give birth to twins of whom he patently could not have been the father, a slight which naturally he did not forgive.

After Madame de Balbi's dismissal Louis, who was quite impartial as to whether his favourites were male or female, gave his favour to the Comte d'Avaray. At least a male favourite could not make him a laughing-stock as Madame de Balbi had. Avaray was, however, forced by his health to leave England for a warmer climate and Louis felt his loss far more acutely than his Queen's. He solaced himself by writing long letters, keeping his absent friend in touch with events at home and abroad and, of more immediate interest to them both, the progress of his old enemy, gout.

Hartwell might be only a small country house but the strictest etiquette prevailed there. It had been arranged to provide the maximum accommodation for the household and Charles Greville, who paid a visit with his father to the King, said it resembled a small town rather than a gentleman's residence, especially since some of the servants had set up small shops in the outhouses.

Louis received the Grevilles graciously in his own apartment, hung with portraits of his martyred relatives, but their attention was focused less on the décor than on the obese body of the King who swung himself backwards and forwards in a manner resembling the heaving of a ship, which made the elder Greville feel seasick.

The dinner they were served was very plain and Louis himself did the honours. After the meal was over each of the ladies folded up her table napkin, tied it round with a piece of ribbon and carried it away. An exiled king must look to his laundry bills. Yet every time the King entered or left the room his sad, red-eyed niece, the Duchesse d'Angoulême, rose and made him a low curtsy, which the King never failed to acknowledge.

Dinner was followed by whist at which the King played for threepence a point, while the courtiers played billiards or ombre. At eleven o'clock the King, and consequently the rest of the company, retired to bed and, in spite of the shortage of rooms, he graciously invited the Grevilles to stay the night.

It was all very dull and the etiquette of Versailles in the midst of such genteel poverty pathetic or absurd, whichever way you chose to look at it. Auguste de La Ferronays found it stifling.

For Albertine life, during Auguste's absences at Hartwell or abroad, was monotonous and lonely but she made no complaint, always waiting patiently for his return to Manchester Street. There were his long letters to look forward to although they must often have distressed her with his patent unhappiness and fears for the future.

She was much occupied with her children. Charles took a precocious interest in the death of Louis XVIII's Queen and knew by heart the names of the people who attended her funeral and their precedence. He was old enough to be sent to school and was put *en pension* with the Abbé Fouquet at Fulham as so many of the émigré schools were now closed. It was, in fact, a very bad school in spite of its good reputation but the La Ferronays would not have dreamed of sending their son to a Protestant establishment. Little Pauline, who was so fat that Louis XVIII called her his resemblance, Alfred and the baby, Albert, remained at home but Albertine still felt the loss of Adèle and Félicie.

Her pre-occupation with the children did not, however, absorb her completely. She had her music and she found a new distraction in taking a course in astronomy with an enthusiastic Abbé, who had invented an ingenious machine which showed the whole of the planetary system and worked on springs like a clock. The King subsequently bought the machine but Albertine never discovered what happened to it and she always regretted that it was lost.

When she could afford it and was invited by her friends, Albertine took short journeys—to Hampstead for a change of air, to Richmond to stay with Lady Acton, who came to London after the death of her husband, Sir John Acton, and with whom the La Ferronays became very friendly. She went also to visit the Sheldons near Oxford and to the Isle of Wight.

When the Royal ladies came to England she and her mother and Félicie went, of course, to Hartwell to pay their court and she was full of emotion at meeting the Duchesse d'Angoulême again whom she had last seen as a child at the Tuileries. Albertine thought her charming and good-looking in spite of her reddened eyes and she behaved to the Montsoreau ladies with the graciousness she reserved for her friends of happier days.

At Hartwell on this occasion Félicie de Montsoreau attracted the attention of the Comte de Blacas, who had taken the place left vacant by d'Avaray in Louis XVIII's affections. Blacas immediately asked for Félicie's hand in marriage but the Comte de Montsoreau thought the favourite's position too insecure to warrant his giving his consent, although as Félicie was now nearly thirty it seemed unlikely that a better *parti* would present himself. The Comte remained adamant in face of all attempts to persuade him otherwise and Félicie was condemned to sit out her days in a corner of the drawing-room at Manchester Street.

It was at this time that something portentous seemed to be about to happen. Two mysterious Vendéens called on de Berri and managed to persuade him and La Ferronays to set out with them for the West of France, which they intended to do without the Comte d'Artois' knowledge.

De Berri wrote to Auguste from Hartwell about the project.

'I received your letter this morning, my dear Auguste, and I thank you for your good advice. I find all that you say very wise and reasonable and, what pleases me more, yet another proof of your attachment to me but, my friend, your remarks are too late and are useless. Everything that you say I have already told myself. I have never shared your confidence in the success of our expedition. I firmly believe that we are going to our death and that is why I will not draw back. You know only too well, my dear Auguste, the absurd things which have been said about us; you know how much we are reproached with not having fought with the Vendée and with not having mingled

our blood with that of the royalists. The lie must be nailed and
you are too much my friend to counsel otherwise.

'You know my opinions about civil wars and those who fer-
ment them. I should count myself traitor to the King, traitor to
France and the most guilty of men if, for the sake of my own
glory or my own personal interest, I tried to rekindle war and
bring on the head of that faithful Vendée the disasters which
have already been the price of its devotion to our cause.

'But, since we are assured that the royalists, tired of the
oppression under which they are living, have decided to take up
arms again, as they tell us, and they are asking for a prince,
nothing will prevent my going to join them. I shall fight at their
head, I shall die in their midst, and my blood shed on the field of
honour, watering the soil of the fatherland, will at least remind
France that the Bourbons exist and that they are worthy of her.
You, my friend, and my old Nantouillet, will share my fate. I
do not pity you. You will be buried at my side.

'Your idea of going before me to sound things out and verify
the state of affairs lacks common sense and you know me well
enough to be very sure that I shall never consent to my friend's
exposing himself to a danger which I should not be sharing
with him.'

But the Comte d'Artois got wind of the expedition and put a
summary stop to it and there went de Berri's good intentions. It
was, however, perhaps just as well that Artois intervened as the
Vendéens had no credentials and were possibly Napoleon's
answer to the Cadoudal plot.

This letter of de Berri's, published only after his death, does
much to rehabilitate his reputation and is a pleasing tribute to the
affection and esteem in which he held Auguste de La Ferronays.

After this abortive attempt at action which might so easily have
ended in disaster Artois kept a careful eye on his son's activities
but no opportunity offered for further enterprise on his part.

Tranquillity, however, never wore out its welcome in the lives
of the La Ferronays. After Auguste's departure from Sweden a
terrible crisis had arisen.

Beaten by the Russians and the Danes and an object of execration
to his own people, Gustave IV was imprisoned in his palace and

forced to abdicate. Then he, too, took the road to exile. He wandered in mind and in body for a year across Europe until suddenly he appeared at Hartwell, seeking the hospitality not of the Prince Regent of England but of the King of France since, as he said, 'I lost myself for his cause. I come to throw myself into his arms after my defeat. I can find shelter nowhere but with him.'

Auguste was much affected by the plight of a king who had shown him so much personal kindness and favour and he asked the Duc de Berri to allow him to be attached to the King's service. It was a thankless task for poor Gustave suspected everyone around him and his behaviour was far from normal but it was natural to Auguste to offer himself without thought of gratitude or reward in accordance with the principles of chivalry.

At last the former King of Sweden decided to return to Europe and begged La Ferronays to accompany him, a pleading he was unable to resist. He recognised that Gustave had sacrificed himself for the Bourbons and, if they were unwilling to succour him further, it was incumbent on him to act as the King's champion.

This time the British Government acted as his friend by forbidding him to accompany Gustave, who perforce had to leave England alone, to drag out an even longer exile than the Bourbons whom he had nobly done his best to aid.

Albertine had taken this prospect of a new parting from Auguste with fortitude but she was particularly glad at this moment that he was obliged to remain in England for suddenly there was an upsurge of feeling against the émigrés. No one knew how or why it arose but now in London where they had always felt so secure there was a hidden terror. Every day the word 'Death' was written on the La Ferronays' door and every morning brought news of some murder, waylaying or mysterious crime. The Comte and Comtesse d'Antraigues were both found murdered and the *Morning Post* was inclined to consider it a political crime.

'We are little inclined to place any confidence in the reports that the Comte d'Antraigues was by no means so attached to the interests of this country as many of the distinguished characters by whom he was countenanced were induced to suppose; but as we have so many foreigners among us and as too many of them may reasonably be suspected of being disposed to favour the news of our inveterate enemy we trust that Government will be firm and resolute in its endeavours to ascertain the true character of the departed French nobleman.

'The interests of the country demand a rigid scrutiny into the truth of the rumours alluded to; for if he was not deserving of the confidence and protection which he experienced we should have strong reasons indeed to be suspicious of many other foreigners who appear in a more questionable shape.'

The *Morning Post* was wrong. An unbalanced servant was responsible for the double murder and all its journalistic eloquence was wasted but its attitude indicates the atmosphere of suspicion with which the French in England were regarded at this time.

Completely inexplicable was the murder of some neighbours of the La Ferronays, quiet and innocent people with no connection with politics. Another family, of merchants, had their throats cut and even their little bird in a cage was battered to death, yet nothing was stolen from the house.

In the evenings in quiet Manchester Street the La Ferronays family would hear dreadful cries. The Duc de Berri seemed particularly menaced, being continually followed as he went his way around the neighbourhood. Auguste never left his side and finally the Comte d'Artois forbade the Duc to go anywhere on foot.

Who was responsible? Disaffected British or agents of Napoleon? No one ever found out for, as suddenly as they had begun, the attacks ceased.

XVI

The Last Years

Events in Sweden after the deposition of Gustave IV had taken a curious turn. His successor had no son and the prince nominated as his heir died of apoplexy. The Swedes had to look around for a future king and their choice fell surprisingly on that ardent republican and Marshal of France, Jean-Baptiste Bernadotte, Prince of Ponte Corvo. The parvenu Bernadotte could not resist the lure of a throne when it offered and he accepted the invitation to become Prince Royal of Sweden.

So far from throwing in his lot with his chief benefactor, Napoleon, Bernadotte, with a prudence and self-interest which did him no credit as a man of honour, stood outside the Emperor's orbit and did not, when the time came, hesitate to take up arms against France, the country of his birth, nor to cast greedy and ambitious eyes on its crown when Napoleon laid it aside. This, however, was for the future.

Now Bernadotte's aloofness from Napoleon and the traditional friendship of Sweden for the Bourbons, together with the French attack on Russia in 1812, all combined to make it seem to Louis XVIII and the Comte d'Artois a politic moment to find out how they stood with the Swedish and Russian monarchs and what might be the chances of a restoration should the unforeseen happen and Napoleon be defeated by Alexander I.

Although he had no training in diplomacy and his whole life had been spent with the Army of Condé, in rushing up and down the high roads of Europe on one abortive quest after another, or in dancing attendance on the Duc de Berri, Auguste de La Ferronays was chosen for this mission. His selection, rather than that of an experienced diplomat, may have been due to the small amount of faith the Princes had in the outcome of the embassy with which they entrusted him and also, no doubt, because he thought little

of travelling across Europe at war and was accustomed to risking
his life in dangerous enterprises.

Auguste's only fear in accepting this mission was that his
inexperience in diplomacy might jeopardise its success and so
damage the Bourbon cause but it was not in his nature to refuse
or retire from a task to which he was called by honour and duty.

Before he set out on his journey the little circle in Manchester
Street celebrated the Duc de Berri's birthday with a comedy,
The Caliph, in which Auguste played the title rôle with great
success and in a costume in which, to the adoring eyes of
Albertine, he looked extremely well. It was a long time since they
had all felt gay enough for theatricals but now there seemed to be a
lightening in the atmosphere and there seemed also to be an omen
in the music.

Someone had lent Albertine a volume of songs, newly brought
from France. She had played some of them over and turned to the
next one with no more interest than that it was new when, to her
astonishment, she found that the refrain was sung to the old and
dear tune of *Vive le Roi, vive la France*. These notes, coming from
France, seemed to her so astonishing that she attached to them an
importance greater than they possessed, seeing in them a presage
of restoration. She ran round the house to share with the others
her surprise and emotion. On such slender hopes do exiles live.

The song had enormous success in England among the émigrés
but first it ensured the success of the evening at Manchester Street
where it was sung by all the actors with enormous enthusiasm.

Then Auguste had to leave but this time the parting was not so
painful to Albertine as events became so absorbing that her heart
and mind were fixed on them.

Auguste, after a tempestuous crossing of the North Sea,
arrived in Stockholm to find again the society which had so
pleased him on his previous visits, both for its own charm and
because it was so different from that in which he moved in England.
He developed a great enthusiasm for Madame de Staël, whom he
met for the first time in Stockholm, finding that in her salon more
ideas were discussed in an hour than in a month at Hartwell. This
charming and handsome man, with his melancholy and lustrous
dark eyes, fascinated Europe's leading blue-stocking, never impervious to masculine charm. She admired in him a man patently

endowed with high intelligence and great gifts of character who could have earned distinction in the service of the Emperor Napoleon yet who chose to lead the life of a poor disregarded exile from the disinterested motives of loyalty to his Princes and his principles.

La Ferronays was, in his turn, charmed by Madame de Staël, who did her best to help him in his efforts to obtain an interview with the Prince Royal whom, however, he did not succeed in meeting. Instead he met a man who was destined to be the greatest formative influence he encountered in Sweden. He was named Camps, a man of humble origin but foster-brother to Bernadotte and now his aide-de-camp, and the ruthlessness of his logic cut sharply into Auguste's ideas though neither he nor anyone else could make the smallest alteration in his ideals.

Bluntly Camps informed Auguste that his mission would be unsuccessful. Everywhere he would find Austria across his path and Napoleon's father-in-law, Francis I, was unlikely to embark on any course of action calculated to prejudice his daughter's position. Alexander of Russia neither would nor could recognise Louis XVIII as King of France. About Francis Camps was wrong. He did not hesitate finally to join with the Allies in ousting Marie Louise from her Empire and her son from his throne. In other words of advice Camps struck nearer home.

'Your King,' he coldly told Auguste, 'forgets a little too often that for twenty years he hasn't been King of France. The word "usurper" which he constantly uses doesn't now mean anything. By giving everyone the place his intelligence and talent merit the revolution has changed the world. France has grown older and matured not by twenty-five years but by a century. It is only you émigrés who do not realise it.'

Both Camps and his master, Bernadotte, men whom the Revolution had made, were living proof of the truth of his words which Auguste made no attempt to deny.

'Your masters had neither the strength nor the courage,' Camps continued, 'to preserve their crown and they no longer have any rights. If ever you do go back to France you will have to shed your antiquated ideas and your prejudices. You must accustom your-selves to hearing and to speaking the strong language which is now used in Paris . . . and you will have to leave everything as you find it. The only reform that there is to be made is of your-selves.'

Auguste was shattered. He disliked Camps' language and even more the tone he used but he was abashed and appalled when this man of the people who thought so straight and who spoke so rudely put into words the half-formulated feelings which he had scarcely dared to admit to himself.

As usual he poured out his feelings to Albertine.

'How far we are in England from seeing things in their true light! How badly we judge what is happening outside ourselves and our prejudices! We are still at the point where we were surprised by the Revolution. While everything in the world has changed we remain stupidly proud of our blood and our educa-tion . . . we insist on believing ourselves superior to the men of the revolution. He whom I have just seen has proved to me the contrary. It is true, of course, that his elbows are not as rounded as those of Monsieur de Vaudreuil, nor does he bow so low, but in contrast he makes a greater impression. His conversation is always serious, but then men of his world think deeply.

'I warn you that the most able of us would not be able to stand up in argument for a quarter of an hour against the most minor official of the least important office of the remotest part of the Empire.'

Although Auguste did not know it Burke had said much the same thing nearly twenty years previously. He, too, thought that it was energy and enterprise which were wanted rather than experience. He was writing at a time when England was suffering defeats at the hand of France:

'In a case like ours I have no opinion at all of old men. If nothing can be done by the young, nothing can be done at all. I verily believe there is not in the Government of France nor in any of its armies a man above five and thirty.'*

Auguste could not linger in Stockholm for Camps to re-orientate his thinking for he had to accomplish the next stage of his journey. He travelled to St. Petersburg heavy-hearted, arriving in

* British Museum, Add. MSS. 9828.

April, 1813, to find that, in spite of Napoleon's attack on Russia and the débâcle of the Grande Armée, Alexander was still under the spell that Bonaparte had cast over him and Auguste did not even succeed in seeing the Czar.

Part of his mission was to sound the Empress Dowager on the prospect of obtaining the hand of one of the Grand Duchesses for the Duc de Berri though it was scarcely likely that she, who had rejected the Emperor Napoleon as a son-in-law at the height of his power, would entertain the project of a matrimonial alliance with this poverty-striken and frivolous Prince whose matrimonial adventures were the gossip of European courts and whose future was so uncertain. At this moment the upstart Romanoffs, securely seated on the Russian throne, could indulge the luxury of looking down on the ancient Bourbons, dispossessed of their heritage.

Auguste La Ferronays had looked for no success here. He was too inured to the rebuffs with which de Berri met on his excursions into the marriage market to hope that he could obtain for his master a Grand Duchess as a bride.

Doggedly he pursued his objectives but his attempt to win over to the Royalist cause the French officers, prisoners-of-war, whom he met in Russia, suffered a like check. What to the Grande Armée, beaten and in captivity though these remnants were, was the prestige of a Louis XVIII, who had never led a charge in battle, compared with the scintillation of their Emperor who had led them to a hundred victories, or what to the soldiers of Napoleon mattered an exiled Bourbon king? To many of them Bourbon was nothing but a name, remotely connected with French history and, as for kings, Napoleon made and unmade them at his will.

Nothing now was left for Auguste but to turn back from this, his first embassy, with only failure to report. He could have made his way back to England again via Sweden and the North Sea but he chose rather to return in the wake of the armies now marching into Germany for the final scenes in the last act but one of the Napoleonic drama.

At Dresden, not surprisingly, he fell ill with fever to which he nearly succumbed, worn out as much by disappointment as by the illness itself. Happily the remedies with which he was treated proved efficacious and Auguste set out once more in quest of the Czar until finally he caught up with him at Leipzig after Napoleon's defeat there.

Alexander I most courteously informed him that, at the moment, circumstances did not permit of his acceding to the wishes of 'Monsieur le Comte de Lille' nor, he added diplomatically, to follow his own inclination since the Allies were at this moment entirely dependent on Austria and it was unlikely that the Emperor Francis would act in a way to damage his daughter's interests.

It was small consolation to Auguste when Alexander earnestly confided in him that it was his belief that legitimacy was the only basis on which peace and tranquillity in Europe could be founded. His last word, as he graciously dismissed Auguste, was to urge the Royalists to do all they could to increase the number of their partisans in France.

Before he left Leipzig Auguste was once more received by the Czar who gave him letters for the 'Comte de Lille,' an appellation which must have made La Ferronays grind his teeth, and reiterated his friendly feelings towards the Princes. He even expressed his regret at being unable to accede to the wishes of the Duc de Berri with regard to one of his sisters.

Personally Auguste had a great success with the Czar and was told by Nesselrode that His Imperial Majesty had said that, if ever the King (though no doubt he said 'Monsieur le Comte de Lille') were in a position to send another ambassador he hoped it would be the Comte de La Ferronays. Neither of them could have thought that this wish would ever come true.

Back to England travelled Auguste once more, bearer of empty promises and emptier compliments, but with a heavier weight on his mind. Until now he had confided his changing ideas about the present and the future of the émigrés only to Albertine but if, through all the vicissitudes, all the political ineptitudes and tergiversations of his Princes, La Ferronays had kept silent he no longer felt he had the right to do so.

He had been sent out of the hothouse that was the emigration in England to sound opinion in the outside world and it was his duty to report faithfully on what he had seen and heard, however unpalatable it might be to his masters. It would be rendering them the worst possible service to conceal from them what the world thought of them and their actions since it was because they were so often misinformed about that opinion that they did and said things that were judged ill or which showed them in a prejudicial light.

His welcome at Hartwell, however, was less critical than he had feared. The King was too accustomed now to wait on events and perhaps too resigned to expect much of any one démarche, and the entourage was indifferent. They were growing old and no doubt Auguste's boundless energy of mind and body wearied as much as his marked indifference annoyed them. They could not share his ideas which had developed in a world remote from the country house in Buckinghamshire, a world where men thought and acted, not vegetated.

'What energy the revolution has unleashed,' he wrote to Albertine from Hartwell, still dazed from his encounter with Camps, 'and what powerful ideas, although it has at the same time destroyed all moral principles. What an iron hand and what genius will be required to dominate it! Alas, my country is very dear to me but once again I ask, shall we be able to live happily there?'

Auguste was almost alone in his apprehensions. It was June, 1813, when he disembarked in England. Wellington had gained his great victory at Vittoria and was preparing to cross the Pyrénées. Although Napoleon fought brilliantly at Bautzen it was a rearguard action and the Allies were pursuing him fast.

Breathlessly the émigrés followed the campaign with mingled emotions of hope and sadness. The unconquered armies of France were going down before the enemy and they could not rejoice whole-heartedly at the humiliation which their country, to which they remained so devoted, was suffering. Just as in 1792, when they had admired the valour of the revolutionary armies in the field even when they defeated the émigrés, so now they deplored the loss of France's glory.

Although, in the view of Sir Morton Eden, brother of Lord Auckland, the émigrés,

'if restored to their country to-morrow, will not become wiser, nor would a moment hesitate to enter into new wars to recover what may be taken from France at the peace,' a prophecy which was destined to be unfulfilled, it was asking too much of them not to remember that they were Frenchmen.

Louis XVIII himself, when asked to patronise a celebration of the battle of Leipzig, replied with great dignity,

'I do not know if the disasters which are overtaking the French army are one of the means by which Providence intends to restore the legitimate authority but neither I, nor any of the princes of my family, can rejoice at events which are so great a sorrow to our country.'

There were some, as Madame de La Ferronays records, who were human enough to rejoice at the prospect of their own liberation but they were greatly reproached by their fellows for so doing.

Auguste himself was less concerned with the victories than with the sufferings of the army in retreat, recalling only too well what defeat meant to the troops. He could hardly be dragged away from the map on which he followed the campaign. But more than anything else he regretted that the Royalists were not represented in the events which seemed likely to restore the monarchy, sharing the fears once expressed by Pitt as to the dangers of a restoration in which the émigrés had no part.

'They have conquered without us,' he mourned.

No one shared Auguste's sorrow to this extent.

The Regent suddenly discovered how attached he was to the King of France and invited him to the Queen's birthday ball at Carlton House.

Louis wrote maliciously to d'Avaray about the invitation and the fluctuations in George III's health which caused a postponement.

'Without boasting, I and all my family are invited!'

The Regent seemed determined to make up for any omissions of the past with regard to Louis XVIII. The walls of Carlton House were covered with hangings embroidered with fleur-de-lys and all the emigration was invited.

Entertainments on a Royal scale had long since ceased to be within the capacity of the poor émigrés and the problem of what they should wear was an embarrassing one. The ladies at least were able to borrow from their English friends the necessary dresses of white, trimmed with silver and gold, and the three Prince of Wales feathers and veils to pin in their hair. Happily panniers were not worn at the Prince's court and the high-waisted dresses then in vogue could be pinned up to fit them. Madame de La Ferronays doubted if they were very elegantly arranged but the fashion of the day only demanded that dresses should be tight in front and bouffant behind.

The gentlemen were not so fortunate. Etiquette required either uniforms or evening dress, neither of which they possessed. They were able to hire suitable costumes and although they must all, according to Albertine de La Ferronays, have presented a very odd appearance the evening passed off very well and to find themselves at Carlton House was a good augury for their return to the Tuileries.

Now real hope of restoration was in the air and, to compensate for their many sorrows, the Montsoreau family had one domestic happiness. The Comte de Montsoreau relented towards the Comte de Blacas and he and Félicie were married by one of the priests of the Chapel of the Annunciation.

As their hopes grew brighter the emigration became more and more agitated. Nobody knew what might happen as excitement mounted and, as the newsboys called out second and even third editions of the papers, the émigrés rushed out into the streets for the latest news. When they set out to exchange New Year greetings they were scarcely able to get out their good wishes to each other, so choked were they with hope and expectation.

Was it, could it, be the end?

XVII

The Restoration

After years of doubt, frustration and disappointment the moment had finally come for the Bourbons to shake off the choking bonds of exile and take possession again of their heritage. The Allies, however, still hesitated as to what form the future government of France should take and the British Government still cautiously held back from giving the Princes its blessing to join in the last stages of the war. At last it could refrain no longer and permission was granted for the Princes to leave London on condition that their departure was unannounced and that they travelled incognito, using only the public stage.

First to go, as was due to his seniority, was the Comte d'Artois. He embarked at Yarmouth at the end of January, 1814, and landed near the Hague, whence he immediately issued a proclamation to the French people, urging them to recognise the benefits of a restoration of their legitimate ruling house. The proclamation caused little stir among a nation menaced by invasion and whose Imperial house of cards was tumbling about its ears.

Nor was Artois' presence welcomed by the Allies and he was forced to move up and down the French frontier along their lines of communication, treated with indifference and allowed to remain only on condition that he did not carry arms and wore neither uniform nor cockade. The Allied sovereigns themselves affected to ignore him and the cause of the Bourbons still hung in the balance.

At last Paris fell and Napoleon abdicated. It now became a matter of urgency for the Allies finally to make up their minds. After many hesitations they came down on the side of a Bourbon restoration, the principle of legitimacy victorious, while the signal was thus given for 'Europe's wormy dynasties to rerobe themselves in their old gilt, to dazzle anew the globe!'

They found Artois a white charger and, still supple and elegant in the uniform of the National Guard in spite of his fifty-seven years, he rode into Paris on April 12th, 1814, in glorious spring sunshine, at the head of a glittering cavalcade led by the Emperor Napoleon's renegade marshals, Ney, Marmont and Moncey. His exile had lasted three months short of twenty-five years.

Artois' departure from England was followed by that of the Duc d'Angoulême, who set off for the Pyrénées to join the Duke of Wellington. It is believed that to Angoulême belongs the credit of converting the Duke to the Bourbon cause.

De Berri and La Ferronays were to go direct to Northern France and on January 30th they mounted the stage for Wey-mouth, bound for Jersey and thence for Normandy! The winter that year was very severe, the worst for many years. Snow was piled high in the streets and round the coasts storms raged ceaselessly. Artois and Angoulême had got away just in time. More than once de Berri's carriage was overturned but he and his companions escaped unhurt.

With France so near and events moving so rapidly de Berri and La Ferronays were nevertheless impotent against the weather. Already Angoulême was at Bordeaux and Artois at Vesoul. Impatient and fretting to be away de Berri and his faithful Auguste were stormbound for weeks in Jersey.

At last the winds dropped and de Berri and La Ferronays were able to embark on the cutter, *Eurotas*. As they approached Cherbourg, still doubtful of their welcome, although a delegation from the city had invited the Prince to land there, they saw the tricolour fall from the fort and the white flag of the Bourbons hoisted in its stead. A salvo of artillery greeted the arrival of the admiral's barge to which de Berri had transferred and, as it came into port, he leapt ashore, crying, 'France!'

England itself was in a state of delirious excitement. The long war was nearly over; Boney, the tyrant, beaten. The citizens of London prepared to give a great reception to old 'bungy Louis' on his way home to France. Now he was no longer 'bungy Louis' but *Louis le Désiré*, the stout old gentleman who had lived among them so quietly and to whom they now looked to consolidate the peace which the Duke of Wellington had done so much to win and for which the whole world craved.

It was April 20th, 1814. In Piccadilly the crowds were dense as the Life Guards trotted up and down, trying with difficulty to exact order from the chattering, excited throng, whose enthusiasm was quickened by the martial tunes the regimental band was blaring out. From every window and balcony, even from the parapets of the houses, heads craned out, watching the show. The long street looked like a drift of hawthorn with something white decking every house. On the walls of Devonshire House were hoisted the colours of France and England, mounted on flag-staffs, the arms embroidered in gold and silver on the richest white silk. Not a family of any respectability appeared without the white cockade, the Bourbon symbol, and they hummed the tune which was all the rage, *The White Cockade*.

'England no more your foe, will bring you aid,
When France shall welcome home the White Cockade.'

Early arrivals saw a magnificent procession sweeping along the road. First came a detachment of the 11th Dragoons, then an immense train of carriages and horsemen, and finally the travelling carriage of the Prince Regent, driven by his postillions in white jackets and white hats, and three outriders in the Royal livery, the Prince himself in full regimentals with his Russian and English orders.

Out past the Paddington turnpike, through the village of Kilburn and beyond the town of Edgware, so bedecked with flags, stars and ribbons that it looked like a vast fair, galloped the Royal carriage and its escort until they reached the village of Stanmore and with a clatter of bit and bridle drew up at the *Abercorn Arms*. Here, too, the decorations were white but less sophisticated than in town.

'Ludicrous but significant decorations graced the roadside; children's white frocks, women's aprons, and in some instances other garments of the prevailing colour were proudly dis-played.'

As the Prince stepped out of his carriage he was greeted by the Duchesse d'Angoulême. There was some delay and the committee of welcome grew anxious. After all Louis was not young and perhaps all the emotion of the last few days had been too much for him? At last cheering was heard in the distance and the King's carriage came in sight, drawn not by horses but by Englishmen harnessed between the shafts. Lord Sheffield would not this time have disapproved. Enthusiasm touched delirium.

The Prince greeted the King and together they took their seats in the Prince's carriage, drawn by eight cream-coloured horses. A sharp order and the procession of six Royal carriages, each drawn by six bays, set out for London. At five o'clock in the afternoon they drew up outside Grillon's Hotel in Albemarle Street, off Piccadilly, and at the same moment the Duke of Kent's own band crashed into 'God Save the King.'

The people huzzaed and the ladies in the windows waved their white handkerchiefs. Louis took the arm of the Prince who conducted him into the hotel with the greatest tenderness. He offered his formal congratulations 'in the most impressive and affecting manner' for which Louis returned thanks and for the protection he had enjoyed and the kindness and attentions with which he had been treated during his residence in this country. Then he took off the cordon and ornaments of the Order of the St. Esprit and hung them round the Prince Regent's neck.

Although the old King was fatigued with the excitements of the day he could not yet retire. The duties of Royalty required that he should receive a large company, the Mayor and Aldermen of the City of Westminster, the émigrés and their ladies who wished to take an English farewell of the King before meeting him again at the Tuileries, and members of the *ton* who desired to be presented to him and to the Duchesse d'Angoulême both from curiosity and to ensure a cordial reception at the Court in Paris.

Fanny Burney, or rather Madame d'Arblay, was among those in the throng in the front room at Grillon's to be presented. She had come with Lady Crewe, who had been a prominent member of the English ladies' committee of relief, in the expectation of meeting the Duchesse d'Angoulême but Marie Thérèse had remained with her father-in-law, the Comte d'Artois, at South Audley Street. Although Madame d'Arblay wished to retire Lady Crewe pushed her forward and she found herself being greeted by Louis XVIII with great warmth and in English.

Louis seized her hand and repeatedly assured her of his happiness in meeting her, indeed he had long wanted to do so since he had been charmed and entertained by her books which he had

read and re-read. He seemed unwilling to let her go and interrupted her curtsy to take her hand again.

If he could not equal his brother in elegance of face and figure
Louis yielded nothing to Artois in graciousness.

On the following day the Prince Regent gave a Dress Party in
Louis' honour and returned his compliment by investing him with
the Order of the Garter.

A day or two later Louis, accompanied by his niece and his
faithful entourage, set out for Dover and France.

Soon the Princes were followed by a stream of émigrés from
all over Europe, from Russia, from Germany, from Austria and
from England, those for whom at last the *chemin de l'honneur* led
homewards. Behind them were years of humiliation, uncertainty,
discouragement, hardship and distress. Before them were the
question-marks of the future but at least it would be a future lived
in France.

As they stood on the decks of the ships which were carrying
them from England, surrounded by the poor bundles of their
meagre possessions, and the white cliffs receded into the spring
haze, a land breeze brought the sound of bells from France, bells
which gave out a different sound from those they had heard so
long for it seemed that they *spoke in French*. And, as they stepped
ashore at last perhaps many, like the Comte Auguste Ferron de La
Ferronays, stooped and kissed the soil of France.

The children gazed with awe on the country they had never
seen but which they had been taught to love. Their parents were
filled with an indescribable emotion, the joy at seeing their own
country again shadowed by regret for the friends, the associations
and the graves they left behind. For many England was still the
reality, France the illusion.

Tearing himself away almost reluctantly from Somers Town
the Abbé Carron addressed a farewell letter, whose words must
secretly have been echoed by many, to his 'benevolent friends, the
citizens of Great Britain.'

'Noble and sensitive souls who deigned to welcome and, for
more than twenty years of exile from his native country,
treated as a brother, cherished as a son, this poor stranger,
obscure citizen in his own country who was, and ought to have

remained, unknown in yours. Magnanimous English, I found your country hospitable as my own native soil. During these long years you, my adoptive parents, showered on me the benevolent care of a father and the tender solicitude of a mother.

'Overwhelmed with your kindnesses I am dragging myself away from your shelter, from my numerous colony, from the little France of Somers Town. Providence condemns me to this great sacrifice which to me is like a new emigration . . .'

Here properly ends the story of the emigration, of the twenty-five years of voluntary exile suffered by the Princes of the House of Bourbon and the faithful few who shared it with them till it closed with that Restoration of which they had never despaired, although it had so often seemed that only a miracle would bring it about.

But, less than a year later, when Napoleon, landing from Elba and sweeping on to Paris for what might have been the re-establishment of his Empire although its brief renaissance ended in a Hundred Days, it must have seemed to those who would always be known as 'émigrés' that it was all to begin again.

In Vienna Wellington and Metternich and the ex-bishop, Talleyrand, hastened to rule Napoleon *hors la loi* while the Comte d'Artois with Marshal Ney, who had sworn to Louis XVIII that he would bring the monster back to Paris in a cage, rushed southward from Paris to stem his advance. But Ney, forgetting his promise and his new allegiance, could not resist the appeal of his old master, a volte-face which would bring him to an ignominious death in front of a firing-squad. Nothing now for Artois but to return to Paris and join in Louis' agonised councils at the Tuileries which must have reminded the old King of the decision that had to be taken before the flight to Varennes. Were they to go or to stay? To remain meant civil war at least which was not to be thought of and then, could they count on the loyalty of the old soldiers of the Imperial armies? In the West of France Angoulême and his Duchesse tried to rally the country from Bordeaux but their efforts failed and they were forced to take ship for England.

Just before Easter, 1815, Louis XVIII with the Comte d'Artois and the Duc de Berri, accompanied by his faithful La Ferronays, left the Tuileries by night, escorted by the *Maison du Roi*, the Royal guard whose reconstitution by the Bourbons had so enraged the Bonapartists who were excluded from its *cadres*, and lumbered their way to the North, pursued either in reality or in imagination by the cavalry of Exelmans who had gone back to Napoleon.

As city after city on their route rallied to the Emperor it soon became apparent to the Royalists on that nightmare journey that only across the frontiers would they find safety. Their choice lay between making for the coast and embarking for England or crossing into Belgium where Allied troops were hastily assembling. It was impossible to embark the remnants of the *Maison du Roi* and perhaps there was something too final in once again putting the Channel between themselves and France so they made for the Belgian frontier and finally came to rest at Ghent.

Louis took up his residence at the Hôtel d'Hane-Steenhuyse, home of the Governor of East Flanders, who had already numbered among his royal guests Jerome Bonaparte, King of Westphalia, the Czar of Russia and William of the Netherlands.

The Hôtel d'Hane-Steenhuyse is smaller than Hartwell House but its owner was rich and it was furnished with great elegance in the French fashion, one room, the ballroom, which was used by Louis XVIII for dinners and concerts, being particularly magnificent with a marquetry floor inlaid with precious woods. And there was a little garden into which he could be wheeled out.

Wellington called on the King when he arrived in Belgium and there was much coming and going of high-ranking officers, but there was nothing really for Louis and Artois to do but to wait in impotent idleness while their fate rested in the hands of the Allies. True, de Berri made a show of martial activity and drilled his handful of troops to the ill-disguised mirth of the British soldiery.

The émigrés could not, as heretofore, rejoice at the initial success of French arms at Fleurus and Quatre Bras for a Napoleonic victory could only mean eternal exile. They were saved by Wellington's great victory at Waterloo on June 18th and they went back to France, protected by foreign bayonets. This time there was no opposition among the Allies for there was no alternative to the Bourbons and they stayed in France for fifteen years.

Louis XVIII with his Charter did his best to rule as a constitutional monarch but, as La Ferronays had realised, it needed an iron hand and genius to rule the French people. There were too many warring elements to be reconciled—the republicans, whom Napoleon kept in check because he, too, was a child of the Revolution; the émigrés, disappointed of their hopes of regaining the positions and the property which had been theirs; the discontented and disbanded soldiers of the Imperial armies who, on their scant half-pay, had nothing to do but brood on the glories of the past to the disadvantage of the melancholy present, time's revenges for the same misery endured by so many representatives of the *ancien régime* during their years of exile.

Life was perhaps most difficult at Court where those of Napoleon's marshals and high officers of state, who had made their submission to the Bourbons, rubbed uneasy shoulders with the Faubourg St. Germain, which had always been in covert opposition to the Emperor and had now come back into its own, and the returned émigrés who arched their proud but threadbare backs at the *noblesse de l'Empire* while their wives were snubbed by the Duchesse d'Angoulême. At Court it was the Bonapartists who now represented the *ancien régime*. Their situation was summed up pithily by the former washerwoman, the Maréchale Lefebvre, Duchess of Dantzig, who no doubt had once taken in the aristocrats' washing, when she said of the Tuileries:

'On y allait quand c'était chez nous. Maintenant que c'est chez eux on ne se sent plus chez soi.'

Many of them found the perfume of the lilies overpowering after the sweet fresh smell of Imperial violets and their ears, and those of France, which were attuned to the *Chant du Départ* and *Veillons au salut de l'Empire*, refused to be reconciled to the musical bombardment of *Charmante Gabrielle* and *Vive Henri IV*. How tired they all became of Henri IV!

In Vienna the little King of Rome was being ground into an Austrian prince and in far-away St. Helena the Emperor was fighting his last battles with that unworthy enemy, Sir Hudson Lowe. There were sporadic attempts at risings by the half-pay officers, and the Royalists attempted a terrible vengeance in the South, but Wellington sat vigilantly in the British Embassy in Paris, in the house where the beautiful Pauline Borghese, sister of Napoleon, had entertained her many lovers.

The Bourbons held on. Louis XVIII from his wheel-chair his limbs now quite useless, managed to keep the monarchy going. It suffered an unexpected blow when de Berri, who had at last found a bride in Caroline of Naples, was assassinated on February 13th, 1820, on his way to the Opera to see one of his favourite dancers (for marriage had done nothing to change de Berri's way of life). He left behind him a daughter and a posthumous son who, as Henri V, became the white hope of the Bourbons.

If de Berri had in his lifetime repeatedly cast away opportunities for acting like a Prince he knew how to die like one and, as his life ebbed away in the incongruous setting of an ante-room at the Opera, urgently begged the King to spare the life of his assassin.

He was buried with great pomp in the basilica of St. Denis, where he had so lately attended a requiem mass for Louis XVI and Marie Antoinette, but to the spectators who knew on what slender life-lines the monarchy now existed the chants, the tolling bells, the cannon booming out over the silent coffin, all the grandeur and all the pomp seemed to celebrate not the funeral of a prince but the obsequies of the monarchy.

With de Berri's death what little life there had been at Louis XVIII's Court seemed to vanish though hope revived with the birth of the young Duc de Bordeaux.

Louis himself was completely given over to the influence of his last and latest favourite, the Comtesse du Cayla, who imposed her political will on the ageing King.

In 1824 Louis XVIII uttered his last witticism as he painfully whispered to his doctors,

'Allez-vous-en, charlatans (Charles attend).'

Chateaubriand, the zealous Royalist, published an obituary pamphlet of Louis which the *Annual Register* castigated as

'perhaps the most perfect specimen of nonsensical, bombastical, antithetical flattery of the dead and the living, that was ever exhibited to the world.'

But Louis had been a good King. A man of the eighteenth century, he had done his best to accommodate himself to the changing circumstances of the nineteenth and the ten years of his reign had given France an opportunity to heal the great wounds in her pride and economy left by the last two savage years of the Empire.

In the Pavillon de Marsan, the wing of the Tuileries where he lived, Charles-Philippe was indeed waiting and his accession was greeted with some apprehension since he had once more become in the eyes of the people the symbol of intransigence and reaction. Neither he, nor de Berri while he lived, was popular, although the French looked with an indulgent eye on de Berri's amours. Angoulême was on the whole rather liked but he did not figure much in the public eye, while the Duchesse d'Angoulême was pitied and respected but not beloved. She was a constant reproach to the Parisians and a living reminder of the days of the Terror, which they would now willingly have forgotten. They might build a *Chapelle Expiatoire*, dedicated to the memory of Louis XVI and Marie Antoinette, but Marie Thérèse de France would still avert her eyes if by mistake her coachman drove past the spot where the heads of her parents had fallen into the executioner's basket.

Artois, too, inspired the French with a guilt complex. Because of his loyalty to the companions of his exile he represented to the nation the old hatreds, the old doubts, the old ideologies and the old quarrels. And then, too, the dead hand of Louise de Polastron influenced the history of France. Charles remained faithful to his promise to her and as devoted to the Church as to her memory. Not even in the interests of the dynasty would he admit the possibility of marrying again after de Berri's death. And the little Abbé Latil, now a Cardinal, *éminence rouge* as well as *éminence grise*, who had received Louise's last confession and brought the Comte d'Artois back to the Church, was always at his side to encourage him in a piety which had almost degenerated into bigotry.

A not wholly welcome reminder of Louise came to Charles after his return to France. Adhémar de Polastron's emigration had ended in 1801 but he had lost his fortune and in later years was forced to appeal for help to the very man who had destroyed his domestic happiness. Artois did what he could for him but de Polastron dragged out the rest of his life in near-poverty and obscurity.

His fate was not unique. Through the years of Louis XVIII's reign the émigrés had been treated shabbily, constantly promised an indemnity which failed to materialise. Louis preferred to run the risk of antagonising some hundred thousand former émigrés rather than inciting forty million Frenchmen to revolt.

From the moment of their return their circumstances were difficult. At an early moment after his return to France in 1814 the Abbé Carron had written to John Wilmot:*

'My worthy and venerable Friend,
I am trying to find means of founding here an establishment which will recreate my dear and well-beloved Somers Town but I am finding very great difficulty as everyone here is in financial distress and I have already experienced many rebuffs in trying to re-assemble and bring up my dear little émigrés.'

Nobody really expected in the early days of his return to walk back into affluence but as the years went on without bringing any recompense the émigrés became embittered. Yet the situation was one of great difficulty, demanding infinite tact and patience to resolve. The laws which had confiscated the aristocrats' property could not now be expunged without upsetting the whole social fabric. This they themselves realised and they did not ask for the restoration of their own lands, long since passed into other hands, but they did demand, in the name of the sacrifices they had made, some compensation for what had been torn from them without, in their eyes, the shadow of legality.

Their appeal to the King was simple.

'How do you expect to maintain among us,' they asked, 'the sacred fire of honour and the chivalrous fidelity which illuminates all the pages of our history when, after thirty years of misfortune, you neglect and forget those who have grown old in the camps and are covered with wounds received in your service?

'We do not ask the restoration of our paternal roofs and the lands which for so many centuries our fathers watered with their blood and sweat. We ask only for an indemnity, for which legitimate aspiration we are treated as criminals. It is thirty years since we were destituted of our lands, our homes and our chattels. Scarcely a tenth of the men who were victims of their fidelity remain. Soon all will have disappeared.'

* British Museum Add. MSS. 9828

Even the Germans after the war of 1939–45 had to recognise that they owed some material reparation to those whom they had likewise despoiled, although to the dead of the gas chambers no reparation can be made. The French could not indemnify the victims of the guillotine and the *noyades* but they owed restitution to the émigrés. Charles X was determined to repair his brother's neglect but, although no one can deny that he was actuated by a spirit of justice, it was on this rock that the Bourbon monarchy foundered.

XVIII

Aftermath

So in 1830 revolution came again to France and the aged Charles X set out once more for exile, by way of Lulworth to Holyrood. The people of Edinburgh were glad to see their old friend again and he stayed with them for two years, but then in the restless way of exiles, he moved on. Angoulême was with him and the Duchesse and the two grandchildren on whom all the hopes of the Bourbons were now centred. If there had been two restorations might there not be a third?

Lord Liverpool who, as Prime Minister, had had dealings with him, found that there was a great similarity between Charles's character and that of many of the princes of the Stuart family. He was a perfect chevalier but had no quality which belonged to a king or a prince in difficult times.

For Madame de Lage, who had shared his splendours and his miseries, he truly belonged to a royal race, such as had never been seen before and would never be seen again, not only for its dignity but for its kindliness. They were devoted heart and soul to their people, she said, but this devotion had made them weak.

Madame de Lage had again taken the *chemin de l'honneur* in 1830 for she would not stay in a country which had renounced its Bourbon kings. She visited Charles in Austria where he had now settled. They talked about the old days at Versailles and in England and about Louise whom so few people remembered now. The old King was unwilling to let Blimonette go.

Then Charles died and Leopold of the Belgians wrote to his niece, Queen Victoria, that:

'He was a good man and deserving to be loved, an honest man, a kind friend, an honourable master, sincere in his opinions and inclined to do everything that is right.'

205

But Leopold added that he was blinded by certain absolute ideas.

Of that joyous company at Versailles before 1789 only Stéphanie de Lage remained, and yet while she lived the ghosts enjoyed a vicarious existence. She wrote to her daughter,

'Croyez-vous que je ne parle pas et longtemps à ma pauvre mère, à Madame de Polastron et aux autres? Je me promène des heures entières dans ma chambre, toute avec eux . . . j'ai' des amis qui n'existent plus; mais ils ne finiront tout à fait qu'avec moi.'

Then Madame de Lage died and there was no one who remembered.

On the throne of France sat that dull citizen king, Louis-Philippe. He had got what he and his regicide father had always coveted and schemed to get, the French crown. But he could not keep it any more than his cousins of the older branch and, in 1848, he, too, took the road to exile again but for him it was no *chemin de l'honneur* and it never led back to France.

Then came the brief glory of the Second Empire and once again a Napoleon ruled in France and after that the French got their Republic back, one and indivisible, but often so sorely divided against itself.

Perhaps if Angoulême had not been so retiring, if the assassin's knife had not struck down de Berri, if Louise de Polastron had lived, if Charles X had possessed a little more statesmanship, if La Ferronays' voice had been heard more clearly, if Henri V had accepted the tricolour . . . if, if, if . . . another king might sit on the throne of France.

On his return to France Auguste de La Ferronays remained in his position as first gentleman of the chamber to the Duc de Berri. Albertine had been delayed in England until September, 1814, because she was expecting the birth of another child and it was not until the baby, Fernand, was five weeks old that she had the joy of returning to France. With her travelled her *femme de chambre*, the baby's wet-nurse and a maidservant and they all settled down in the Rue de Varenne in the Faubourg St. Germain.

When de Berri married, Albertine was appointed mistress of the robes to his wife and the La Ferronays moved into a magnificent suite at the Elysée where the young ménage set up house. Albertine had formed one of the delegation sent to fetch the Princess on her arrival in France from Naples but, although by birth and upbringing she was entitled to her place at Court and she had moved among princes from her childhood, the years of exile had only increased her natural timidity, making her over-anxious to do the right thing, a zeal which caused a good deal of criticism among the intriguers of the jealous Court circle.

De Berri was only too anxious to reward the friends about whom he most cared and when his wife expected her first child he appointed Madame de Montsoreau as its *gouvernante*. The child died and a stupid quarrel in which La Ferronays supported his mother-in-law over the rights to its layette, which traditionally belonged to the *gouvernante*, caused a rupture between him and the Duc.

Where his pride was concerned Auguste did not stop to think of how he was going to provide for his large family, but de Berri could not let his old friend fade into oblivion nor into poverty since he was only too well aware that the La Ferronays were not 'enervated with the secure possession of wealth.' Through his intervention Auguste was first nominated as Ambassador to Denmark and then to St. Petersburg so that the wish Alexander I had expressed at Leipzig was unexpectedly fulfilled. So Auguste de La Ferronays returned to the Court of the Romanoffs where he remained from 1819 until 1827, not as the humble representative of 'Monsieur le Comte de Lille' of Hartwell House near Aylesbury in the county of Buckinghamshire but as Ambassador of His Most Christian Majesty, Louis XVIII, King of France and Navarre.

His compatriot, Chateaubriand, too, went back to the scene of his poverty and humiliation but as French Ambassador to the Court of St. James's. It was during his embassy that he spoke at a dinner of the Royal Literary Fund and deplored the fact that he had not known of its existence during the days of his penurious emigration since he might have applied to it for aid.

As distinctions came crowding upon the two Bretons these days must have seemed to them farther away than a few mere years of time. The young private soldier without a shirt was now a General, a Peer of France, a chevalier of the Order of the

St. Esprit and on his breast blazed many Russian Orders, bestowed by the Czar.

It was at St. Petersburg that Auguste learned of the death of the friend of his youth and his maturity, the Duc de Berri, whom he had not seen since the day of their fatal quarrel. But de Berri had not forgotten him and from his death-bed he sent Auguste the Cross of the Legion of Honour which he was wearing on his coat. On hearing the news of the assassination Auguste fell into a dead faint, remaining insensible for some hours, and the shock affected his heart so that from now on his robust health began to decline.

In 1827 La Ferronays was recalled to France by Charles X to succeed Chateaubriand as Foreign Minister but it was too late to save the King, obstinately bent on reaction, from his destiny. Finally Auguste's health succumbed to the strain he had been putting on it for years and he resigned from the Ministry to become Ambassador in Rome but he had been a very short time in office when the Revolution of 1830 once again swept the Bourbons out of France. For Auguste there was no alternative to resigning his appointment and remaining in exile, while Chateaubriand followed the Duchesse de Berri to a new campaign in the ever-faithful Vendée.

Auguste's last years were spent in Italy and only twice did he cross the Alps to re-visit his beloved France. His daughter-in-law, wife of the Fernand whose birth had delayed Albertine's return, has left a picture of the ageing La Ferronays, but it is scarcely a kind one. Madame Fernand belonged not to the nobility but to the *haute bourgeoisie* and, because of the inferiority of her birth, the La Ferronays had not welcomed the connection.

Their daughter-in-law repaid their coolness by the rather cruel sketch she made of their home at Lucca on the occasion of the visit she made to them on her marriage. After that she seems to have seen little of her parents-in-law. She patently felt ill at ease with them, criticising in particular their Italian brand of piety, for Auguste had found again the faith which had for so long deserted him and, according to Madame Fernand, was in a great state of religious exaltation.

'My mother-in-law,' she wrote in her Memoirs, 'has still a

pleasing face but one might almost call her hunch-backed as her neck is very short and she has heavy shoulders on which her head seems to rest.'

She had to admit that her character was full of sweetness and that her piety, which was sincere and natural, did not partake of the quality of intransigence of her newly converted father-in-law.

Auguste obviously did not care for Madame Fernand, finding her neither pretty nor intelligent, but hers was a new face in their circle and he talked to her of his youth, recreating those days of drama as he mused aloud more to himself than to her. He, who had spent a life full of action, was bored to death by the inaction to which he was condemned by his unshakeable loyalty to the Bourbons.

The La Ferronays' circumstances were not easy and their family was large, two more daughters having been born to them after their return from England, Olga and Eugénie. The Czar, however, insisted that Auguste accept a pension from him as a token of friendship which he continued to Albertine after Auguste's death.

About her sister-in-law, Pauline, Madame Fernand de La Ferronays' comments were far more acid. Pauline had married an Englishman, Augustus Craven, who was in the Diplomatic Service, but who does not seem to have made a great success of his life, although their marriage was of the happiest. When their finances became strained Pauline turned to writing and her novels were much admired by Queen Victoria and crowned by the French Academy. She is still remembered for her touching story of family devotion and Catholic faith, *Récit d'une Sœur*.

The La Ferronays were at Rome when suddenly, on January 17th, 1842, with no intensification of the heart symptoms from which he suffered and with no illness Auguste de La Ferronays died. Like his father he was buried far from France in foreign soil. He lies at rest in the Church of Sant' Andrea delle Fratte at Rome.

To Pauline Albertine wrote of that horrible moment which had been her *idée fixe* for forty years.

'This terror, my dear child, has possessed me from the moment I became his. "My God, if I lost him!" has been the cry from the depths of my heart every moment of my life. I have never had an hour of security, practically not an hour when I could forget this thought—never has my grief about it ceased for long. He was the whole point of my life.'

Her only consolation in his loss was that his last years had been spent in the full and whole-hearted exercise of his religion.

Chateaubriand has enshrined his own life and thought in lapidary prose which is familiar to all. La Ferronays' is a name that most of the world has forgotten and he is revealed to us only in those letters which show perhaps more clearly than any formalised literature the character of the man, his steadfastness and loyalty, his gaiety and his charm, his receptivity to new ideas although he never sought fresh allegiances.

Chateaubriand's words may stand as his epitaph.

'Everyone respects my noble colleague and friend, and no one hates him, because his character and mind are upright and tolerant.'

After Auguste's death sorrows crowded upon Albertine. The children of whose future he had despaired grew up to do him great credit but one after the other they died in their youth. First Albert died, and then in quick succession the two youngest daughters, Olga, who had always been frail, and Eugénie. Those who were left and their descendants have always held by the true line and, from generation to generation, have been found responding to the call of duty and of honour in the tradition of which Auguste de La Ferronays was so notable a follower.

Much of Albertine's time was now spent with Pauline and perhaps to recapture the magic of her years with Auguste she wrote for her children an account of her life and her years of emigration. They are written in a fine eighteenth-century hand in two elegant calf-bound volumes but it is Auguste's story they tell more than Albertine's. She finished her story in 1846 and now there was nothing more for her to do but to await the happy moment when she would rejoin Auguste.

It was in November, 1848, six years after his death, that the moment came. She was living with Pauline in Baden and her last illness was brief.

She asked at the end for the crucifix to which her husband had clung as he lay dying and only as she took it did she let drop from her hands the framed portrait of Auguste which at night she put under her pillow and which she had held until this final moment.

The cemetery of Boury-en-Vexin lies on the outskirts of the straggling village. Luxuriant hedge-rows border the steep lane which leads to it. The countryside is rich and peaceful, the houses hidden in the valley. A few miles away a white château stands out in sharp relief against the dark woods.

On one side of the cemetery there is a walled enclosure entered by simple wrought-iron gates into which the rust is eating. In summer a tangled pink rambler rose sprawling over them brings a shock of colour to the grey stones. Here and there scarlet poppies start out of the sandy paths between the graves.

A large Russian cross dominates this private burial-ground and looms over the flat headstones into whose marble the years have eaten so that the names on them are scarcely legible. Pious hands of a later generation have ranged new marble tablets on the old walls so that the names and legends of those who lie buried here may prevail a little longer against the defacing ravages of time. Eugénie, Albert, Olga, . . . the dates show how brief were their lives.

One tablet holds the place of honour, recording the Comte de La Ferronays, born in 1777, died in 1842, father and husband of these others. His body lies exiled in death from his beloved France, as for so many years in life, and in far away London the graves of Félicie and Adèle, who did not live to eat the bitter bread of exile, have vanished. Yet one feels that his heart must linger here in the Pays de Vexin, a part of France that was old when Paris was young.

The family of La Ferronays made their home at Boury-en-Vexin for a brief eighteen years until the old loyalties sent them into exile again, but now it is their last long home. The vast rooms of their château are nearly all empty and desolate, though the chapel where they worshipped with such piety remains as they left it. In the village church every trace of their short residence is preserved with loving care. Boury makes a cult of this by-gone family.

Time moves slowly in the heart of rural France yet a hundred years have passed over sleeping Boury since the château was sold and no one living can now remember Auguste or Albertine de La Ferronays. All that remains of them is a worn prie-dieu in the Church and those old headstones. What quality was in this family that to these simple villagers who knew them not they are not dead but only sleep under the protection of the great Russian cross?

The Comte Auguste Ferron de La Ferronays died full of honours gained in the service of his country but other men have reaped richer rewards than he and stand out more boldly in their country's history and lie forgotten. The peasants of Boury know nothing of ambassadors or foreign ministers or men who walk with Princes. They keep faith with the past by cherishing and revering the memory of chivalry. It is not to the honours of Auguste de La Ferronays that they pay their humble tribute but to the shining honour of which he was the essence.

Postscript

Since the Israelites fled from Egypt and oppression by Pharaoh men have taken up their staffs and moved on until they found a climate favourable to the free exercise of their conscience and where they could live their lives in peace.

Later the Wandering of the Nations, the Pilgrim Fathers, the Huguenots of France and the Jacobites of England made the uprooting of peoples from their homelands a familiar part of history. In our own times refugees from Poland, White Russians fleeing from red revolution, victims of Nazi persecution, displaced persons, have become an integral part of the political scene. We find new names to re-dress an old story.

The French emigration of the eighteenth century was only one in this long series of movements of population under duress but the French émigré differed in one vital respect from modern refugees. He found a happy ending to his exile with faith triumphant, hope justified. The White Russian has long known his dream of the restoration of a Czarist Russia to be a dream. Polish independence is an illusion. Refugees from Nazism cannot return and build new lives on charnel-house foundations in a country where six million corpses have found few graves.

The French émigrés, too, nourished a dream but it was a dream which came true. It is of small moment now how dangerously slender was the thread on which their hopes were hung for the thread became a rope and that rope their life-line. And if, during these long and painful years, the émigrés cherished memories of the France they had known few of them truly believed that they would find it again as they had known it, but hope feeds on memory and they lived by hope. So the men and women who had kept faith with their ideals went home, not slinking back, hat in hand, begging asylum in their own country, but with the white cockade of the Bourbons in their hats, the white flag of the Bourbons at the head of their march and all the air perfumed with the lilies of France.

In the face of our present and personal knowledge of so many exiles it may seem idle to have dwelt on this faded tale of the past. What can it teach us that we do not already know, what chord can it strike that has not become wearisome by repetition? The answer is that, if we deny the past its right to be heard, we can never profit by the lessons of history and there is much that can profitably be learned from the French émigrés.

It is a cheap jibe hurled at the heads of the Bourbons that they learned nothing and forgot nothing. Let the lie be nailed once and for all. This remark was never made about the Bourbons. The Chevalier de Panat is reputed to have said,

'*No one* has learned anything and *no one* has forgotten anything,' and he said it in 1795 when the emigration had another twenty years ahead of it, during which time both the Bourbons and their adherents learned a great deal. To argue otherwise is to believe that a hundred thousand Frenchmen lived during their exile in a vacuum.

They learned of liberal institutions and liberality of heart; they learned to wear their poverty and their heartbreak under a smiling face and they learned that true charity may be found even in a traditional enemy. Their enforced travels at a time when new ideas and new concepts of philosophy and literature were circulating widely brought them into touch with men of varied ways of thought and different political outlook. The French with their lively native intelligence could not remain impervious to these influences and the effect on them was shown on their return to France by the growth of liberal ideas in politics and the new Romantic approach to art and literature. For many thousands of Frenchmen the emigration was a great intellectual adventure and to suggest that, once they had re-crossed the frontiers of France, they threw away all that they had learned is absurd.

Naturally men like Neuilly and La Ferronays and Walsh, who were adolescents when they left France, were more susceptible to new ideas than the men of Versailles who had reached maturity under the *ancien régime*. To ask them to be equally receptive to new influences was perhaps demanding that water run uphill but even the older generation could not remain wholly indifferent to the atmosphere of the foreign countries in which they lived.

Although the younger men grew up and were educated under the impact of new ideas they did not therefore turn their backs on the old loyalties. Auguste de La Ferronays spent far more than half his life abroad but he remained not only entirely French but also a convinced Royalist. If the Neuillys and the Falaiseaus and the La Ferronays came to believe that their fathers had made mistakes they did not feel that their attachment to their cause was mistaken. The ideals to which they all remained faithful must have had some enduring and mystical attribute to retain the allegiance of men of such intelligence. That France, except for a brief interlude, for sixty-five years after the Restoration maintained a monarchical form of government is an indication that attachment to monarchy was not essentially reactionary.

In a narrower sphere, too, the émigrés profited by their misfortunes. Those who had previously lived in great state were constrained by their slender resources to live as bourgeois surrounded by their children who, instead of being sent away to school or convent, benefited by a family life which they would not have enjoyed in France. Family life, too, took on a new complexion through the drawing together of husbands and wives. Before the Revolution the marriage tie in France was very lightly held by the nobility. Marriages were made at an early age, often when girls were still in their convent schools, and family considerations were the only criterion for the alliance. Now, during the years of emigration when the family was the only unit, bonds between husband and wife grew closer and, even when the tie was not one of marriage, it gained a force which often hallowed it.

For the émigrés exile was less of a trial of political strength between themselves and the revolutionaries than a test of character and few of them had cause to be ashamed of the way in which they met the challenge. As their years of emigration receded many of them set down their experiences so that some memorial should remain of their exile and why it had been undertaken. They wrote mainly for their children and grandchildren and not for publication, and they told their stories with modesty about the part they themselves had played, with simplicity about their privations but with pride of their devotion to the point of honour.

They recounted the hazards of leaving France and their frustrating journeys, their losses and sacrifices and they lived over again the battles in which so much blood was spilt. They recalled the varied traditions of foreign countries and the diverse welcomes they had received. All these recollections stimulated the imaginations and touched the hearts of the younger generations, ensuring that they would be handed down as the most glorious lessons of honour in their great traditions.

The most glorious lessons of honour . . . how cynically we now use the word, but there are times when it wins its rightful response.

Was Charles de Gaulle, the *Condé de nos jours*, ridiculed for adopting as his device the very motto of the Legion of Honour, *Honneur et patrie*? He was not sneered at but applauded when he thundered that, if France capitulated in face of the enemy, she would have done with honour. But General de Gaulle was following closely in the footsteps of those Frenchmen for whom the point of honour was all, following a national tradition, the tradition of a country even more conservative than our own.

It is fashionable to condemn conservatism as the enemy of progress, but without conservatism progress would be impossible. If each generation did not conserve its own achievements to hand down to the next man would never have advanced beyond the state of tilling the ground with a stick. It is through tradition that the generations link hands with the past and stretch them out to the future.

'Si vos pères n'eussent pas été généreusement fidèles aux antiques mœurs, vous n'auriez pas puisé dans cette fidelité native l'énergie qui a fait votre gloire dans les mœurs nouvelles. Ce n'est entre la France du dix-neuvième siècle et la vieille France qu'une transformation de vertu.'

Chateaubriand was speaking to the nineteenth century but what he said is equally valid for the twentieth. It is always dangerous to make historical parallels but those between 1792 and 1940 are too striking to avoid. In 1940 the Free French showed that devotion to honour and duty did not die with but, as Chateaubriand said, stemmed from the *ancien régime* and through it to a more distant but no less chivalrous past. Democracy had learned some of the virtues of aristocracy.

Particularly in Brittany do the old virtues die hard, its rugged landscape producing a vigour of purpose alike to defy the harshness of the soil and to defend the craggy ideals of liberty and honour. Chateaubriand, the poet of the emigration, was a Breton; Auguste de La Ferronays, the modern paladin, was a Breton; Thierry d'Argenlieu, the monk turned sailor, was a Breton; the *fusiliers marins*, who glorified the unknown name of Bir Hacheim, were for the most part Breton fisher folk who, rough and uneducated as they were, knew instinctively and by heredity that in 1940 the right road lay out of France, the old road, the *chemin de l'honneur*. The name of Pierre Bonsard is one that history does not know but he should have his place in it along with the unknown Vendéens and Chouans who fought dourly for their God and their King, this simple sailor from the Ecole Navale at Brest who, brandishing a pistol in either hand, threatened to shoot those who would not accompany him to England in 1940 to carry on the war for France. And there were those descendants of the 'tigers savaging their mother's bosom' who chose a German prison rather than compromise with tyranny in the shape of the 'Occupying Power,' that anodyne name for the bestial forces of Germany.

One might for Brittany paraphrase Racine:

> 'S'immoler pour son nom et pour son héritage
> D'un enfant de Bretagne voilà le vrai partage.'

But if the children of Brittany were outstanding and are outstanding in their fidelity they would not arrogate that virtue to themselves exclusively.

And let us not deprive those English of the eighteenth century of their honourable place in the émigrés' history for they gave not only their purse but their heart. If, in modesty, we do not accept the encomium of Jean-François de La Marche, Bishop of St. Pol de Léon, that:

> 'the generosity of the English nation surpasses all the instances of benevolence recorded in the history of nations'

let us not deny our ancestors their part in maintaining that tradition of relief of distress abroad and political asylum at home which is one of the proudest glories of the English people but which was not the creation of the twentieth century.

'En Angleterre même, l'estime et la sympathie entouraient les Français. Le roi, d'abord, voulut les leur marquer. Chacun des membres de sa famille en fit autant. D'autre part, les ministres et les autorités, ne manquaient jamais l'occasion de témoigner leurs bons sentiments. Mais on ne saurait imaginer la généreuse gentillesse que le peuple anglais lui-même montrait partout à notre égard.'

These are not the words of some forgotten French worthy, long tumbled into dust. They were written by General Charles de Gaulle* of the reception given to him and his troops after the fall of France, a moment in time which has the greatest significance for us all, but they show that, as Chateaubriand said, fidelity to the old traditions creates the climate for the new.

History has been harsh to the émigrés, judging their conduct misguided. Their champions have been few. For every Antoine de Saint-Gervais for whom the French emigration was noble in its origins, glorious in its course, honourable in its misfortunes, useful in its consequences and an embellishment to the pages of French history there have been many Montrols who heap on the heads of the émigrés the ten plagues of Egypt.

'This precipitate abandon, these unsuccessful attempts to return to France by force of arms, have been the origin of all French misfortunes. Thirty years of war abroad, anarchy and terror at home, these are the bloody fruits of the emigration. Yes, all that France has suffered, all that she has lost, her sons, the great men for whom she is still mourning, a million of her children killed in the Vendée and on every battlefield, this is what she owes to the émigrés.'

If Monsieur de Montrol's sweeping statement represents the judgment of history then that judgment is not only factually but morally wrong for the crime of the émigrés was to dare to resist tyranny and injustice and such resistance is always justified. If

* *Memoires de Guerre—l'Appel.*

Montrol believed that the émigrés oppressed the French people when they were in a position to do so, which is more than arguable, then they paid a hundredfold for their errors. To ascribe to them all the vicissitudes of the Revolutionary and Napoleonic wars is laughable.

Antoine de Saint-Gervais and Montrol were historians contemporary with the emigration. A more balanced judgment comes from a historian of our own days, Fernand Baldensperger, who writes with the objectivity of a hundred and thirty years later.

'These people suffered for a cause which history has in fact repudiated. But why should they lose the benefit of their sufferings because after their time the course of events has proved that they belonged to a world which had begun to vanish.'*

But to Napoleon may go the last word which withholds judgment but recognises the great virtue of the emigration.

'France opposed their actions while admiring their courage. All great devotion is heroic . . .'

In the light of history it is idle to dare to hope that never again will people be forced to leave their homes involuntarily under the goad of oppression and threat of annihilation. Except for insignificant groups this is a fate which the British people has been spared. We do not as a nation or part of a nation know what it means to drag out long years of exile, often in bitter poverty and in drab and humble surroundings, when nothing had prepared us mentally, morally or materially for such a reversal of fortune. The lot of this nation has been the more fortunate one of succouring and supporting those in a kind of distress to which it is itself a stranger.

Since all this lies outside our national experience we must ask ourselves, before we adopt the bitter adverse judgments of their opponents, what we would have done in the place of the French émigrés and all the others, whether in spite of momentary lapses we should have shown the same courage in adversity, the same fortitude in privation and the same steadfastness of purpose.

In writing this brief story of a long exile it is my hope that I

* *Le Mouvement des Idées pendant l'Emigration.*

have in some slight measure restored to the French émigrés something of the benefit of those sufferings which has been denied to them by posterity and for which they sought no recompense but the knowledge that they had been true to their ideals and faithfully served their God and their King.

Taking the lesson they have taught us into the future we could do far worse than adopt their device,

Mon âme à Dieu
Ma vie au roi
L'honneur à moi!

APPENDIX I

Note on the Chapel of the Annunciation, Little King Street, St. Marylebone*

After the Restoration the Chapel of the Annunciation was not forgotten by the Princes who had worshipped there. In 1815 it was by letters patent from Louis XVIII designated a Chapel Royal and endowed with a handsome grant, enabling the clergy to withdraw the seat tax and open the chapel freely to French, English and Irish without distinction.

Throughout the nineteenth century the Chapel fully merited its title of 'Royal' for, as one by one the dynasties in France fell victims to new revolutions and the sovereigns fled again to exile in England, they again found in it a spiritual home to remind them of the France they had left and which they would for the most part never see again.

Changes in government and particularly the institution of the Third Republic, which divorced Church from State, brought corresponding changes to the Chapel. The official grants ceased and the clergy had to make it self-supporting. They had once hoped to buy the freehold of the building but it was entailed in the Portman Estate and, even had this not been so, it would have been impossible to raise the money. Finding three thousand pounds to renew the lease and repair the building presented a sufficiently great problem.

Cardinal Manning came to the rescue, opening a subscription list, on which figured the names of the Empress Eugénie and the Orléans Princes. The Chapel was re-dedicated by Cardinal Manning under the name of St. Louis de France. To raise further funds the Abbé Tourzel, nephew of one of the founder priests, wrote a pamphlet history of the Chapel which was sold at the price of one franc or one shilling.

Somehow the little Chapel managed to struggle on although the centre of French life in London had long since moved westwards and French Catholics found their new church of Notre Dame de France in Leicester Square more spacious and more convenient.

In Little King Street the Titian presented by Louis-Philippe still hung above the altar and in appearance the Chapel remained as it had been in the days when half the hierarchy and half the Royal family of France knelt within its walls.

* Now Carton Street

When in 1910 the Abbé Tourzel died the Chapel had to close its doors. It passed first into the hands of the Anglicans and then the building fell on evil days. Its furnishings were scattered and during the First World War it was used as a toy factory and then became a furniture store.

In 1946 the Western Synagogue found a home there when its own buildings were bombed and it remained a consecrated house for ten years. But now the building has again been put to secular use and one memorial of the French émigrés who for so long made London their home has been lost.

Of their chapels only the little building in High Hampstead which, built in 1816, was never properly an émigré chapel remains and the Church of St. Aloysius in Phoenix Street, Somers Town, the still-living memorial of the Abbé Carron.

Parliamentary Grants to French Refugees*

		£	s.	d.
1794	*February 14th* (Supplies Granted by Parliament for the year 1794.) On account of the French refugees	27,692	4	6½
1795	*February 23rd* Relief of the suffering clergy and laity of France	98,410	o	o
1796	*May 2nd* French refugees	129,350	o	o
	December 22nd To make good money issued for the relief of the suffering clergy and laity of France	140,090	o	o
1797	*April 25th* To make good money issued to the Secretary to the Commissioners for relief of the suffering clergy and laity of France	31,000	o	o
	June 26th Towards the relief of the suffering clergy and laity of France for 1797	180,000	o	o
	November 23rd For relief of the suffering clergy and laity of France	168,000	o	o
1798	*April 24th* To make good money issued for relief of the suffering clergy and laity of France	12,677	12	1
1799	*March 16th* For relief of the suffering clergy and laity of France, Toulonese emigrants and American loyalists	226,000	o	o

Carried forward £1,013,219 16 7½

* Source: *Annual Register.*

		£	s.	d.
	Brought forward	1,013,219	16	7½

1800 *February 4th*
For relief of the suffering clergy and laity of
France, Toulonese and Corsican emigrants,
certain Saint Domingo sufferers and American loyalists ... 242,798 5 1

February 4th
For relief of the suffering clergy and laity of
France, Toulonese emigrants and American
loyalists for 1799, over and above the estimated sum ... 7,574 6 5

April 1st
To make good money issued for the relief of
Toulonese emigrants, not included in the
estimate for 1799 ... 900 0 0

1801 *April 27th*
For relief of the suffering clergy and laity of
France, Toulonese and Corsican emigrants,
certain St. Domingo sufferers and American
loyalists ... 208,772 0 0

1801 *November 20th*
For the relief of the suffering clergy and laity
of France and American loyalists ... 69,000 0 0

1802 *May 27th*
For the relief of the suffering clergy and laity
of France, Toulonese and Corsican emigrants, St. Domingo sufferers and American
loyalists ... 173,535 0 0

December 14th
For the relief of the suffering clergy and laity
of France, Toulonese, and Corsican emigrants, etc. ... 191,584 17 6

1803 *December 13th*
For relief of the suffering clergy and laity of
France, Toulonese, Corsican and Dutch
emigrants and American loyalists ... 149,121 0 0

1805 *February 14th*
For relief of the suffering clergy and laity of
France and American loyalists ... 135,721 12 0

£2,192,226 17 7½

		£	s.	d.
1806 *March 25th* Brought forward	£2,192,226	17	7½
For the French, Toulonese and Corsican emigrants and American loyalists	143,849	17	0
May 22nd For Protestant dissenting ministers and French refugees	10,336	3	0
1807 *January 26th* For the relief of the suffering clergy and laity of France, etc.	140,199	17	0

1808 An account showing how the monies remaining in the receipt of the Exchequer on the 5th day of January, 1807, together with the monies paid into the same during the year ended the 5th of January, 1808, have been actually applied; so far as relates to Miscellaneous Services

	£	s.	d.
For the French clergy and laity, Toulonese Corsican and Dutch emigrants and American loyalists, 1806–1807	133,119	2	7
Protestant dissenting ministers in England and for the relief of the poor French Protestant clergy and laity for 1806–1807	9,370	5	0
For the deficiency of the grant, 1806, for the relief of the suffering clergy and laity of France, Toulonese, Dutch and Corsican emigrants, and American loyalists, 1807	1,432	13	6
For the deficiency of the grant *anno* 1806, for the Protestant dissenting ministers in England and for the relief of the poor French Protestant clergy and laity, 1807	377	8	6
1809 *Appropriation of the British Supplies* Distrest laity and clergy of France	160,382	2	0
1810 *Appropriation of the British Supplies* Emigrant clergy and laity of France	161,452	2	0
	£2,952,746	8	2½

In the tables of Public Expenditure from the years 1811 onwards the *Annual Register* does not break down 'Miscellaneous Services' in detail but there is no reason to suppose that Parliamentary grants were suddenly withdrawn.

Bibliography

Archives of the French Chapel Royal.

British Museum Add. MSS 18591, 18592, 9828.

Public Record Office T 93, Papers relating to the French Clergy Refugees in the British Dominions.

Minutes of the Committee of Subscribers.

Letter Books.

Lists of Emigrés.

Lists of Subscribers.

Souvenirs d'une Pauvre Vieille by the Comtesse de La Ferronays (unpublished).

The Annual Register, 1789–1815.

Anti-Jacobin Review and Magazine, 1798–1801.

Boyle's Court Guide.

Dictionary of National Biography.

Gentleman's Magazine, 1789–1815.

Hansard, 1789.

Laity's Directory, 1789–1795.

The Morning Post.

Abrantès, Mémoires de la Duchesse d', Chez Ladvocat, Paris, 1831.

Antoine, A: *Histoire des Emigrés Français depuis* 1789 *jusqu'en* 1828. L. F. Hivert, Paris, 1828, 3 vols.

Ashbourne, Lord, *Pitt: Some Chapters of His Life and Times*. Longmans, Green & Co., London, 1898.

Auckland, Journal and Correspondence of William, Lord. Richard Bentley, London, 1862.

Baldensperger, Fernand: *Le Mouvement des Idées dans l'Emigration Française* (1789–1815). Plon-Nourrit et Cie, Paris, 1924.

Bellew, The Honble. Mrs., *Charlotte-Jeanne: a forgotten episode of the French Revolution*, Nineteenth Century and After, *No.* 382. December, 1908.

Bertaut, Jules: *Les Belles Émigrées*, Flammarion, Paris, 1948.

Bessborough, Lady and Her Family Circle, edited by the Earl of Bessborough. John Murray, London, 1940.

Bishop, Maria Catherine: *A Memoir of Mrs. Augustus Craven (Pauline de La Ferronays)*. Richard Bentley and Son, London, 1894.

Boigne, Mémoires de la Comtesse de. Plon-Nourrit et Cie, Paris, 1907.

Boutet de Monvel, Roger: *Les Anglais à Paris* 1800–1850. Plon-Nourrit et Cie, Paris, 1911.

Brissot, J. P., *Mémoires* (1754–1793) *publiés avec étude critique et notes par Cl. Perroud.* Alphonse Picard et fils, Paris, 1911.

Broc, Vicomte de: *Dix Ans de la Vie d'une Femme pendant l'Emigration, Adélaïde de Kerjean, Marquise de Falaiseau.* Plon-Nourrit et Cie, Paris, 1893.

Brown, Walter Edwin: *Saint-Pancras Open Spaces and Disused Burial Ground.* Town Hall, St. Pancras, 1902.

Bryant, Arthur: *The Age of Elegance.* Collins, London, 1950.

Burke, Edmund: *Reflections on the Revolution in France,* edited by E. J. Payne. At the Clarendon Press, Oxford, 1898.
Four Letters on the Proposals for Peace with the Regicide Directory of France, edited by E. J. Payne. At the Clarendon Press, Oxford, 1904.

Burney, The Diary of Fanny, edited by Lewis Gibbs. Everyman's Library, J. M. Dent & Sons, Ltd., London, 1950.

Campan: Journal Anecdotique de Madame, ou Souvenirs Recueillis dans ses Entretiens, par M. Maigne. Baudouin Frères, Paris, 1824.
Memoirs of Marie Antoinette. Hutchinson & Co., 1906.

Cars, Mémoires du Duc des. E. Plon-Nourrit et Cie, Paris, 1890.

Cartrie, Memoirs of the Count de. John Lane, the Bodley Head, London, 1906.

Castelot, André: *Le Duc de Berry et Son Double Mariage.* Sfelt, Paris, 1951.

Cooper, Duff: *Talleyrand.* Jonathan Cape, Ltd., London, 1932.

Chateaubriand, Vicomte de: *Mémoires, Lettres et Pièces Authentiques touchant La Vie et La Mort de S.A.R. Monseigneur Charles-Ferdinand d'Artois, Fils de France, Duc de Berry.* Chez Le Normant, Paris, 1820.
Mémoires d'Outre-Tombe. Bruxelles, 1848–50.
Atala, René, Bibliothèque Larousse, Paris.

Chuquet, Arthur: *Souvenirs du Baron de Frénilly.* Plon-Nourrit et Cie, Paris, 1908.

Clinch, George: *Marylebone & St. Pancras, Their History, Celebrities, Buildings and Institutions.* Truslove & Shirley, London, 1890.

Cobban, Alfred: *A History of Modern France,* Vol. 1. Penguin Books, 1957.

Costa de Beauregard, Marquis: *Souvenirs tirés des Papiers du Cte. A. de La Ferronays* (1777–1814). Plon-Nourrit et Cie, Paris, 1900.

Craven, Mme. August: *Récit d'Une Sœur.* Didier et Cie, Paris, 1868.

Dobrée, Bonamy: *The Letters of George III,* edited by. Cassell & Co., Ltd., London, 1935.

Farington, Diary, edited by James Greig. Hutchinson & Co., London.

Fauche-Borel, Mémoires de. Moutardier, Paris, 1829.

Forneron, H., *Histoire Générale des Émigrés.* E. Plon-Nourrit et Cie, Paris, 1884, 3 vols.

Fox Bourne, H. R., *English Newspapers.* Chatto & Windus, London, 1887.

France, Secret Memoirs of the Royal Family of, by a Lady of Rank. H. S. Nichols & Co., London, 1895.

Gaulle, Général Charles de: *Mémoires de Guerre: L'Appel.* Plon, Paris, 1954.

Gontaut, Mémoires de Madame la Duchesse de, Gouvernante des Enfants de France pendant la Restauration, 1773–1836. Plon, Paris, 1892.

Greatheed, Bertie: *An Englishman in Paris: 1803, The Journal of,* edited by J. P. T. Bury and J. C. Barry. Geoffrey Bles, London, 1953.

Greer, Donald: *The Incidence of Emigration during the French Revolution.* Harvard Historical Monographs, No. 24, 1951.

Greville, Memoirs, edited by Henry Reeves. Longmans, Green & Co., London, 1896.
Diary, edited by Philip Whitwell Wilson. William Heinemann, London, 1927.

Gronow, Reminiscences of Captain. Smith, Elder & Co., London, 1842.

Guichen, Vicomte de, *Le Duc d'Angoulême.* Emile-Paul, Paris, 1909.

Halévy, Elie: *England in 1815.* Ernest Benn, London, 1949.

Hart, B. H. Liddell: *The Letters of Private Wheeler,* edited by. Michael Joseph, London, 1951.

Jausions, P. A., *Vie de l'Abbé Carron.* Paris, 1866.

Jullien, Rosalie: *The Great French Revolution.* Sampson Low, London, 1881.

La Ferronays, Mémoires de Mme de. Librairie Paul Ollendorff, Paris, 1899.

Lally-Tollendal, Trophime-Gérard de: *Défense des Émigrés.* Chez Cocheris, Paris, 1797.

La Marche, Jean-François de, Letter of the Right Rev., Bishop of Léon. Printed by J. P. Coghlan, No. 37, Duke Street, Grosvenor Square, London, 1793.

Langlade, Emile: *Rose Bertin, La Marchande de Modes de Marie Antoinette.* Albin Michel, Paris, 1911.

Larochejaquelein, Mémoires de Madame la Marquise de. Chez L. G. Michaud, Paris, 1822.

Las Cases, Comte de: *Mémorial de Ste. Hélène.* Garnier Frères, Paris, 1823.

La Tour du Pin, Marquise de: *Journal d'une Femme de Cinquante Ans.* Berger-Levrault, Paris, 1951.

Lebon, André: *L'Angleterre et l'Emigration Française de* 1794–1801. E. Plon et Cie, Paris, 1882.

Le Brun, Vigée, *Souvenirs de Madame.* Charpentier et Cie, Paris, 1869.

Lockitt, C. H.: *The Relations of French and English Society* (1763–1793). Longmans, Green & Co., London, 1920.

La Gorce, Pierre de: *Louis XVIII.* Librairie Plon, Paris, 1926.

Louis XVIII, Correspondance Privée et Inédite de, Pendant son séjour en Angleterre. H. Tarlier, Bruxelles, 1830.

Mémoires d'une Dame de Qualité sur. Mame et Dalaunay-Vallée, Paris, 1829.

Lubersac, Abbé de: *Journal historique et réligieux de l'Emigration.* London, 1802.

Lucas-Dubreton, J., *Le Comte d'Artois, Charles X.* Librairie Hachette, Paris, 1927.

Malouet, Mémoires de, publiés par son petit-fils le Baron Malouet. Didier et Cie, Paris, 1868.

Montlosier, Comte de: *Souvenirs d'un Emigré* (1791–1798). Hachette, Paris, 1951.

Montrol, M. F. de: *Histoire de l'Emigration* 1789–1825. Ponthieu et Cie, Paris, 1827.

Neuilly, Souvenirs et Correspondance du Comte de: Dix Années d'Emigration. Charles Douniol, Paris, 1865.

Petrie, Sir Charles: *Lord Liverpool and His Times.* James Barrie, London, 1954.

Plasse, F. X., *Le Clergé Français réfugié en Angleterre.* Palmé, Paris, 1886.

Portalis, Baron Roger: *Henry-Pierre Danloux, Peintre de Portraits et Son Journal durant l'Emigration* (1753–1809). Pour la Société des Bibliophiles Français, chez Edouard Ranir, Paris, 1910.

Puisaye, Comte Joseph de: *Mémoires qui pourront servir à l'histoire du parti royaliste durant la Révolution.* Londres, 1803–8.

Reinach-Foussemagne, Comtesse de: *La Marquise de Lage de Volude,* 1764–1842, Perrin et Cie, Paris, 1908.

Reiset, Vicomte de: *Les Enfants du Duc de Berry.* Librairie Emile-Paul, Paris, 1905.

Louise d'Esparbès, Comtesse de Polastron. Emile-Paul, Paris, 1907.

Rosebery, Lord: *Pitt.* Macmillan & Co., London, 1893.

Rougé, Comte A. de: *Le Marquis de Vérac et ses amis.* E. Plon-Nourrit et Cie, Paris, 1890.

Salvemini, Gaetano: *The French Revolution,* 1788–1792. Jonathan Cape, London, 1954.

Savigny-Vesco, Marguerite: *Une Fresque Romantique, Les La Ferronays.* Editions Sésame, 1958.

Timbs, John: *Curiosities of London*. London, 1867.

Tourzel, Abbé: *La Chapelle française à Londres, Saint-Louis-de-France, 21, King's Street, Portman Square*. Imp. De Soye et fils, Paris, 1886.

Turquan, Joseph: *Les Favorites de Louis XVIII*. Montgrédien et Cie. Paris.

Vaudreuil, Correspondance intime du Comte de Vaudreuil et du Comte d'Artois pendant l'Emigration (1789–1815), edited by Léonce Pingaud. Plon, Paris, 1889.

Victoria, Letters of Queen, 1837–1861, edited by A. C. Benson and Viscount Esher. John Murray, London, 1908.

Vivent, Jacques: *Charles X, Dernier Roi de France et de Navarre*. Le Livre Contemporain, Paris, 1958.

Walford, Edward: *Old and New London*. Cassell, Petter & Galpin, London.

Walpole, The Letters of Horace, edited by Mrs. Paget Toynbee. Clarendon Press, Oxford, 1905.

Walsh, Vicomte: *Souvenirs de Cinquante Ans*. Au Bureau de la Mode, Paris, 1845.

Walter, Gérard: *Le Comte de Provence*. Editions Albin Michel, Paris, 1950.

Weiss, Charles: *History of the French Protestant Refugees*. William Blackwood and Sons, Edinburgh and London, 1854.

Windham, Diary of the Rt. Hon. William, edited by Mrs. Henry Baring. Longmans, Green and Co., London, 1866.

Yorke, Henry Redhead: *France in Eighteen Hundred and Two*, edited by J. C. A. Sykes. William Heinemann, London, 1906.

Young, Arthur: *Travels in France during the years* 1787, 1788 and 1789. Bury St. Edmunds, 1792–4.

Index

INDEX